Literate Community
in Early Imperial China

SUNY series in Chinese Philosophy and Culture
_____

Roger T. Ames, editor

Literate Community
in Early Imperial China

The Northwestern Frontier in Han Times

CHARLES SANFT

SUNY PRESS

Cover painting by Sarah Moore (from the author's collection).

Published by State University of New York Press, Albany

For information, contact State University of New York Press, Albany, NY
www.sunypress.edu

Library of Congress Cataloging-in-Publication Data

Names: Sanft, Charles, 1972– author.
Title: Literate community in early imperial China : the northwestern frontier
    in Han times / Charles Sanft.
Description: Albany : State University of New York Press, [2019] | Series:
    SUNY series in Chinese philosophy and culture | Includes bibliographical
    references and index.
Identifiers: LCCN 2018036278 | ISBN 9781438475134 (hardcover : alk. paper) |
    ISBN 9781438475141 (ebook)
Subjects: LCSH: Chinese language—To 600. | Chinese language—Writing—
    History. | Literacy—China—History.
Classification: LCC PL1077 .S26 2019 | DDC 895.1/001—dc23
LC record available at https://lccn.loc.gov/2018036278

10 9 8 7 6 5 4 3 2 1

to Hsiu-yi (again)

Contents

Acknowledgments

This project would never have happened without the support and advice of many colleagues and friends, all of whom have my gratitude. Miranda Brown helped me work out my ideas over the course of the project and subsequently read and commented on the manuscript in various forms. Miyake Kiyoshi's 宮宅潔 scholarship had a deep influence on this project, and he answered questions and gave me advice during the course of research and writing. Michael Hunter read the manuscript and offered much incisive advice in writing and in conversation.

Ma Yi 馬怡, whose work is a model of rigor and engagement with detail, generously took the time to meet with me and read Han letters together with her students. Thomas E. Burman and Martin Kern gave me reading suggestions that decisively influenced the course of my research. Christopher Foster offered both suggestions and encouragement for this project. Mélodie Doumy facilitated my viewing of Han writing strips from the northwest in the collection of the British Library. Olivier Venture and Robin D. S. Yates graciously shared their time and research materials with me. Enno Giele first introduced me to excavated materials as sources for Han history, and his works are prominent in my bibliography.

I had conversations and email exchanges with a number of scholars about aspects of the book, which helped me tremendously. In this respect, I wish to thank Anthony Barbieri-Low, Raffaella Cribiore, Mark Csikszentmihalyi, Nicola Di Cosmo, Lothar von Falkenhausen, Michael Puett, Matthias Richter, Edward Shaughnessy, and Ori Tavor.

This project benefited from two seminars, and I wish to thank all those involved. The first was a *Fragments* seminar at the University of Michigan, Ann Arbor, which Miranda Brown and Ian Moyer organized. I am grateful to Roger Bagnall, who traveled to be there and whose ideas contributed so much to my own thinking. My appreciation extends to the University of Michigan faculty members who made the seminar challenging, exciting, and enjoyable, particularly Susan Alcock, William Baxter, Erin Brightwell, Katherine French, Piotr Michalowski, Sonya Özbey, Hitomi Tonomura, and Thomas Trautmann. The University of Tennessee Humanities Center hosted a seminar discussion of the completed manuscript. My thanks to Lai Guolong 來國龍, who flew in to take part; Gregor Kalas, who read and commented on the entire manuscript; and Megan Bryson, Maura Lafferty, and Brad Phillis, who gave many recommendations for the manuscript in the course of our conversation—or conversations, rather, as I have been fortunate to talk with each of them about the project outside the seminar, too. Finally, S. E. Kile deserves a special prize for participating in both seminars and marking corrections and suggestions throughout the manuscript.

I gratefully acknowledge the generosity of the American Council of Learned Societies, which granted me a fellowship for the completion of this book. My research and writing also received support from a University of Tennessee Chancellor's Grant for Faculty Research, a faculty fellowship at the University of Tennessee Humanities Center, the University of Tennessee Jefferson Prize for Faculty Research, and from the Department of History at the University of Tennessee.

The roots of this book reach back to my postdoctoral fellowship at Kyoto University, which the Japan Society for the Promotion of Science made possible. Tomiya Itaru 冨谷至 was my host there, and his erudition and energy remain an inspiration. Without him, this book would not have been written.

Fragments: Interdisciplinary Approaches to the Ancient and Medieval Pasts will publish a version of chapter 1, and some of the translations in chapters 3 and 8 previously appeared in *Early China* and *Renditions: A Chinese-English Translation Magazine*. My thanks to the editors for permission to include that material.

Introduction

. . . what people do with language is more instructive than what they know about language or believe they do with it.

—Linda Brodkey, *Academic Writing as Social Practice*

Text defined society in early imperial China. It did so before and after, too. But in the first centuries of empire, the position of text changed, and those changes resonated throughout society. Men and women at every social level interacted meaningfully with text. This book examines some of those interactions.

I argue in this book that the military bureaucracy of Han-era China brought soldiers and others from different regions and placed them in a literate community in the northwestern border region. There the soldiers encountered text, worked with information transmitted in written form, and heard various sorts of texts read. They were part of the textual culture of the realm.

Text has a long history in China, but the first imperial dynasties leveraged it in new ways. China entered the early imperial period in 221 BCE with a declaration of unification, which the First Emperor of Qin 秦始皇 (r. 221–210 BCE) promulgated throughout the realm in written form. The universal government of the Qin dynasty was a bureaucracy, and the Han dynasty (206/2 BCE–220 CE) inherited and refined that system.[1] It functioned on the basis of text and played a key role in the dissemination of text throughout the realm.

M. T. Clanchy has written about the fundamental role religion played in spreading literate culture in medieval Europe. In Europe, the needs and requirements of the Christian church—its teachings, its authority, its controversies—gave shape and impetus to the development of textual civilization.[2] Document bureaucracy played an analogous role in early imperial China.

During the early imperial period, religion was an important part of Qin and Han culture. But there was no institution to act as a driving force in the development of textual culture. Religious practices varied and were often highly localized. While government was involved in religion, in that it promoted specific observances and prohibited others, there was far more variation across geographical area and social position than there was consistency. As Ori Tavor writes, "early Chinese religion is a particularly amorphous entity, as it lacks many of the features modern scholars view as fundamental—a canonical set of scriptures, organized clergy, or a fixed pantheon."[3] The situation changed after the arrival of Buddhism, but the spread of textual culture happened another way.

In contrast, the early bureaucracy, the governance that depended upon it, and the documents it produced, were universal influences. The bureaucracy, in theory at least, brought the whole of the Qin and Han realm under a single system, with its center at the capital. Its workings teemed with text; its documents were in front of all eyes. Religion was part of the bureaucracy, but as one matter among many.[4] When Buddhism spread to and within China, it brought with it new texts and inspired new traditions, and contributed to the spread of forms of writing. Buddhism came to influence China in many respects, including written culture.[5] But Chinese culture was already textual prior to its advent.

Due perhaps to text's central position in their governance and society, the first imperial dynasties in China dominated written culture in unprecedented ways. The Qin took measures that the critical historiography of the Han denoted as "the burning of books"—a putative destruction of much previously written knowledge.[6] Contemporary and later writers celebrated the establishment of scholastic offices dedicated to specific texts under the Han.[7] The Han period saw the creation of China's first universal history, *Historian's Records* (*Shiji* 史記), which was also arguably the first important example of synthesizing historiography in China. Later in the Han came the first dynastic history, *Han History* (*Han shu* 漢書). These works evinced new meta-conceptions of text as a tool for shaping perceptions of the past and the present.[8] Written forms of literary and intellectual expression were well established. And, of course, Chinese governance was, throughout the period (and after), a document bureaucracy. Officials read and wrote as part of their work. These things deserve the attention historians have given them. In this book, however, I want to look beyond the boundaries of formal officialdom.

The best-known forms of text in early China were the province of particular groups, all of whom were power holders or elites of various sorts. Previous studies have usually focused on the ways these groups engaged writing. Their members were often literate in a very full sense. They read and they wrote, often at a very high level, and in doing so drew from deep sources of shared textual culture. Those writers and their textual modes played a decisive role in the development of historiography and literature in China. For the most part, the texts that later historians study and take inspiration from were the same ones early historians, literati, and officials wrote and read. Those depictions remain definitive to the present. They also represent a narrow part of society.[9]

The pictures that emerge from studies in the inherited mode—sometimes consciously, oftentimes not—carry over social structures that inhere in those conceptions and their modern descendants. As Ruth Finnegan puts it, "Interpretations of the past which, perhaps quite innocently, fall in with current power relationships are to be found everywhere."[10] Or, as Alice Yao has written about early China specifically, "the privileging of one source material may also reprise unstated power relations."[11] It was power holders who were literate in the ways that came to matter for most historians and later readers, and they have often ended up being the focal points of scholarship. I want to examine other aspects of society, which requires making some shifts.

This book is distinctive in two main ways. First, it argues for a way of thinking about the roles of text in Chinese society during the Han period that differs from its predecessors'. I propose an expanded understanding of what people did with text and concentrate on interaction with it. This approach encompasses a broader social scope than has been usual in considering paleographic texts. In place of concentrating more or less exclusively on officials and literati, which has been a common way to approach these things, I seek to consider more members of the community. This conception and its relationship to scholarship within and outside early China studies is the topic of chapter 1. The second way this book differs from its predecessors lies in its choice of source material. Most considerations of the topic have concentrated on literary or historical forms and transmitted texts. Here I am going to consider what is in essence a case study comprising documents that record the lives and activities of military personnel and the people around them in the northwestern border region of the Han.

While this book takes the form of a case study, it is not a narrow one. I do not restrict myself to a single site or small set of sites. I draw from paleographic records from throughout the four command-eries that defined the northwest border region in Han times. The Han did not occupy the areas at the same time or in the same way. I briefly discuss the background of the region and the characteristics of the Han presence there in chapter 2.

In this study, I give limited attention to institutions as institutions, because many scholars have already treated them. Previous scholarship on the source materials I use has generally taken one of two forms. The first of these is institutional history; the second is collection and translation. The truly seminal work of Michael Loewe combines both modes, and some later scholars have followed his example.[12] When translation is not the goal, institutional modes of history writing dominate. Often institutional studies concentrate on what the documents tell us about bureaucratic offices and practices. I draw a great deal from institutional history throughout my study. But by applying a different approach, I hope to do something distinct.

For the historian—in other words, someone fundamentally concerned with written records of the past—the northwestern border area offers things that other areas in China do not, or not in the same way. The first such thing is the very documents that I study. Despite recent finds and publications of early imperial paleographic sources, the materials now available represent only a small fraction of what once existed. The northwest border area provides us a sizable part of that fraction, because the military bureaucracy and the people who staffed it produced a lot of text and the climate of the region helped to preserve it. I talk in chapter 2 about their forms and contexts. There I also consider certain key institutional factors, especially the system of conscription that brought people from hundreds of miles away to the border region, then released them to return home when their service was done. The bureaucratic documents record particular types of information about the Han people in the northwest and what they did, which enables me to study their activities as members of a group, if not individually. Here we have more information than we do elsewhere.

This point has important implications for my study. Most of the paleographic texts that have contributed so much to our understanding of early Chinese history and culture in recent decades come from tombs. Many tombs have been excavated; according to Susan N. Erickson, for the Han period alone, "some thirty thousand, as estimated in 1999."[13] But only a small percentage contained written materials: Alain Thote calculates that just 119 tombs have produced texts, a figure that includes some pre-Han sites.[14] The contrast with the northwest is stark, as no few locations in the region of Juyan produced documents. Some produced thousands of strips, while most contained far fewer.[15] While the differences between tombs as a group and the northwest border region sites preclude direct comparison, the figures reflect that the northwest border region under Han occupation was rich in text.

The northwestern area has particular characteristics that contribute to my analysis. The region was far removed from the centers of culture and politics. Being located as they were on the edges of Han-controlled space, the border stations were remote by any standard. And the dry climate of the region preserved the documents for later historians, without the involvement of editors and compilers over the intervening centuries.

Deduction and Evidence

Over the course of this book, I go beyond collecting and relating information to make inferences and interpretations concerning aspects of Chinese society in early imperial times. The potential for misinterpretation in deduction and related processes is inevitable. The picture will also continue to evolve over time as archaeologists continue to add to the available body of text and the material record. I nevertheless believe that an interpretive method is the best.

Interpretation has not been the usual mode of inquiry in Chinese history over the centuries, including the most recent one. Much scholarship concerning Chinese history adheres to an approach that is more descriptive and antiquarian than historiographical. Scholars taking the descriptive approach gather, catalog, order, and relate the content of their sources. Institutional history as pursued in the Chinese context often epitomizes this mode; it conveys abundant detail about sources and what they tell us about things like specific official positions, structures, processes, and procedures. Details by themselves are not meaningful, however. What substitutes for acknowledged interpretation in many cases is tacit acceptance of existing concepts and wisdom. A historiographical approach, in contrast, seeks to make larger arguments about the past. Scholarship in this mode engages in acknowledged interpretation as a way to better understand its subject. Details and sources are always important, even as they become part of the larger argument and narrative rather than ends in themselves.[16]

This description of two approaches to studying the past is obviously simplified, and the best scholarship usually incorporates aspects of both. In this book, though, I consciously choose to prefer the historiographical. It is my goal to make a larger argument about the place of text in early society, not only examine individual examples. Making judicious deductions about the situation on a clearly delineated and supported basis is likely to create a better picture than is otherwise possible.

The focus on descriptive and institutional approaches to history is in some respects a reaction to the difficulties of studying antiquity. The nature of early history means that historical fact is inevitably less certain than an idealist would like. Confirmation on the basis of multiple sources, as a historian of later times would demand, is usually not possible.[17] In the context of the early imperial period in China, a small set of texts, above all the *Historian's Records* and *Han History*, provide the bulk of available information. No few scholars have written on their basis alone, and all study of the period bears their imprint. This leaves the modern historian, skeptical and concerned about sources and reliability, with a decision to make about how to work. Institutional history and descriptive modes provide certainty and are thus appealing.

Descriptive and institutional modes of engagement, which concentrate on cataloging, compiling, evaluating, and translating sources, are conceptually similar approaches to the uncertainties of early history. Many scholars devote themselves to writing institutional history in more or less this fashion: extracting, arranging, and discussing details about systems and positions. Such work has immense value in increasing our understanding of the past, especially since it has developed into an important means of incorporating newly excavated materials into historical accounts. I draw from institutional history extensively in this book. That scholarship also leaves space for developing the sort of historiographical analysis and arguments that I seek.

Another approach to the problem has been to seek a solid basis among archaeological data. Yet, while archaeology in China has enriched our understanding of history, to turn history into a subordinate or ancillary of archaeology (or vice versa) would do justice to neither. They are separate, if overlapping, fields of inquiry. And, as Nicola Di Cosmo has put it, "If historical questions are investigated exclusively from an archaeological perspective, and thus removed from a deeper and broader understanding of the historical context, their interpretation may suffer from distortions due to an exclusive focus on material evidence."[18]

I would be a bit more emphatic than Di Cosmo in asserting that while history and archaeology inform each other, they are distinct. They can enrich but do not negate each other—even when they challenge each other. Such contact between the fields can be very productive. To quote Lothar von Falkenhausen, "The tension between texts and archaeology is potentially a fruitful one, because it enables us to broaden the scope of inquiry and ask new questions about ancient China."[19] This book is one product of contact between history and archaeology, in that it makes extensive use of archaeologically recovered materials. But it does not place archaeology in a position of absolute authority over history, or the other way around.

The final alternative way of dealing with early history's uncertainties that I would like to discuss is remaining silent and waiting for proof to emerge. This has real appeal, for one who is silent commits no error. Yet I do not think it is a feasible approach. No one knows what sorts of new sources may emerge in the coming years and decades. Waiting for evidence may prove interminable. And when archaeology has provided new data in the past, the sources often do not contain the exact information a historian would want. That seems likely to be the case in the future, too. In the meantime, I argue, remaining silent is not really possible. Even if one forgoes participation in the active and exciting international conversations about the history of early China that are happening now, silence would not mean saying nothing. The discursive space is not empty: a body of conceptions informed by centuries of historiography and editorial work fills it. To say nothing is to accede to those presentations and those ideas.

The preponderance of evidence suggests reality was different from the traditional picture. There is reason to think that received conceptions need revision. In my view, the historian's choice is not between patient silence on the one hand and risky deduction on the other. The choice seems to be between perpetuating the errors and prejudices of centuries and engaging in acknowledged interpretation. In this book, I choose the latter course.

This is not to condemn any other approach out of hand. Great scholars have worked in various modes. It is simply that I want to do something else. Part of that is redefinition of interaction with text, which is a key part of my argument. But more than just that definition is in play. Thinking about the past—especially the distant past—calls for something different than what has gone before.

Brief Summary of Chapters

Here I will briefly sketch the content of this book's chapters, saving detailed discussion and citation references for the respective sections of this book. I have already mentioned some of what chapter 1 does. It is there that I propose both to think in terms of interacting with text rather than literacy and to frame the discussion in terms of a community rather than individuals. Chapter 1 lays out the reasoning behind my approach, connecting it to and differentiating it from existing scholarship in early China studies. Some of the conclusions that guide my reasoning come from scholars working in other fields. One of those other fields is the study of textual culture and literacy in Europe and the Middle East during late antiquity and medieval times. Writers such as papyrologist and paleographer Roger Bagnall, paleographer M. C. A. Macdonald, and medievalist M. T. Clanchy provide important interdisciplinary support for my contentions about how to think about text and its place in society.

Many scholars have considered this question in terms of literacy in the sense of a person's ability to read and write at a certain level. Oftentimes those discussions treat scribes and others whose jobs required them to be able to read and write. We should, however, avoid imagining interaction with text in terms of a sharp distinction between professional literates, who read and wrote, and everyone else, who did not. Rather we should expect people's abilities to have existed on a spectrum.

At the low end of that spectrum were those who encountered text only insofar as it was read aloud and explained to them, or as it was written down on the basis of what they said. This was not a zero level of engagement, which the text-soaked environment of the early Chinese empire precluded, but a low level. At the other end were highly educated scholars and officials, and those who were both. They could read, compose, write, and comprehend text at a high level—activities that required extensive knowledge of the script, literature, and history of their intellectual environment. Most people fell somewhere in between these two extremes.

For the purposes of discussion in this book, I separate reading and writing. This more accurately represents the historical (and present) situation, as these activities are distinct. Research in fields ranging from neuroscience to literacy education indicates that learning to read is much easier than learning to write. I propose the military bureaucracy of the northwest region created conditions conducive to learning to read.

The combination of posting and reading aloud of text developed a spectrum of comprehension among the population of the early empire, some of whom could and did read; some of whom read along; a majority of whom combined listening with some degree of reading, however slight; and some who relied on listening alone. It is important to remember that persons who did not write still participated in the creation of text by dictation. As comparative research reminds us, dictation is a legitimate means of content creation and is not invalid or inauthentic.

While the distinction between written and oral transmission is an important one, even more important is the recognition that for most persons in Han China, there was not a black-and-white separation between the two. Rather, people lived in groups—communities—in which they interacted with text orally or through written transmission according to their abilities and interests. The sources from Han China will probably never permit us to reliably calculate a broad literacy rate for early imperial China. That does not prevent us from considering how people interacted with text.

Chapter 2 gives a brief overview of the arid northwest context of the documents I treat in this book. Those details aid the reader in understanding the rest of the book but constitute a limited part of the discussion. The chapters that follow the first two work out the implications of my mode of engagement by considering different types of materials. Each chapter treats one type or set of types of text, each itself illustrating different types of interaction with text. While these may seem to align with genres of texts, it is not the purpose of this book to argue for the historical integrity of those groups as groups. While some bear similarities to types that appear in the earliest extant textual groupings, others are absent from those lists.[20] Rather than asserting that the sets of texts I treat were genres in their contemporary context, I use them as a way to structure my consideration and presentation of the primary sources. Those sources come to us without intrinsic order, and I need to give them some order for the purpose of discussion. While I do not doubt the sources I study could contribute to a study of early textual genres, that is a separate issue.

Chapter 3 begins the study of the sources by considering examples of posted texts. These are of two main types. One of these types is the regulations outlining the signals that soldiers used to communicate across distances by means of fire, drums, flags, and so forth, to convey information. Local-level authorities disseminated the standards, which soldiers needed to know for signaling. The function of the border defense system required this knowledge, and we have documents indicating that soldiers' knowledge was checked. The other type of posted texts is imperial edicts, which conveyed commands from the central government, and which in several extant cases incorporated elevated, literary language. Many examples of posted texts contain instructions that required the contents of the texts to be posted in public places and communicated to the populace.

Both of these types were available to the soldiers who formed the main audience for the texts I study; both contained and conveyed knowledge that they needed to master. These two created a situation in which learning to read at least some words was likely: the combination of content learned by rote and texts conveying that content would have allowed anyone interested to put the two together and begin to acquire reading ability. Obviously not everyone did this. But the most reasonable interpretation, if we consider what we know about learning and reading, is that a meaningful portion did. That already changes how we think about text and its roles in early imperial society.

Chapter 4 introduces statements, marked by the phrase *ziyan* 自言 ("to state oneself"), which represent a different sort of widespread interaction with text. These documents emerged out of oral exchanges between officials and members of the common population. The process by which these documents were created represents a form of dictation. The statements thus record interaction with text for those commoners who made them. Women dictated statements, too, which testifies to their interaction with text in a mode that was, mutatis mutandis, the same as that of men. Women were part of the literate community. There are furthermore statements from non-Chinese persons. These examples demonstrate that the literate community of the region had boundaries that could shift, depending on the situation. The documents I study confirm that, far from being limited to the official scribes and others who fall within conventional definitions of literacy, persons from throughout and even beyond Han society also interacted with text in early China.

One important manner of interacting with text in Han literary practice was creation by assembly, in which a creator selected and combined existing written material in a new way. Some of the most famous and important texts in Chinese history came into being around this time and in this manner. Chapter 5 shows that this mode functioned in the border regions, too, where we find composite texts created from locally available source material. The main example text juxtaposes an idiosyncratic imperial pronouncement with a personal letter. Scholars studying it have typically concentrated on one or the other of these aspects of the text, usually the former, and have not considered the implications of the two being alongside each other. As part of this discussion I also look at some example texts that come to us from graves in the northwest region. These examples concern the "king's staff" (*wangzhang* 王杖), which Han practice granted to men of advanced age as a symbol of special status and attendant privileges. The documents we have contain various texts and appear to have been assembled by individuals for personal purposes. Creating composites was an important mode of interaction with text that the borderlands shared with the center.

Chapter 6 considers texts that direct the reader in how to do things. For this reason I call them *practical*. The best example of this type is a short text on evaluating swords. Its content was of interest to soldiers, and its form also seems to be something that would be accessible to inexpert readers. Its structure is simple and explicit, its grammar is elementary, and its reasoning very straightforward. In this case, again, I bring in consideration of some texts that archaeologists excavated from graves to help illustrate what is distinctive about the northwest example. The most important counterpoint is that of a text on the evaluation of horses, which employs a complicated structure, recondite formulations, and difficult vocabulary. It implies an educated readership just as much as the text on evaluating swords suggests a less-cultivated audience. The chapter ends with discussion of a text on the brewing of beer that straddles the boundary between practical writing and ritual classic.

That text is not the only example of a classic among the documents from the border region. Chapter 7 discusses examples from *Analects* (*Lunyu* 論語) and other canonical texts. The chapter title refers to its subject as cultural texts; however, rather than canonical, as much of what we find in the documents does not correspond to classics, or the classic content is embedded in other material. There is perhaps no really satisfactory way to label these texts: most possible labels would necessarily or potentially be anachronistic, exclude certain materials, pass a judgment upon them, or simply confuse the matter. But these texts embodied cultivation in a way distinct from other types of text, and so I label them cultural. This is intended as a description, not to assert that they form a generic type. Among the texts from the northwest we find, for instance, material that appears in the *Book of Documents* (*Shangshu* 尚書), as well as texts that quote *Book of Odes* (*Shijing* 詩經) poems, a common occurrence throughout received literature. The settings, however, differ from the previously known examples. There are also narratives that relate to figures and accounts familiar from received literature, albeit in different guises. These things reflect the border regions' connections to the literary culture and community of the center, despite their physical distance from it.[21]

Chapter 8 is in some respects the culmination of the book. Its topic is letters that officials working in low rungs of the bureaucracy exchanged. While the letters usually concern matters connected with official work, they existed outside the usual bureaucratic processes for creating and circulating documents and adopted a more personal tone.

They thus mark a development in interaction between individuals through text at a low social level, within the context that soldiers and others also occupied. Indeed, no few of the letters bring in by name persons who neither created the content nor were named as recipient(s). Such letters illustrate relationships that were maintained through and by means of text, even when the persons involved were outside of the binary relationship of creator and recipient. The letters demonstrate the extent of the literate community. Importantly, here again I show that the community included women, who were addressed in some instances by title and other times by name, and sometimes brought into the official matters that letters treated. As a social group, women fall outside the usual definitions of literacy in early imperial China. Yet they, like other non-officials, were part of the literate community and had meaningful interactions with text.

This project has broad implications for our understanding of early imperial society. Because the primary source material I work with comes from a limited geographical area and provides a spectrum of information not available elsewhere, the main part of the monograph does not treat its wider ramifications. I wait to engage them until the conclusion, where I push my interpretations further than elsewhere. One of the important, broad implications of this study is that we should expect there to have been much more interaction with text—more reading, in particular—in early imperial society than scholars have often assumed. Widespread interaction with text was a characteristic of society in early China and helped shape it then and in later centuries. The first step in arriving at this recognition is the conceptual framework that is the topic of chapter 1.

Chapter One

Interacting with Text in Early Imperial China and Beyond

I'm quite illiterate, but I read a lot.

—Holden Caulfield

In *The Catcher in the Rye*, Holden Caulfield tells us that he is both illiterate and a reader, and it is irony, for Holden's is the voice of the novel.[1] For Holden, "literate" implies facility with writing, something he claims to lack. Distinct from that is the ability to read, which he admits having. Because the usual definition of literacy encompasses equally reading and writing, his assertion becomes a paradox, one of the many that characterize Holden throughout the novel. Angst-ridden teenaged inconsistency aside, though, Holden is on to something. He dissociates writing from reading and is right to do so.

In this chapter I consider and reconsider conceptions of interaction with text—not because the usual conceptions do not reflect our experiences as literates. They often do. Rather, I do this because studying the distant past calls for something else. Commonplace understandings of literacy concentrate on the ability—or lack thereof—of an individual to read and write. Here I provide a conceptual foundation for thinking in broader terms, larger sets, and different configurations, and explore some of the implications of those shifts.

This chapter makes the case for considering reading, including reading aloud; listening to others read aloud; writing; and dictation as different ways of doing one thing: interacting with text. For the

1

purposes of my discussion, this approach replaces the more common interest in the ability required to single-handedly create text as the measure of literacy. While scholars often treat reading as a skill to be learned only with great difficulty, here I show that reading may be more easily acquired than is often assumed.

Nor am I content to consider the subject only in terms of individuals' abilities in reading and writing, which is the standard mode of inquiry for literacy and related topics. I propose thinking instead about groups—communities—and contexts in which oral and textual transmission existed and intermingled. Doing this offers a workable solution to the difficulties and limitations of early sources. As an approach, it is more suited to the context of antiquity generally, and ancient China specifically, than concentrating on individual persons is. These things constitute the basis for my consideration of the Han military bureaucracy and its texts in subsequent chapters of this book.

Starting Point

Literacy in early China, as in other parts of the world, has received attention from many scholars. Much of the research concerning premodern societies has concentrated, expressly or not, on the relationship between exceptional individuals, elite classes, power holders, and the written word. This concentration is probably inevitable, at least in China. Those persons and groups created the texts that form the main part of history—and indeed high culture generally.[2] In this way, they shaped and continue to shape our perceptions of the past. But those texts necessarily represent a small segment of society. The argument in this book concentrates elsewhere and seeks to better understand the experiences of persons with little power, at the edges of the empire.

In this book, I draw from interdisciplinary examples. This is my way of working with the limited sources available concerning non-elites in the Han period. Considering other cultures and contexts provides a way to analyze the information and arrive at reasonable conclusions. Roger S. Bagnall and Raffaella Cribiore provide an example of this approach. They make use of "comparative evidence," along with consideration of context, to deal with what they call "a lack of density in the documentation" about their subjects, ancient

Egyptian women.[3] Wang Haicheng, in his study of writing and text in early China and other cultures, both argues for and demonstrates the usefulness of examining different cultures and drawing conclusions on the basis of those comparisons.[4] I consider the borderlands as the site of a literate community in Han times, a literate community comprising individuals from what can, for lack of a better term, be called non-elite classes.

Two Models of Literacy

I want to disclaim at the start the idea that every person in ancient China was capable of understanding, much less creating, every sort of text. That is not my argument. The barriers to creating, or fully comprehending, literary texts were extremely high in early China. Michael Nylan has described, for example, the rare combination of talent and erudition that Yang Xiong 揚雄 (53 BCE–18 CE), one of the great writers of the Han period, drew upon to compose his masterworks. Yang's imagined audience consisted of people whose levels of facility with text were, if lower than his, still very high: "Yang Xiong's ideal readers were those sufficiently learned and cultivated to engage in serious reading, transcribing, and composing of texts packed with classical allusions." To create or fully understand elevated literature in early China demanded mastery of a large body of knowledge. The textual corpus was already extensive, if organized very differently than it would be later. Those texts were the source of imagery, allusions, and phrasings, and their study also helped the reader acquire vocabulary and skills that both reader and writer needed. But meeting the standard that Yang Xiong set, or just appreciating his work completely, was beyond most people. The part of society with the resources required to develop those capabilities was small.[5]

Nor was it easy to become a qualified writer of even quotidian stuff in early times. Miyake Kiyoshi 宮宅潔 and others have written about the very high standards someone had to meet to hold the official position of scribe (shi 史). According to legal statutes from the second century BCE, those requirements included the demonstrated ability to read and write at least five thousand characters and to work with eight different scripts. Miyake, like some other scholars, understands five thousand in this context to mean five thousand distinct characters.[6]

That would give a Han scribe a vocabulary approximately equal to that of a modern Chinese person who has studied literature or history to an advanced level. Such a person typically knows around five or six thousand characters. This exceeds the vocabulary of an average person in modern China, which usually runs to between three and four thousand graphs.[7] Other researchers believe that the figure five thousand refers to a text comprising that many graphs in total, rather than five thousand different characters.[8] Either way, the statute requires a scribe to have a very substantial written vocabulary.

A person who hoped to pass for scribe would need to invest a great deal of time and effort in preparing to meet those requirements. And there were significant hurdles to doing that. As K. E. Brashier describes the situation, these difficulties arose from multiple sources. One of these was attitudes. Not everyone valued canonical or literary learning. More concretely, it required resources that were not available to everyone, in particular access to exemplary texts and a knowledgeable teacher, as well as free time for study.[9] Those requirements limited who could achieve a scribal level of facility with reading and writing.

Most scholars who have considered questions of literacy do so with one or both of these two models in mind. They may envision a literato, or potential literato, possessing exceptional talent and learning, at work among the classics and canons—in other words, a Yang Xiong or one of his readers. Or they may conceive of the question in terms of scribes and officials, whose station required them to master a vocabulary subject to quantification and verification. Without disagreeing about the position and characteristics of literacy in elevated culture and in official service, I suggest that working with a more nuanced conception of interaction with writing and written material will allow us to understand a part of early society beyond those groups.

My Proposal

The shift in understanding I propose has a number of aspects to it. Part of the shift concerns the definition of literacy, which is a complicated matter. Intrinsic to the matter of defining this difficult concept as I would like to, however, is considering the relationship between text and the human mind. There is recent research about the mind that undermines some of the commonsense assumptions that undergird prior studies. In what follows, I will discuss conceptions of literacy and the relationship of text to the human mind and suggest that a new approach can change how we think about early China.

In order to arrive at a better understanding of how text functioned in early Chinese society, I want to frame the terms of my discussion of literacy differently than my predecessors, in two main respects. First, I concentrate most of my consideration on the consumption of written information through reading and listening and do not give reading and writing equal space. Second, I conceive of the matter not in terms of individual capabilities but instead as a characteristic of a *community*.

Most scholars, usually but not always tacitly, focus their considerations primarily or entirely on individual persons and individuals' skills, interests, and life circumstances. This is in fact what trying to establish a rate of literacy does, only on a larger scale: to figure a percentage is to calculate the number of individuals with a particular characteristic within a larger group. This approach has parallels in early sources. As I have noted, the standards Han scribes needed to pass were based on the capabilities of a given man and his suitability for a position in the bureaucracy.

Nonetheless, thinking in terms of groups is more illuminating and more suited to the premodern context. The understanding of interaction with text that I propose thus revises commonplace understandings by breaking down the association between reading and writing and by considering literacy at the level of the group, rather than the single person. Communities are of course composed of individuals, and I will not avoid all discussion of individuals. But I want to place the weight of my attention on the group, rather than the persons that comprise it.

Getting at Text in Early China

Many scholars have acknowledged that deriving a workable definition of literacy in a premodern context is tricky. How much a person has to know to qualify as "literate" varies across time and place and among languages. Most importantly for the study of antiquity, the sources from the distant past that are available to us do not lend themselves to providing the kind of evidence most researchers seek when trying to understand literacy.

Evelyn Rawski opens her widely cited study of literacy in late imperial China with the assertion that "One of the most difficult problems confronting students of premodern literacy concerns the definition of the term."[10] Robin D. S. Yates refers to an absence of "evidence to determine exactly what constituted 'literacy' for the lower orders."[11] Enno Giele has acknowledged the difficulties in defining literacy and deciding who had it in early imperial China, alluding to the fact that standard modern definitions are not well suited to the study of early history. Giele suggests a number of different ways of understanding the question, depending on the specific context.[12]

Tomiya Itaru 冨谷至 deems it *impossible* to articulate a workable standard for literacy in the case of early China due to the various types of facility with text that existed and the difficulty of understanding them on the basis of our limited sources. Particularly important for my discussion here is Tomiya's insistence that in this context reading ability and writing ability are fundamentally distinct, a point that the paleographer M. C. A. Macdonald has made more generally.[13]

This is a crucial shift. Literacy as most people commonly conceive of it concerns both abilities, reading and writing, and historians apply the same conception to antiquity.[14] Wang Haicheng, for example, asserts that in early China "Basic literacy acquisition has two goals: the ability to recognize graphs and the ability to write them."[15] Yates argues that in early China commoners needed "to be functionally literate, meaning able to meet the state's demands for competency in reading and writing."[16] I derive much inspiration from Yates's discussion and his attention to commoners, in both specific and general aspects, and I agree, "ordinary members of the population in Qin and Han times could have possessed basic literacy skills."[17] Indeed, in this book I go further than that, if in a somewhat different direction. My argumentation, though, takes another form, and asserting a distinction between reading and writing is one aspect of that.

Scholars who use the word "literacy" in a sense that combines reading and writing have good reasons for doing so. After all, the dictionary definition of the "literacy" in English does the same.[18] Nor is this fusion unique to modern times: the Han standards for scribes I mentioned already, for instance, set out requirements that specify reading *and* writing at least five thousand characters.[19] Official positions other than scribe also required their holders to have writing ability, alongside basic accountancy and familiarity with laws. Some such positions called for a familiarity with law and performing tasks that entailed writing, implying reading ability without necessarily spelling it out. The exact level of facility these requirements connote is uncertain, as they do not provide a standard for judgment. But there are numerous examples of personnel records of various sorts among the documents reflecting the importance of combined skills in reading and writing.[20] The problem is that looking only at this type of capability is too narrow, as the following example demonstrates.

One approach to looking at literacy rates, which considers the question in terms of official requirements, would be to use the number of holders of official positions requiring literacy as a proxy for the number of literate individuals in Han society. An example study in this mode extrapolates to suggest a rate of literacy among the male population in Han times of around 1.4 percent.[21] There are, however, limitations to this sort of approach, which also tell us something about the limitations of thinking in terms of reading and writing as the standard for all interaction with text. It necessarily leaves out activities outside official contexts and sets aside the possibility of reading ability only. Furthermore, the very functioning of the Han bureaucracy shows that we cannot use the standards to judge literacy, even if we are thinking about writing ability in institutional terms. For there were official positions that required literacy but not scribal status, just as there were low-ranking military bureaucrats who were not scribes and yet routinely worked with text.[22] Given the high standards and other qualifications that applied for scribes in the official bureaucracy, there must have been no few such persons whose work put them in contact with text without granting them formal status.

If this sort of extrapolation is to have any broader meaning, it must rest upon an assumption of even distribution. That is obviously not the case across so great and varied a territory as the Han empire and thus represents another limitation. There may well have been areas whose inhabitants were unacquainted with writing; we would have few documentary traces of those people, and they would fall out of the record, except perhaps as population figures recorded by government officials. In such places, the number of officials could more or less equal the number of literate persons.

That proportion does not define the number of persons who were able to interact with text everywhere, however. For as the sources of this book show, there were places where the proportions of literate persons was demonstrably higher than this sort of extrapolation would suppose. The border region military apparatus is a concrete example of such a context, a point I will come back to in the next chapter.

Despite the prevalence in the past and the present of a view that takes literacy, in the sense of competence in writing and reading, as the standard for delimiting the ability to interact with text, it leaves the scope of consideration too narrow. In the case of early imperial China this perspective derives from a focus on official duties and requirements, on the one hand, and on literary achievement on the other. Breaking away from these two modes, which have dominated previous studies, requires us to reconsider how we conceive of literacy in some important respects.

Scholars who have considered literacy in early China often treat writing and reading in this context not merely as linked but as more or less interchangeable as terms of analysis. They switch back and forth between them as needed to make a point, conflating the two. When one of the two receives more attention than the other, it is writing. The reason is clear enough: writing leaves visible traces, while reading does not. Discussing reading thus requires us to hypothesize on the basis of imperfect information, while writing's traces give us something concrete to describe. This historiographical problem is not limited to premodern China. Konrad Hirschler confronted the problem of reading's tracelessness in his study of medieval Arabic literature. His response was to look closely at the sources available from a defined chronological period and reason on that basis, rather than bringing in a modern conception of what he would like to find.[23] I attempt something similar in this book.

For those who see reading and writing as fungible, however, the safer option has always been preferable. This, too, applied also in early times: "being able to write," *neng shu* 能書 in the parlance of the Han bureaucracy, was testable and documentable in a concrete and durable fashion that being able to read was and is not. Yet while reading and writing are connected, they are two very different abilities.

Reading ≠ Writing

Writing and reading obviously have an intrinsic association: without the former, the second cannot exist; without the second, the first has little meaning. But in terms of skills and abilities, reading and writing are very different. Combining them, as prevalent understandings of literacy do, works to obscure or minimize their dissimilarities.

The basic fact of this difference is, I think, familiar to anyone reading this book. I am surely not the only person to have gotten used to typing Chinese with a phonetic method and then experienced some dismay when the pencil is back in the hand and the strokes do not always flow as they once did, and should. Something similar happens when I, who am used to relying on automatic correction when typing English, need to spell a word myself and cannot remember the spelling and need to look it up, or, worse yet, *commit an actual misspelling*. These things are simply not at issue when thinking only about reading, which is to say thinking about recognizing rather than generating words. A foreign language that one has only a reading knowledge of, or that one commonly reads but does not often speak, makes this point poignantly. Trying to write, or just speak, a language one is accustomed only to read can be humbling.

These common experiences help show that reading and writing are distinct, yet as examples they do not suffice. We need to remember how difficult the physical acts connected with writing are. They stand in stark contrast to reading, which—mental activity aside—is, in physical terms, a matter of looking. A particular kind of looking connected with a particular kind of cognition, certainly, but all things the human body does by nature. More on this in a moment.[24]

Jean-Pierre Drège has discussed the processes of learning to read and to write in medieval China. As he describes it, the acquisition of writing was more or less simultaneous with learning to read but was separate from it and pursued at a different pace. Formal instruction in reading began with engaging full texts under the tutelage of a teacher; the primary method was memorizing edifying material. Developing the ability to write began with first learning how to hold the writing brush. The student would then proceed to tracing simple characters and, eventually, to mastering word lists. In this process, the separation between reading and writing was clear and reflected an essential distinction between the two activities. For reading, there was no need to learn a new physical skill. Students could skip directly to advanced mental activity, namely, learning complex material by heart. There was no particular need to be selective about the Chinese characters that the students would learn to read. It is perhaps counterintuitive, but experimental research shows that the relative complexity of characters in terms of strokes seems to have no clear influence on the recognition of graphs. Any text the teacher chose was fair game, and the most useful vocabulary items would emerge naturally through frequent appearance.[25]

Learning to write was (and is) the opposite of this, in many respects. Writing calls for new physical skills, in addition to proficiency in the composition of characters. The initial difficulty in writing characters made it necessary to begin writing with simple graphs. The emerging appreciation during the Han period of calligraphy as a visual art, and not merely a useful skill, added yet another difficulty for learners.[26]

The need to distinguish between reading and writing is not specific to Chinese or any of the writing systems derived from it. M. T. Clanchy stresses the technical gulf between writing and reading in European manuscript cultures. He lists a specific set of skills required for writing that the modern world more or less obviates—things like using an early writing implement to form legible script. Reliably creating recognizable words is hard, and was so even in a context that did not put much weight on standardized orthography. Writing calls upon faculties that reading does not.[27] An examination of the past cannot forget this. And while Clanchy's context is European, these things are not different in kind from the writing of Chinese in early times. Both experience and history thus show that writing is harder to learn and more difficult to do than reading. Distinguishing between the two is crucial for an accurate understanding of how people interacted (and interact) with text.

All this is not to say that no members of the common classes wrote in early China. Anthony Barbieri-Low, for example, has described how handworkers such as potters made use of writing to mark their products with their names and those of their workshops.[28] But acknowledging the separation between writing and reading leads my analysis in different directions than previous studies.

Reasons and Means for Learning to Read

Disentangling writing and reading permits me to bring out several characteristics specific to reading. Some existing studies of literacy in early China concentrate on how practical utility motivated people to become literate. Scholars often conceive of that utility in terms of working with documents as part of official service as a scribe or other bureaucrat.[29] Historians, in other words, have often approached the question by considering what use a potential reader/writer would have for literacy or, by extension, what they would do with a certain text or genre. In the context of China's early governance, which was already thoroughly bureaucratic in nature in the Qin and Han periods, this utility has furthermore been understood primarily in terms of acquiring an official position. *Literate* was equated with *employable as an official*; *worth reading* was equal to *useful in one's work*.

This concentration on specific types of concrete utility reflects the general tendency among people to treat the written word as separate and removed from the rest of life, as something a person would not tangle with unless there were some concrete and discernable benefit to gain thereby.[30] Scholars conceive of engaging text as something special, something that requires a specific reason before it will happen. Historians, primarily concerned with written records of the past, embody this broader tendency.

The demands of historiography furthermore call for reasons that lend themselves to clear articulation. Immediate practical utility, identifiable in terms of institutions and official duties, has a strong appeal that has led to it becoming a primary mode of analysis. And practical utility can undoubtedly be an important motivation for learning to interact with text, now as in the past. Yet reading is much more than a mere tool of gainful employment.

M. C. A. Macdonald has cataloged assumptions about human interaction with text and writing, demonstrating their limitations. One such assumption, directly germane to this book, is the notion that utility must be the reason for literacy. Macdonald discusses an oral society that remains primarily oral despite the presence of writing: its members handle important work orally, even though the society possesses writing. For members of that group, writing serves only nonserious, even ludic, purposes. That is of course an extreme case. But the underlying point is important for the discussion here. Literacy need not be utilitarian, either primarily or exclusively. Macdonald also discusses another case that suggests nonutilitarian motivations for writing: ancient nomads who marked the landscape they dwelled in with graffiti. These graffiti had no directly practical purpose. They were a form of expression or entertainment. As Macdonald writes,

> Literacy, it seems, added an extra pastime with almost end-
> less possibilities. . . . writing in these societies fulfilled a
> real need in the lives of individuals, not in the practical,

material and economic spheres with which we are accustomed to associate it, but as a creative antidote to hours of solitary boredom.[31]

Text is not merely a tool for concrete or remunerative purposes. It can be a source of enjoyment, and this has at times proven an important impetus for expanding text consumption.[32] Text can alleviate boredom and become a creative outlet for those without other possibilities but with time on their hands. Mark Edward Lewis has examined this question in the context of early China, arguing that it is a mistake to think of facility with text as leading only to an official career.[33]

The notion that doing something with text must necessarily require an immediate and tangible benefit results from assumptions about writing's distinctiveness. The usual idea is that writing, unlike spoken language, is not part of innate human nature—that it exists outside us and our inherent characteristics.[34] Yet there is real reason to challenge this idea and to think of text as a natural phenomenon. Although Macdonald's study is a historical and philological one, his analysis in this respect meshes with results from empirical research in the fields of neuroscience and psycholinguistics.

Neuroscience and Psycholinguistics

The conception of writing as unnatural treats it as a system that exists outside the evolved mind. Of course the associations between words and their referents are, as a rule, matters of convention and exist as a system within human groups. One might thus think of writing as unnatural. That does not mean, however, that text itself is intrinsically separate from humans, nature, or human nature. Just the opposite.[35]

Neuroscientist Stanislas Dehaene has demonstrated that text has an intrinsic relationship with human nature. He discusses at length how written language depends on the human brain's built-in ability to recognize and interpret forms in the natural environment. When people developed writing, they did so without realizing it, in a way that relied on making use of neural circuitry that evolved for other purposes. Writing emerged in forms that interface with the brain's features. Shared characteristics among texts, including alphabetic scripts and others, such as Chinese, provide evidence for this. All

have common shapes and other traits that work with the systems of
our brains. Images of what happens in the brain during reading confirm this understanding. Insofar as it built upon our evolved brains,
reading is an essentially natural activity.[36]

Frank Smith spent his career studying the processes of learning
how to read. In his influential book *Understanding Reading*, Smith
arrives at more or less the same conclusion that Dehaene does by a
different route. Writing from a psycholinguistic perspective, Smith
concentrates not on the evolution of the abilities that permit reading
but rather on the process of learning how to read. Psycholinguistics,
according to Smith, holds that reading is just another form of learning, and that learning is both natural and universal among human
beings. It is not so much learning that needs explaining as it is *not*
learning that is exceptional and in need of explanation. This applies
for reading as for any other form of learning.[37]

Evidence from other fields supports Smith here. Research indicates
that evolution predisposes humans toward certain kinds of learning,
just as it does all higher organisms. The types of learning that humans
are predisposed to include precisely the kinds of shape recognition
that reading entails. This empirical evidence is independent confirmation of the same tendencies toward learning that Smith points to.[38]
Learning and learning to read are natural.

Motivations for Learning to Read

For Smith, learning to read is part of a process of seeking to understand the world around us. People learn not only to amass information for practical use, immediate or otherwise, or because another
person commands it. People learn because our nature implants that
desire in us. Learning in and of itself can bring pleasure, and reading can be part of this. Reading can provide enjoyment and thus be
something that serves as an end in itself, and not only for literati.[39]
This recalls Macdonald's work on text being a means of amusement
among nomads, who had no other concrete use for it.

As Smith explains it, several factors are required for the acquisition of reading ability, and I will refer to them in the remainder of
the chapter. The first of Smith's factors is for a person to understand
that text contains information, has meaning, and is important in the
world around him or her. Once that happens, in the presence of

text and with the availability of assistance when needed, people can learn to read.[40] Not every person will do so, and not every time, but enough people enough of the time. Looking for absolutes and black and white distinctions is both artificial and impracticable when dealing with human behavior, now and in the past. The available evidence reflects that the requirements Smith names were present among the military outposts guarding the northern borders of the Han dynasty. The preponderance of evidence suggests that at least some of the people there must have learned to read.

Text was important in early China and textual culture enjoyed tremendous prestige. As Martin Kern writes, "Toward the end of the first century BCE, two centuries after the establishment of the Chinese imperial state, writing began to assume a supreme status of cultural expression."[41] This prestige existed in the border regions, too. For the conscripts, who had been registered by bureaucrats in their home areas, sent by bureaucrats to the border, and who served within a bureaucratic military, the importance of writing for their lives cannot be doubted. If there were any possibility of doubt about that importance, contemporary reading practices meant that every soldier, conscript or otherwise, was aware of exactly what written text was—a record of language—and what it offered, which included immediate and utilitarian applications, as well as other purposes. That satisfies the first of Smith's criteria. The other criteria were present as well, as the subsequent discussion will show.

Text and Orality

I would like to shift now and consider the relationship between writing and speech. It may seem natural to juxtapose the two and place them in opposition to each other. But text has never displaced orality, especially in manuscript cultures. Textual transmission did not (mostly) replace oral transmission until late in history. The two supplemented and lived alongside each other. Thus, when we think about writing and speech in the context of early China, we must think in terms of overlap and connection.

Walter J. Ong stresses the close relationship that writing maintained with spoken word transmission in manuscript cultures, where "Writing served largely to recycle knowledge back into the oral world." Using text as a means of recording and transmitting information did not end the close connection to speech. "Manuscript cultures remained largely oral-aural even in retrieval of material preserved in texts." Only with the advent of printing did this relationship begin to shift.[42]

Histories of specific example cases reflect the overlap that Ong describes in more abstract terms. They also demonstrate that the period of overlap was lengthy. One primary theme of Clanchy's *From Memory to Written Record* is the languid pace of the shift from oral to written culture in medieval England. Clanchy describes how text only slowly acquired an authority and importance that exceeded that of speech.[43] Gregor Schoeler describes a comparable process in early Islam, where oral and aural transmission retained authority long after the advent of widespread textual culture. The final shift that gave primacy to writing came only late, and at the instigation of governmental and religious authorities.[44]

Textual and oral transmission mingled in China, as well. Kern analyzes inscriptions on bronze vessels created to mark the bestowal of official positions in preimperial, Western Zhou China. Those texts were created and then read aloud as part of the rituals for installing officials. The result was what Kern calls a "complex interplay between the oral and the written performance of text." The creation of a text recording granting a position did not replace the spoken, and thus heard, aspects.[45] Li Feng has endorsed Kern's views in this respect, further arguing that bronze vessels record only a portion of these "appointment inscriptions," as only some were inscribed on bronzes. More existed on perishable materials and have been lost. All were read aloud.[46] While epigraphic and not manuscript sources, the extant texts in these cases served the same purpose that Ong asserted for manuscripts, namely, "to recycle knowledge back into the oral world."[47] This interplay was not limited to these Zhou dynasty contexts. Bu Xianqun 卜憲群 and Giele call attention to the important role oral communication had as an adjunct of document bureaucracy in the early imperial period, as well.[48]

Audible Text in Early China

There was a more general close relationship between writing and speech in early China. The philosophical text *Master Zhuang* (*Zhuangzi* 莊子) famously asserts that "Writing is nothing but speech" 書不過

語.[49] *Master Han Fei* (*Han Feizi* 韓非子) uses similar phrases to express the idea that "Writings are talk" 書者, 言也.[50] This was more literally true in its time than it is—or may seem—now. Reading aloud was the standard mode in early China, as it was elsewhere in the ancient world.[51] The very words most often used meaning "to read" in classical Chinese, *du* 讀 and *song* 誦, implied reading aloud.[52] Silent reading was exceptional.[53] In such a context, texts would not be created with the expectation of silent reading; they would be created to be read aloud.[54] And they were. Tomiya has described the result as an "environment of recitation" under the early imperial bureaucracy.[55]

The connection between reading and reading aloud was so strong in early China that it became fixed. The *sound of reading*—that is, the sound of reading aloud—became metonymy for the study of text and evidence for the same.[56] It could likewise stand for education in a more abstract sense. In *The Weighing of Arguments* (*Lunheng* 論衡), Wang Chong 王充 (27–97) relates how Confucius's disciple Zilu 子路 was so boorish before he came under the influence of the Master that when "he heard the sounds of reading aloud" 聞誦讀之聲—which is to say the sounds of learning—he responded by blowing a raspberry.[57]

Scholars who have talked about reading aloud in premodern China have often done so with a focus on the person doing the reading and the connection, or lack thereof, to an author.[58] But it is also reasonable to conjecture that overhearing text read aloud—the same overhearing that let someone know there was studying going on—could have resulted in the transmission of information outside of this pairing. A classic example of the phenomenon comes in a well-known absurdist story from the *Master Zhuang*. There we find the account of a ruler who was reading in his hall. Because the ruler was reading aloud, a wheelwright named Bian 扁, at work carving a wheel, overheard him. "What are you reading?" the wheelwright asked, and he learned that the lord was reading the philosophy of sages. Bian then derided his lord's reading material as the "dregs" of dead men who had tried and failed to convey the ineffable through words. The story of Wheelwright Bian remained current into the Han dynasty and made its way, with changes, into compendia such as *Master of Huainan* (*Huainanzi* 淮南子) and *Han's Exoteric Commentary on the Odes* (*Hanshi waizhuan* 韓詩外傳).[59]

In this story, the transmission of information did not occur through overhearing alone. Bian needed to ask what his ruler was

reading. Still, the account suggests a conception of interaction with—
and about—text that was neither completely oral/aural nor solely
through writing; it was both. This story is especially illuminating for
the discussion here because of the connection it makes between reading, hearing, and hierarchy. For while the lord responded with anger
to Bian's audacity in critiquing his reading material, no version of
the tale remarks in any way on the fact of a handworker listening to
his ruler read unbidden; none questions the propriety of overhearing.
This might at first seem unexpected, but it is in fact natural. After
all, in a society like early China, with no particular expectation of
privacy, overhearing would be inevitable and ubiquitous. Nor was
commenting tartly when overhearing one's sovereign read limited to
Zhuangzian wheelwrights. It happened at the Han court, too.[60]

Smith reminds us that in order to learn to read, a learner needs
someone who can answer questions. As I have discussed, many officials
in the Han military bureaucracy knew how to both read and write, and
ordinary soldiers had contact with at least some of them. I describe
the structure of the military governance in some detail in the next
chapter. For now, it is enough to note that the lowest functioning
organizational unit was the squad, which consisted of three to five men
under a squad leader. Squad leaders had bureaucratic tasks—recording and reporting—that called upon them to write.[61] At the level
above the squad leader, there were other low-level officials, including
scribes and assistants, whose positions required writing facility. All
of these professional literates worked with text as part of their tasks.
I will return to these things in the next chapter. For now it suffices
to note that their presence meant the soldiers of those squads had
someone to whom they could address questions about text, especially
that most basic one: "What are you reading?"

Speech into Text

My approach in this book decenters writing, but writing remains an
important part of the picture I present. After all, this study treats
texts, which imply writing. The Han military bureaucracy required its
officials to write, which included keeping records down to the level
of the squad. Thus, just as a person could overhear another person
reading—by default, reading aloud—one could as well see someone

at work with a brush and ask, "What are you writing?" The step to dictation—"Will you write . . ."—is a small one.

The role of dictation as a mode of interacting with texts is important and often misunderstood. For dictation is a valid means of interacting with text, not one inferior to others. As Clanchy discusses, dictation is frequently treated as something that indicates a lack of literacy, because many moderns assume that only someone who could not write would not do so. There is furthermore the common assumption that a dictated text does not represent the voice of its begetter, that it is not that person's creation. But historically, these things have not been the case. In medieval society, which Clanchy studies, dictating was legitimate, perhaps superior, to writing oneself: "the most educated did not often write (they perfected the art of Latin dictation)." The act of "writing," in current understanding, subsumes two tasks: the creation of content in words and the writing down of those words. But creation and writing are different. The fact that someone composes by means of dictation and does not write out a text does not mean the text is not, or was not, that person's composition.[62] Thus, while it seems that the women creators of the letters that Bagnall and Cribiore study at times—maybe often—did not themselves wield the writing implement, their letters nonetheless preserve those women's voices.[63]

Just as hearing text read aloud was a valid way of accessing that content, so was dictation a legitimate mode of creation. This is but another facet of the close relationship between text and orality in manuscript cultures, and it applies in the context of Han China, too. In many cases we do not know who wielded the writing brush to create the text in front of us. That does not diminish the value of these pieces as products of meaningful interaction with text and valuable records of experience and voices. Yates has discussed the role of dictation, and I wish to go still further than he does in giving this mode of text creation a larger place in the life of the literate community.[64]

Getting to Text

Among the conditioning factors that Smith names, the final one is the presence of written material, without which learning to read is, naturally, impossible. David Johnson also broaches the question of access to text in his discussion of Chinese popular literature in medieval and later times. Johnson is alert to the existence of the ability to work with text at varying social levels and argues that as books became widely available, "The increased accessibility of books stimulated the growth of literacy, especially moderate literacy." Johnson argues that the lack of easy contact with text in early China worked against the spread of literacy and the emergence of popular literature in that time.[65]

I agree with Johnson that simple access to text would result in increased literacy, perhaps of a limited sort. But Johnson supposes that broad accessibility came only with the emergence and expansion of print culture. Excavated materials from the northwest indicate that, at least in certain contexts, access to text came much earlier than printing.

As will become clear in the course of this book, a variety of texts were present in the northwestern border region in Han times, all of which were potential reading material. These included not only bureaucratic documents, though those were there, too. This is one context in which we can have clear evidence of members of the common classes in proximity with edicts, poetry, letters, classics, and discursive texts, as well as documents. And as Donald Harper has recently noted, hemerological texts, a type of text that existed in many places across the realm, also emerged from the northwest.[66]

The example texts archaeologists have found are wood and bamboo writing strips from trash heaps, neglected corners, and sometimes latrines.[67] The small size of the military posts, the existence of explicitly public text, and the relaxed attitude about written materials after their creation meant the soldiers had material for reading, if they wanted it. Officially disseminated texts could constitute primers, whether or not they were so intended; the contents of trash heaps, if nothing else, would provide additional potential reading material. It takes little imagination to suppose that texts so lightly disposed of also made their ways into various hands as they made their slow way to disposal (and eventual recovery). Readings of various types, frequent listening, and overhearing would work toward developing a community around and permeated by text. This was the literate community that emerged in the desert northwest under Han occupation.

The Power of Boredom

A final ingredient is not among those Smith names specifically, although he does allude to the role of interest, and that is boredom. Macdonald notes the possibilities writing offered as a pastime to desert dwellers.[68] This is undoubtedly important for this book, for the local environment that the Han soldiers lived in was similarly bereft of ready amusement.

The level of readily available diversion was, in general, certainly lower in Han China than in the present. Yet the situation in the desert regions must have been dull by even Han standards. The conscripts lived temporarily separated from their families and ordinary lives, in a sparsely populated region of arid wastes. Staring into those same wastes and watching for the approach of enemies figured largely among the soldiers' duties. Actual armed conflict with the enemy was rare. This created an environment in which the stimulation that learning to read offered would have stood out against the austere and stony backdrop of the wastelands, providing impetus that was widely shared: the need for something to occupy one's mind. There is some evidence of entertainment among the archaeological remains of the soldiers' posts, but not much: there are indications of music, simple painting, exercise, dice, and board games, all in limited quantities.[69]

One might well doubt the appeal of, say, a name register or an equipment inventory as reading material. But under the conditions of the frontier, the mental exercise of working through the written version of one's signaling standards or a particular imperial edict would doubtless have appealed to some. And some of the texts were not governmental in nature: literary narratives, poetry, and technical texts were also present, all of which would have another sort of appeal.

The context of military installations in the border regions worked to mitigate the resource constraints that I have mentioned. Subsequent chapters of this book will show in some detail the kinds of texts that soldiers had to see and to read. And, as I discuss in the next chapter, while far from idle, the soldiers had time in which they could learn, if they chose. Their most important duty, after all, was manning watchtowers. Soldiers' and officers' schedules included time for rest and allowed them regular days off.[70] The presence of literates at least at the level of squad leader, even if we temporarily set aside other soldiers, meant there was someone who could teach or at least answer questions and read aloud to them.

This is not to say that every soldier learned to read, or that most did. Any sort of black and white, yes or no assertion in this respect would oversimplify a complicated situation. My analysis provides good reason to think that a significant number must have acquired some ability to meaningfully interact with text, including through reading. We should not imagine a stark distinction between those who read and those who could not. Rather, we should conceive of each individual as possessing abilities that existed along a spectrum with innumerable gradations between absolutely nothing and absolutely everything, between those able to read every text themselves, those who only listened or spoke, and those whose abilities lay between these two extremes.[71] The last was surely the largest group. The likelihood that most persons would have at most acquired what would be for us in the present a very limited ability does not mean this was without consequence. As Ong notes, "It only takes a moderate degree of literacy to make a tremendous difference in thought processes. . . . A little literacy goes a long way."[72]

Determining an exact number or percentage of individuals who could read is an insoluble problem. Conceiving of a range of ability, a spectrum that stretches without a definite break between the two extremes, further complicates posing the question by precluding any easy resolution. Placing an individual at a specific location on that spectrum would require information that is, in nearly all cases, lacking. There is, however, a better approach than this focus on individuals' abilities, an approach that both averts these intractable problems and better fits the intellectual context of early China. That is to think in terms of the group rather than only of its constituents.

Individual Literacy versus a Literate Community

We in the modern world generally conceive of reading and writing in terms of a person's competency, a conception that has influenced how scholars think about the past. As Nicholas Orme explains, "We think of literacy as a personal skill, because we live in a society that places an emphasis on people as individuals." Things in the premodern world were different. There, the focus was less on the individual and more on the community.[73] This is not to say that the individual was not important in early China.[74] But for people in China of the time, as in other premodern societies, cultural production and dissemination was, generally speaking, a group matter.

Some researchers working in the field of early China have noted the key function of groups in textual culture. Lewis has written that in early China "Learning in solitude may have existed, but the generation and transmission of texts was a collective activity."[75] Lewis concentrates on elevated texts and formal contexts, the provinces of power holders and high culture. This book examines other parts of society, where conceptually similar things were happening, with different texts among different groups.

Thinking in terms of community rather than individuals also provides a way to work around the intractable questions connected with determining rates of literacy.[76] According to Bagnall, it is impossible to know with certainty exactly how many were literate in any ancient society.[77] Yates has made this same point about early China specifically, where even the size of the population remains unclear.[78]

Despite the attention such questions have attracted and the difficulties inherent in addressing them reliably, the available results do not seem to offer correspondingly meaningful insights. This is the case both within and outside China. As Alan K. Bowman, paleographer and historian of the Roman world, writes:

> Attempts at quantifying and measuring literacy in the ancient world face formidable difficulties, and it is much more important and fruitful to consider the ways in which use of the written word was embedded in the institutional and social structures of a society and the functions which depended on that use.[79]

Shifting away from attempting exact quantification does at least two things. It recognizes the limitations of what we can assert about the past. It also invites us to see that other questions, about which we can speak, are more promising.

Macdonald has examined the many different forms interaction with text took on the Arabian Peninsula in premodern times. He finds the question of what individuals were doing is, in most cases, unanswerable at the distance of two thousand years. Macdonald instead considers literacy at the level of the society, saying, "I would define a 'literate society' as one in which reading and writing have become essential to its functioning, either throughout the society . . . or in certain vital aspects, such as bureaucracy, economic and commercial activities, or religious life."[80] Thus, as Bagnall puts it, "a society may be called literate even where a very high percentage of its members are not."[81]

Literate Community

While I follow Macdonald in thinking about literacy at the level of the group rather than the individual, I write in terms of *community* rather than society. The term "community" has a useful flexibility in comparison to society. While society implies a large size and an advanced level of complexity, community can denote a group of persons who are linked together by some characteristic, often simple physical closeness.[82]

I also draw inspiration from Brian Stock's work on the "textual communities" that came into being around religious texts in medieval Europe. In Stock's use, a textual community formed at the intersection of two groups of persons, the literate and illiterate, and a text or set of texts. Like many others, Stock thinks of literacy in terms of the ability to read and write. He adds, however, important additional aspects. One of these is the utilization of text, irrespective of whether someone read it personally. Stock takes into account oral transmission, reading aloud, or otherwise relaying content via word of mouth. The situation in a given community was thus not an absolute distinction between literate persons who could read and nonliterate persons who did not read and had no access to what a particular text conveyed. The situation was rather a blending of two forms of communication, reading and speaking/listening. The content of a text was separate from any particular instantiation of it. Transmission could take the form of text for those who read, and speech for those who did not. After transmission, in whatever form, the text came to constitute the center of the community, a means for it to communicate and to function.[83]

For the modern literate, transmission other than by reading oneself can seem unreliable and untrustworthy compared with the fixity and durability of writing, but this is a product of a particular way of dealing with text and is not universal.[84] It was not necessarily for everyone to read everything—or even anything—by themselves to be part of the literate community, and this participation need not imply some lesser degree of affiliation.

In the case of the Han military community in the northern border regions, there was no single text that defined it. The defining quality of the community was that it comprised officers, soldiers, and families physically present in the region, who lived in close proximity to each other. Texts played an important role in the community, but in a manner unlike the religious writings that Stock considered. These texts were the set of texts of various forms and the practices associated with them by which the community functioned, and which its members consumed in various forms. I contend that in this aspect, as in others, the bureaucracy in early China occupied the cultural space that religion did in medieval Europe and provided much of the developmental impetus that religion did there.[85]

This conception of community connects to the idea of the "script community" that Robert W. Bagley has put forth in his discussion of writing's emergence in China. Bagley argues against the common idea that writing in China developed for religious purposes and suggests instead that writing had its origins in administration. The earliest administrators as a group constituted what Bagley calls a "script community," composed of people who used writing and taught others to do so, including others who were likewise going to become bureaucrats. This community ensured the use and perpetuation of what was then a relatively new form of communication.[86] Bagley's focus is on writing and learning to write. This resembles that of other scholars who consider literacy in early China, rather than my interest in reading and oral/aural communication. Yet in different ways, Lewis, Bagley, and I all recognize the position of the community as a nexus for activity with text. I draw from the definitions of literacy that Macdonald, Bagnall, and others employ. They consider the question at the level of the community and do not seek evidence that a specific individual could personally write. In the same way, I approach my sources with an eye to what they tell us about the function of text in the life and relationships of the community.

As will become clear in the course of this book, the soldiers and their families interacted with each other in different ways. They lived in a general geographical proximity, within which there was regular exchange of information. They knew or could know each other by name. This is not to say that there was no link to a larger structure, and in the conclusion I explore those possibilities. But that larger structure was not constitutive of the community I study.

The word "community" may call to mind Benedict Anderson's influential work on "imagined communities." The community that is the subject of my study, however, was not "imagined"—at least not within the context of my study. In Anderson's analysis, people who are in close proximity and personally acquainted with each other are part of a different sort of community than those who imagine theirs into existence.[87]

Conscription and the Literate Community

This book treats a community of people who were in proximity to each other. For many of its members, participation in the community was not voluntary. Those members of the community were present in the region as part of a system of conscription. I will further discuss conscription, including the origins of the conscripted soldiers, in the next chapter. Here I wish to concentrate on the relationship between obligatory service and the community.

I must first note that not all members of the community were conscript soldiers. There were also professional soldiers present, as well as officers. There were men who took money to act as substitutes and do others' service in their place. And there were, at least sometimes, members of groups from outside the Han empire, who allied themselves with the Han out of interest.[88]

Importantly, the families of the soldiers were present, too. Han government policy encouraged the wives and children of soldiers (both conscripts and other) to accompany them on service deployment to the borders. The government maintained records of their presence and provided rations and funds to support them. They were nevertheless, as a rule, not employed by the Han government.[89] As letters I examine in chapter 8 show, their membership in the community went beyond mere presence and included acquaintance with their husbands' and fathers' comrades.

This military context is accessible to us due to a happy conjunction—happy for the historian, at least. The system of required service brought men and, in many cases, their families to the border regions. Han systems of governance were highly bureaucratic in all aspects, including the military. These systems created and deposited a great deal of written material at military posts, which—along with much else—recorded the names of men, their families, and their circumstances. I discuss these records more in the next chapter.

Hsing I-t'ien 邢義田, Miyake, and Yates have all, in different ways, noted that these systems necessarily put soldiers in contact with written information as a means of communication and led to the dissemination of literacy. My project takes inspiration from all three, although this book goes in a different direction from them. Hsing was the first to point to a relationship between military service and learning. He concentrates on what he calls "education" among members of the military, who needed to read things like the codes used in communicating visually across distances.[90] For reasons that I will discuss later, I eschew a focus on education per se. Nonetheless, Hsing's study represents an important insight into the multifaceted impact of military service on society in early China. Miyake discusses a number of types of documents in this context. He considers in particular both written and oral communication of information in the context of military communications standards, the relationship between the two, and how they worked to disseminate knowledge of and about text.[91] This is an important observation, and one that I find echoes ideas from the cross-cultural research I discuss in this chapter. It is also a point I wish to apply more broadly. Yates's consideration of the matter makes explicit some very important points. The most vital of these is the recognition that text—Yates writes in terms of literacy—worked in various social strata, and not only among men, but also among women. While my argumentation is different from Yates's, he and I share these conclusions.[92]

Hsing frames his consideration in terms of education, but I do not limit discussion of interaction with text to education per se, or its results. This is not to say that Hsing is wrong. Clearly, in terms of military training, education is part of what was happening. And there is reason to think education of different sorts was happening within the context of sites that I study. There is evidence of deliberate learning in the border regions, including practice writing, sometimes of specialist vocabulary. Christopher Foster has examined didactic texts used for the purpose of acquiring literacy, fragments of which archaeologists have found at various Han sites.[93]

Despite all that, and without rejecting those conclusions, I concentrate elsewhere. The word "education," formal or not, suggests a particular intentionality, and thinking in those terms would leave this study too narrow. *Learning* certainly happened, including specifically military matters and learning to read. But I want to consider how that was a side effect of other processes, pursued not because of an interest in education and instead out of boredom or any number of other possibilities.

The word education also brings implications of institutional structures with that purpose. Yates notes that we do not have evidence of schools for commoners in Han times.[94] Yet classrooms are far from the only place where learning can take place, including learning to engage textual information. Neither schools nor formal educational processes are required for learning to read.[95] As I have noted, the context of military service in the Han northwest provided other routes to interact with text. Military service would of course be unlikely to be the first time anyone alive during the Han would have seen text. Written household registration was universal and renewed each year, coins bore labels, marketplace goods bore written prices, and craftsmen's wares bore makers' marks.[96] Edicts and other bureaucratic writings that existed across the realm also provided possibilities, a point to which I will return in the conclusion.

Nor would any single individual's ability to access text by reading delimit his or her access to the information therein. Living in a literate community meant that the community's ability to interact with text was the deciding factor, and it is to the community that we should look. This community was not autochthonous, which has the potential to raise questions of how representative it was. Those questions are, I think, simply unanswerable at present, perhaps forever. The preservation of records about the people who once lived here resulted from conditions that do not apply elsewhere. This is not the only place where archaeologists have recovered detailed records of the population.[97] Yet the geographic and chronological dispersal of those records means that we have no way to judge exactly how representative our sample of documents is. As a result, while I discuss the larger implications of this study in the conclusion, I do not seek to make specific and concrete generalizations beyond the community that forms the context of my study.[98] In the following chapter, I consider that context further.

Chapter Two

Contexts and Sources

This chapter provides background on the military presence that left behind the sources for this book. The northwestern border region during the Han dynasty is a good case study for my purposes due to several reasons. The functioning of the military bureaucracy generated written records that preserved information about the persons present, including their names, their hometowns, and, sometimes, what they were doing. The dry climate preserved those records, making them available for us to read. We do not get the sort of extensive information about individuals that would permit a detailed picture of one or more persons. But there is enough detail to speak about the community that was there. That is the level I will focus on.

Scattered finds in other geographical areas dating to the early imperial period indicate that every member of the Han population was subject to recordkeeping. But other Western Han sites do not provide the kind of variety and density of texts that sites from the northwest do. It is thus impossible to show that the records or the population I discuss in this book are representative in this respect. These texts illustrate a single intriguing example, which invites us to think differently about how people in early imperial times interacted with text. I therefore do not seek to generalize my arguments, although some wider considerations come in the conclusion. Future research and new archaeological finds may well provide the information such a project would need.

I intend this chapter to give the reader the information necessary to understand the remainder of the book. It is not a detailed overview of the institutional structure of the region in Han times, something that would fall outside the scope of this book.[1] Along similar lines, in this book I treat a period of more than a century. Inevitably, there were changes to systems and methods over that time, but they fall outside the scope of my study.[2]

This chapter begins with the cross-cultural encounter that brought the Han military to the northwest border region. I sketch the Han military presence in the northwest and the documents that it produced in their physical aspects and contemporary purposes. This chapter ends with a brief discussion of the important archaeological excavations that brought the documents to light and made their study possible.

Contacts at the Border

Conflicts between the people of what would become China and their culturally distinct neighbors date to earliest knowable times and remain a recurring theme throughout the imperial period.[3] Relations along the northern border in Han times were dominated by contacts with the steppes people who lived in that area and further to the north. In the late third century BCE, around the time of China's unification under the Qin, a new confederation emerged on the steppes to become the largest external threat the early empire faced. The Xiongnu 匈奴 were a heterogeneous group of pastoralists who raised horses and sheep on the grasslands of northern Asia. They did not live in permanent buildings and yet were not fully nomadic, either, as they did not roam without pattern or plan. Rather they moved their herds through specific grazing areas over the course of the year and had set locations for gatherings, which were the settings for political and religious activities.

While the groups that comprised the Xiongnu confederation shared cultural traits, they were originally different. The Xiongnu union was political, not ethnic. Although they lacked the ability— and perhaps the desire—to conquer the whole of Han territory, the Xiongnu were superior to the Han in battle. Their warriors were famous for toughness, skill, and mobility. These traits enabled them to carry out raids on Han territory more or less at will. The Han emperors who reigned through the first half of the second century BCE addressed the threat with a series of treaties that sought to buy off the Xiongnu. That approach did not work, but circumstances in the first decades of the Han dynasty did not permit using force to resolve the situation.

The civil war that ended with the establishment of the Han dynasty in the late third century BCE did major damage to the economy, both in terms of direct costs and disruption to agriculture and other forms of production. By the time Emperor Wu 武 (Liu Che 劉徹, r. 140–86 BCE) ascended the throne, the situation was improving, and improvement continued in the first years of his reign. The strengthening economy provided resources that enabled Emperor Wu and his court to adopt a new, aggressive stance toward the Xiongnu and other steppes peoples. Toward the end of the second century BCE, the Han military extended its reach to the northwest and west, beyond the vague borders that had defined the empire previously. This marks the beginning of the primary history of Han activity in the region.

Han forces pushed the Xiongnu back, disrupting the confederation's relations with its allies. By around 119 BCE, the Han had established a level of control over parts of the western reaches. Over the subsequent half century or so, the Han put in place a border defense system. The overall governmental structure of the Han empire centered on administrative districts called commanderies (jun 郡), and they established four new ones in the border regions: Zhangye 張掖, Dunhuang 敦煌, Wuwei 武威, and Jiuquan 酒泉, all within modern Gansu Province and the Inner Mongolia Autonomous Region.

In those areas the Han defended parts of the territory by connecting previously existing sections of walls and building new ones, putting in place a series of watch- and signal towers staffed with officers and soldiers to keep watch on the border. The Han sent conscript farmers to the agricultural lands, established military colonies to supply imperial forces, and set up official postal relay routes to enable the sending of documents. Han civilians also settled—willingly or under duress—in the areas of fertile farmland to take advantage of the soil's productivity and the trade from and through the region.

The Han soldiers in the border region were part of the effort to defend and to extend the Han empire's territory. As Nicola Di Cosmo has pointed out, both aspects were salient, and if anything the latter was more important. The Han project was, despite contemporary rhetoric that portrayed it as defensive, an expansion.[4] The border between the Han empire and the steppes shifted back and forth over the subsequent centuries. Intermittent armed conflict continued, as did the peaceful movement of people across what was, in most places, a theoretical line. In the middle of the first century, the Xiongnu confederation divided into two, with some of its population joining the Han and others shifting their grazing lands further north on the steppes. This particular group never again posed the great threat they once had.

Han soldiers remained in the northwestern border regions into the second century CE. Rather than firm control over the entire expanse, Han power was at best patchy and localized. The weakening of central control at the end of the Han period in the second century coincided with the growing power of other groups of semi-nomads, including the Qiang 羌. The Qiang had long challenged Han governance, and in the shifting dynamics of the border region of the second century they became so potent that they contributed to the end of Han supremacy in the region and the fall of the dynasty that followed shortly thereafter. Later dynasties would also station troops in the area, and indeed there is a substantial military presence in China's western and northwestern wastes even today.

The Han Military Bureaucracy

The commandery was the basic mid-level (i.e., below the empire and above the locality) administrative unit in most of the Han empire. Commanderies are similar to modern US states in some respects: they stand between high-level, central government and local-level authorities, and they vary widely in size and population density. Traditional historiography held that the Qin established thirty-six commanderies after unification in the late third century BCE. More recently, excavated materials have shown that there were in fact more, although the ongoing discovery and publication of documents means that any count is necessarily tentative. The Han later expanded the number of commanderies, reaching some 103 commanderies and princely states (*guo* 國) around 81 BCE.[5]

Commanderies encompassed two main types of administrative structure, one in the interior, away from the borders, and the other in the borderlands. In both, a commandery administrator (*junshou* 郡守), assisted by a large staff, had overall supervisory responsibility for the variety of offices that managed the government of a commandery. In the interior, away from the borderlands, military matters, including things that we would now consider law enforcement, such as combatting gangs of robbers, were the province of the chief commandant (*duwei* 都尉) of the commandery. Other administrative tasks were delegated to prefectures (*xian* 縣) that made up the commandery. Each prefecture had a prefect (*xianling* 縣令) and a staff to administer it and was further divided into districts (*xiang* 鄉) and villages (*li* 里), each with its own staff of officials.[6]

Things were different in the northwestern border commanderies of Dunhuang, Wuwei, Jiuquan, and Zhangye. There, rather than a single chief commandant, a given commandery administrator would have under him chief commandants of several regions (*bu* 部). The regional chief commandants' duties concerned not only military matters but also other aspects of administration, effectively creating a mixed governance. Beneath the regional chief commandants were companies (*houguan* 候官) under company commanders (*houguanzhang* 候官長). The documents from Juyan 居延 record two particular regions, among others, one containing four companies and the other five. One of those regions was named Juyan and also contained a company by that same name.[7]

A company commander's standard salary was, in theory, equal to what a prefect at the low end of the corresponding pay scale in the interior would earn. This suggests the company was approximately equivalent in importance to a prefecture. Like a prefect, each company commander had a staff supporting him, including an assistant (*cheng* 丞), a frontier commandant (*saiwei* 塞尉), a foreman clerk (*lingshi* 令史), a commandant clerk (*weishi* 尉史), and other officials. Most numerous were the hundred or so soldiers that comprised the company. The soldiers formed squads (*sui* 燧, also written 隧 and 隊) of three to five men under a squad leader (*suizhang* 燧長). The squad was the smallest organizational group in the border area. Sometimes several squads would be combined to form a troop (also called *bu* 部). The low officers who commanded these units came from local areas, and the material conditions of their lives were not different from those they commanded. The social ranks of company commanders and squad leaders were, like those of the conscripts, within the range of the ordinary population. Squad leaders drew provisions and a small stipend from government sources at rates that left them strapped. They lived both near their men and very much like them, suffering penury and hardships that were proverbial.[8]

Conscripts and Others

For much of the Han dynasty, male commoners were subject to two years of compulsory military service. One of the years in service was spent training. The other was on active duty, often under the leadership of low-ranking officers in the northwest. There, they formed the main part of the border defense force. The system began before the Han and ended in the first century CE.[9]

The soldiers who guarded the northwest came from many places, often quite far away from their duty stations. Practices of recording and tracking identity in early imperial times provide important details about how far many of them traveled. The bureaucracy used three pieces of information to identify an individual: name, social rank (jue 爵), and location of household registration. The last of these consisted of the name of a village and, if that could be ambiguous, commandery. Unless a person changed his or her place of registration, it remained the same, even if that person was away from home on extended government service.[10]

In keeping with these practices, documents among the Han finds from Juyan that identify individual soldiers record their places of registration and thus their geographical origins. Those origins were dispersed over the Han realm. While some soldiers came from the border region itself, many conscripts came from interior commanderies outside the region. Men representing a large proportion of localities throughout the empire were present among the border defense troops. Paleographic evidence shows that soldiers from some forty-eight commanderies and princedoms were present, hailing from over 170 prefectures and some 670 villages. Specific places that provided large numbers of troops include locations in modern Henan and Hubei, many hundreds of miles from the northwest border. In many cases, only one or two conscripts came from a given village. An intriguingly large number came from the area of the Western Han capital, Chang'an 長安 (Shaanxi). In a few cases, records indicate several soldiers from an area at a particular installation. But the sources do not suggest any systematic attempt to group conscripts according to their regional origins.[11] There was presumably a great deal of variation in the language spoken by people from different regions. As Miyake notes, we do not know how they solved that problem. We know only that they did.[12]

Traditional sources state that men served sometime between the ages of twenty-two and fifty-five. Archaeologically recovered texts reflect the presence of an even broader range of ages, mentioning men from seventeen to sixty-eight.[13] The men's families often accompanied them, and records list soldiers' wives, children, and parents. Like the conscripts, the family members also received food through the military bureaucracy. These provisions, combined with the medical care available to military personnel and, presumably, their dependents, suggest that there were aspects in which life along the border might have held some appeal for families. Policy encouraged and eventually required that family members accompany the troops. The families present in the records, about which we have little information due to source limitations, tend to be nuclear families of a husband, wife, and their child or children. Wives performed important work, including farming and maintaining the soldiers' clothing.[14] As I show in chapter 8, women were very much a part of the life of the literate community in the northwest.

Hans Bielenstein has written on the basis of traditional sources that "When the two years of military service had been completed, the men were discharged and sent home to resume their civilian lives."[15] Paleographic sources confirm this. A permanent change in domicile would have entailed a change to the conscripts' identifying information, which we do not see. There was furthermore specific terminology used for soldiers who were to remain, reflecting that most of the soldiers returned home. Records pertaining to troops traveling between their home areas in those regions and the border zone confirm these movements. When those men went home, they would bring the experiences and knowledge acquired while doing service with them—experiences that included encounters with text.[16]

The Soldiers' Tasks

Common soldiers fulfilled a variety of tasks connected with guarding the border. The most important of these was simply observing for sight or sound of the enemy. The admonition "Assiduously keep a lookout!" 謹候望 appears repeatedly among the documents, and the border guards' diligence in this respect finds mention in early history.[17] The soldiers transmitted information about emergencies, another important duty, and passed along alerts they received from others. (The signaling codes they used for those purposes feature in the next chapter.) The soldiers built and maintained the walls, towers, and other structures in and around where they lived and worked, and the roads that ran in the area. They also constructed and maintained artificial sand flats (*tiantian* 天田) that would show footprints, stockades, and suspended lines as means to detect and deter surreptitious enemy intrusions. Some conscripts lived away from the lines, growing grain to provide for the troops; others worked in armories, granaries, or in the bureaucratic offices and postal service of the military administration. They and their leaders kept records of soldiers' activities, and their performance was checked by visiting officers.[18]

Documents

The documents that I draw upon for my study come to us in the form of trash and other detritus that the Han dynasty military bureaucracy produced and then left behind. They are documents produced by military bureaucrats and soldiers working in offices at the level of the chief commandant, company, troop, or squad, along with those that emanated from border control stations, granaries, and armories.[19]

A *historical* interest in ancient garbage may at first seem counterintuitive. The material objects that dominate such finds are themselves usually the domain of archaeology and art history, after all, rather than history. Roger S. Bagnall, who works in the Mediterranean world, has pointed out that throwing documents away turns out to have been a very good way to preserve them. People in antiquity generally piled trash in out-of-the-way places and left it. That prevented the sort of casual destruction that accompanies frequent contact and use. Documents that would have disappeared over time were in this way preserved. The contents of these trash piles are, however, very irregular, in that they contain whatever people happened to throw away. When this includes documents, as in the case of the sites I draw from, the result is quite different from a systematic archive.

Although it was not random, the preservation of documents as part of trash resulted from a combination of contemporary practice and environmental factors over the course of centuries. This unsystematic manner of accumulation created a "lumpy" material record, with many examples of certain kinds of things and few or none of others, which may not represent the distribution or proportion of documents in the original context.[20]

The Han dynasty northern border follows this same pattern. We have thousands of documents, but as a data set they are extremely lumpy: there are many examples of some types, few of others, and more that we know must have existed but are unrepresented among finds to date. There are surely still more that we are unaware of. This lumpiness rules out any sort of easy generalization. It is also impossible to predict exactly what sort of future lumps archaeologists may find. Thus, while it is possible to describe what archaeologists have found, any general typology is perforce provisional and incomplete.

This has not stopped scholars from trying to enumerate, on the basis of archaeological finds to date, the types of documents that the Han military bureaucracy produced. The variety of approaches scholars use further complicates the creation of typologies. Most categorizations employ some combination of physical description, Han-time labels, content, and other factors. This began with Luo Zhenyu 羅振玉 (1866–1940) and Wang Guowei 王國維 (1877–1927) in the early twentieth century and continues today.[21]

Considering an example typology will help show what I mean about the difficulties of organization. The authors of one representative categorization of materials from the Dunhuang region preface their classification schema by saying, "the meaning of most [of the documents] is clear and classification relatively obvious." They then divide the documents into twenty types, mostly on the basis of content (rather than form or other characteristics), ranging from "edicts" to "other." The numbers of examples of each type vary a great deal. Some types are represented by a single known example, others by a few, and some by many. What they call "registers," for instance, are by far the most numerous, representing a tremendous lump of more than 450 examples. The authors further divide "registers" into fifty subtypes on the basis of subject matter, and a number of those subtypes are divided yet again into sub-subtypes.[22]

I do not criticize this elaborate typology, although its heterogeneous groupings and multiple layers belie the authors' contention that classification is "relatively obvious." The categorization's intricacies reflect the complexity of trying to create a system out of materials that were created with a less than scrupulous adherence to standards, if and when standards existed, and then preserved through the vagaries of refuse disposal. The complexities accentuate the impression of the record's lumpiness. The significant difficulties of interpretation and the variations in the physical forms of the sources, as well as the likelihood of future finds adding to our knowledge of the military bureaucracy, limit the usefulness of a cataloging or typological approach to these documents.

In his discussion of source materials from the northwest, Tomiya Itaru draws attention to the problems and limitations inherent in creating a typology of the documents. Tomiya is mindful of the fact that we are looking at things that were unneeded and so discarded and, furthermore, that the specific examples we see were often copies. He acknowledges that the mediated and intrinsically provisional nature of the data set means that a definitive description is impossible. He seeks rather to understand the documents as bearers of data within a system that generated, stored, transported, and used information. Tomiya's sophisticated analysis does not take as its starting point the physical form or objective content of documents. Instead he makes a primary distinction between documents on the basis of their position in the document flow of the bureaucracy, beginning with the matter of whether they moved. The first set Tomiya considers comprises documents that moved. Some of these texts came from other official installations, including those that arrived for further dissemination to one or more other places. This group includes the documents created at a given office to be sent elsewhere as part of its work, and the labels that directed the movement of documents via the official post. Tomiya's second set contains those documents that did not move, because they were created and retained at a given office. These include records such as accounts, name registers, lists of tasks completed, and more, along with the documents an office needed to function, such as reference texts, calendars, certificates, and labels.[23]

Comparing Tomiya's conception with a purely descriptive approach to categorization helps bring out a shortcoming of the latter. Treating writing strips in an antiquarian fashion—as individual examples—could focus the analysis around enumeration and creating a comprehensive catalog. This would threaten to divorce the documents from their original context.[24] As Tomiya reminds us, this was an information *system*, in which text played a primary role. This system established and maintained two-way connections—real, however attenuated—between the Han government and its subjects, including those in lower social classes in the border regions. An analysis that loses sight of this fact, however thorough it may be, will not grasp the importance of the system.

Tomiya's analysis gives primacy to the movement of information through the bureaucracy, which is a vital point. As a rule, documents were created to record and transmit data and narratives, or to accomplish specific official tasks related to those things. Tomiya's approach keeps the documents in their historical context, treating them as part of a functional system primarily concerned with information. Only a relatively small number of documents do something different. It happens that this book deals with some exceptional examples, as will be clear in subsequent chapters. But those exceptions, too, existed in the larger context of the bureaucratic system.

Much of the documentation from the Juyan and the other commanderies is recordkeeping, accounting, and reporting on the activities of the soldiers who guarded the border. The majority is most evidently the stuff of institutional history. This explains in part the importance of that mode of study in previous scholarship. The fragmentary state of most excavated documents imposes limits on our understanding. Yet among all that remains there is much evidence of the lives of the conscripted soldiers who lived in the Juyan area. One of the core contentions of this book is that the evidence shows that in at least this area, the men in the border regions were part of the broader textual culture of the Han realm.

The Medium

The usual writing medium in Han times was strips of soft woods and bamboo. (Some scholars refer to these as "slips."[25]) Writing strips generally made use of locally available materials. Because the dry climate in northwestern China does not support the growth of bamboo, there are few bamboo strips present among the manuscripts from the northwest; those present necessarily represent imports from distant areas. The great majority are wood.[26]

Researchers have identified a number of the tree species that provided writing media. Tamarisk (*Tamarix chinensis* Lour.) is one, and it remains common in Gansu, Qinghai, and Xinjiang. Another, white poplar (*Populus tomentosa* Carr.), grows widely in northern China, while the particular spruce the soldiers often used (*Picea neoveitchii* Mast.) is found in the mountainous areas of northeastern Hubei, Shaanxi, Shanxi, and Gansu. Willows, including weeping willow (*Salix babylonica* Linn.), grow widely in China, and pines are similarly widespread and furnished writing material. This list of wood types does not represent a catalog of all possibilities. The rule for materials seems to have been to use whatever suitable wood grew nearby, rather than to employ designated species. There are records of the purchase of wood for use as a writing material, although soldiers surely also gathered wood to make writing materials, as well.[27]

Han dynasty wooden writing strips varied a great deal in both size and purpose. The most usual length for writing strips in that period was a bit over twenty-three centimeters, corresponding to one Han foot (*chi* 尺). Width varied more than length. How wide a given strip was depended first on how much writing it was to contain. It was common for a strip to be one to two centimeters wide and contain one line of full-sized script, or two lines of somewhat smaller text, in which case a strip would be somewhat wider. The variation in the dimensions was sometimes meaningful, as an imperial edict would occupy a strip wide enough for two lines of writing despite having only one; the strip would also be longer, about twenty-five and a half centimeters, due to the addition of an extra inch (*cun* 寸, approximately 2.3 cm.) to indicate the importance of its contents. Some of the documents' variation is thus due to the existence of different standards for different types of content, and the lack of conventions for other forms. Further variation arises from the development of standards over time. Even at its strictest, adherence to these standards varied a great deal and for many reasons, not least the natural irregularity of wood. Early recorders often bound strips together with hemp cord to form longer documents, and those strips were a bit more standardized. But there were also many single-strip documents, which tended to vary even more in their physical characteristics.[28]

large parts of Central Asia and nearby areas. In 1907 and 1914 he led the excavation of many small border posts from the Han period in what he and others referred to as the Dunhuang region. Those excavations took place in what had been in Han times Dunhuang and the neighboring commandery, Jiuquan.[32]

A couple of decades later, the Sino-Swedish Expeditions, which also explored Central Asia, carried out archaeological excavations in the Juyan region. While Hedin, as head of the overall project, is better known, Folke Bergman (1902–1946) led and indeed carried out much of the most important early work in the Juyan area himself, including the recovery of the materials known as the "Juyan Han strips" (Juyan Han *jian* 居延漢簡). The cataloging, transcription, and publication of those strips was an international matter, undertaken in collaboration with Chinese scholars such as Lao Gan 勞榦 (1907–2003) and others. The reception of European archaeologists' work in the Juyan and Dunhuang regions is complicated. While Europeans' contributions to archaeology in the region were significant, their work has also been the subject of much criticism in China. In some cases that criticism is clearly warranted, as in the case of the destructive removal of artwork from the Mogao Grottoes 莫高窟 at Dunhuang. In other cases the situation is at least arguably ambiguous. Bergman, for example, went to some trouble to obtain authorization for his expeditions from Chinese officials. From the modern perspective, however, all these activities represent the abstraction of cultural relics from China.[33]

In the 1970s and later, teams of archaeologists from the Gansu provincial museum and other official institutions carried out extensive excavations at sites in what is commonly called the Juyan area. The bulk of the written materials they located constitutes the "new Juyan strips" (Juyan *xinjian* 居延新簡). Archaeological teams from provincial and city-level entities also pursued further excavations at a variety of small sites in the Dunhuang area.[34] In addition, there have been numerous minor finds in these areas, at the sites of watchtowers and other small fortifications that dotted the border region.[35] A final publishing project deserves special attention. Bergman first noted the Jianshui Jinguan 肩水金關 site during his explorations of the area around the Eji'na River. Jianshui Jinguan was a border control station under the Jianshui 肩水 commandant (*duwei*), to the south of Juyan. Excavations there in the early 1970s turned up thousands of strips. A multi-volume series has appeared, making color photographs, infrared images, and transcriptions of the entire corpus available for reference.[36]

Chapter Three

Posted Texts

But while I was sitting down, I saw something that drove me crazy. Somebody'd written . . . on the wall. It drove me damn near crazy. I thought how Phoebe and all the other little kids would see it, and how they'd wonder what the hell it meant, and then finally some dirty kid would tell them—all cockeyed, naturally—what it means, and how they'd all think about it and maybe even worry about it for a couple of days. I kept wanting to kill whoever'd written it.

—Holden Caulfield

The preceding chapters have provided the intellectual and historical contexts for my study and made the case for thinking about forms of interaction with text that go beyond the usual definitions of literacy. In this chapter, I shift to begin looking at sets of excavated texts from the Han border areas. Here I examine the standardized codes by which soldiers communicated at a distance. They attest to the dissemination of information from the realm of writing to the soldiers themselves. Because this information had a direct bearing on the soldiers' central tasks, we can be sure that it reached them. Reports on soldiers' readiness, while few in number, provide further confirmation of transmission. I then move on to consider imperial edicts, copies of which archaeologists have also recovered from northwestern military installations. As I will show, these documents and related materials say explicitly that their contents were for active dissemination by both oral/aural and visual means. The combination of dissemination of the content and the availability of the written form created a situation in which learning to read could occur. These documents thus open the way for the discussion in subsequent chapters.

From a traditional standpoint, which sees text as the province of elites, it might seem possible to argue that the formulas concerning dissemination are not to be taken seriously, and that the instructions were there but no one expected recipients to follow them. In this way of thinking, the common population, including soldiers, obtained functional knowledge of the information texts contained but had access to texts or ideas about text-based transmission. I bookend the chapter with a pair of examples that forestall these criticisms. These examples confirm in different ways both the functioning of the systems that transmitted information by means of writing and that members of the common population knew the contents.

I first consider examples of the codes that the border defense system used for signaling. The functioning of that system required soldiers to know the codes, and there is evidence showing the enforcement of this requirement. The chapter closes with a multilayered edict document, which incorporates content from a statement made by two commoners. That statement shows that commoners received the information in edicts and understood what was supposed to happen. The intervening discussion considers specific example documents that the system relied on and that were made public.

Standards for Signaling

This chapter later examines public texts that had broad applicability and correspondingly wide audiences. I would like to begin, however, with a type of text that had a specific target audience: the standards for signals used along the border. As Hsing I-t'ien has argued, these and other texts were the subject of soldiers' education. Men in military service needed to grasp the information those texts conveyed.[1] While my analysis of the functions involved differs from Hsing's, I concur with him on the crucial point that these were the subject of learning. Miyake also gives these texts a prominent place in his study of literacy and communication through text, and I follow him, as well, in this respect.[2] I just want to go a bit further.

Soldiers and officials at border posts along the northern border of the Han empire had as their primary task the monitoring of the border for the arrival of enemy forces. When a post made a sighting, the troops stationed there transmitted an alert by means of signals, and when a post caught sight of another's signal, they would pass it along. There were six main types of signal in use, which used fire, smoke, and other visible and audible signs. The rules that determined the signals to be used allowed messages to specify the location and size of a given group of visitors. While the basic elements of the system—fire, smoke, flags, and so on—were the same across the region, the specific codes were not standardized and instead varied according to locality. The authorities distributed the relevant forms in written form within the areas of their jurisdiction.[3] The following lines begin one set of signals and give an idea of how these things worked:

> If you sight one or more of the enemy entering the defenses, light one pile of firewood and raise two signals or, at night, two lit torches. If you see more than ten persons outside the defenses, light and raise [signals] according to the regulations for one person [entering] the defenses.

> 望見虜一人以上入塞燔一積(:積)新(:薪)舉二蓬, 夜二苣火. 見十人以上在塞外燔舉如一人塞品.[4]

These regulations continue, specifying the signals for larger bodies of enemy forces and the corresponding signals. Related rules, similar in form and structure, have been found at numerous archaeological sites dating from a period of centuries.[5] Some examples go beyond describing the signals and also specify when signaling should or should not stop, and what should be done in particular situations. For instance:

> If you sight the enemy outside the defenses, or they enter the defenses, and then the enemy goes back and leaves, always lower the signals and stop the fires. If the next watchtower does not lower its signals and stop its fires, someone shall go on foot to pass the message to them. If the chief commandant went out in pursuit and has not yet returned, do not lower the signals.

望見虜塞外及入塞, 虜即還去輒下蓬止煙火. 如次亭未下蓬止
煙火, 人走傳相告. 都尉出追未還毋下蓬.[6]

The directions on this final strip show that regulations governed
everything having to do with signals, down to how to handle the
failure of a neighboring station to cease signaling when it should
and the continuation of signaling when forces remained in action.

Texts for Border Guards

There was no group of signaling specialists who might have had particular jurisdiction over these codes. The regulations were required
knowledge for all troops. As one text puts it, "They shall all read
aloud and understand the individual regulations and only then patrol"
皆諷讀知條品方循.[7] The systems also included provisions for verifying
that the soldiers possessed the required knowledge. There are instances
of ordinary soldiers going on report as not knowing the signal fire
regulations.[8] One specific record tells of a soldier who improperly
forwarded a signal, reflecting that he was supposed to know the system and did not.[9] Accounts like these confirm soldiers needed to be
familiar with the system.

The signaling directives collectively represent a scheme for
rapid response to urgent situations. It explicitly required the various
members of the bureaucratized border defense forces to employ and
decipher a scheme of signals. This information was disseminated and
maintained in written form and soldiers had to know it.

The texts do not tell us everything about how the content of
the system reached the troops. Certainly, we cannot assume that most
or even many of, say, the conscripts would have arrived at the border
ready to read and comprehend a fairly complicated set of regulations.
The command that they "shall all read aloud and understand the
individual regulations" suggests a combination of written and oral
communication. The regulations were crucial information, both for
the imperial government that relied upon the signals for warning
and for the troops who needed to employ the system as part of their
duties. These texts were available in written form, and their contents
were compulsory learning for soldiers. It would have been a relatively
small step for an individual to connect the written texts with their
contents and begin to recognize characters.

The government's need to disseminate information about standard practices extended beyond military signaling regulations. It encompassed the administrative and legal texts that guided people throughout the empire. In the following discussion I examine forms that dissemination took and the contents of some representative examples. The northwestern sites where archaeologists found these texts were military, but similar systems extended beyond those contexts. For while the examples that I will discuss in the next section also come from military installations, the contents of some unambiguously indicate distribution throughout the empire.

Posted Documents

One characteristic form of public text in Han times was the "posted document" (*bianshu* 扁書).[10] While this was not the only public form of text, it has an advantage for the discussion here in that they include formulas marking them as such. One complete example formula reads:

> When the document arrives, clearly and largely post the document in each market, village, government office, bureau, lodging place gate, watchtowers, and within the watchtower enclosures, and cause the officers, soldiers, and people to all recite and understand it.

> 書到，各明白大扁書市、里、官所、寺、舍、門、亭、隧堠中，令吏卒民盡訟知之。[1]

This text culminates with the order to send an official around to verify knowledge among soldiers and officers. Transmission, not pro forma performance, was the goal.

The exact wording of the formulas varied, and damage to the writing media means often only part of the text remains on any given strip. Nevertheless, enough complete examples survive to enable the identification of the core pattern, which consists of three parts: the command to post the document; the locations for that posting; and an order to have ordinary people and government workers, including soldiers, repeat aloud or understand the document's content. The term for these documents, *bianshu*, is a compound of two words. The Eastern Han lexicon *Explaining Characters and Analyzing Graphs* (*Shuowen*

The Recovery of the Documents

This book's sources come mainly from the ruins of the military posts where troops guarding the border lived and served, many of which were simultaneously part of the border-monitoring apparatus that observed and controlled the passage of people and goods. Rather than setting out a precise line to demarcate the border, the system of posts and outposts created a border corridor, within which archaeological sites are now dispersed. The corridor was at its widest some hundred kilometers wide, and even at its most narrow measured some three kilometers. The terrain is variable and includes rocky wastes and sand expanses, as well as mountains and high plains, and is in places quite fertile. There are also marshes, rivers, seasonal washes, and oases. The area is generally arid, however, which helps to explain the preservation of the materials we have.[29]

Most of these documents come from two regions. Archaeologists and historians often refer to the eastern one by the Han-era name Juyan, which derives from a marshy lake in the area. The other important area centers around a modern city that bears a name dating to Han times, Dunhuang. Archaeologists working in those areas over the past century have recovered, along with other vestiges of material culture, many thousands of documents left behind by the military bureaucracy that managed the border defenses. The working of that governance generated texts, which were thrown into trash heaps, tossed away at random, or disposed of in latrines.

The Juyan area has long been famous as a source of ancient manuscripts. A tenth-century collection contains a tale set in the region, which it attributes to an earlier, Tang-era collection. It tells of an uncanny series of events, including the excavation of an ancient enclosure, inside which some illegible "bamboo writing strip documents" were found. The presence of excavated documents in the story suggests such things were known already in Tang times.[30] There are more certain references later in the medieval period, and in Song times antiquarian scholars used excavated textual sources from the region to make arguments about Han history.[31]

Modern excavations in China's desert northwest began at the end of the nineteenth century. Sven Hedin (1865–1952) visited the western reaches of China in 1899 as part of his explorations of Central Asia. More activity in the region came soon thereafter, in the first years of the twentieth century. Marc Aurel Stein (1862–1943) explored *jiezi* 說文解字, ca. 100 CE) defines the first, *bian* 扁, here meaning "posted," as "to write . . . this is text that is written upon doors" 署也 . . . 署門戶之文也.[12] The word for "document" (*shu* 書) can also mean "to write," and both it and "to post" occasionally appear alone in these contexts. While some scholars explain those instances as defective copying, multiple examples and the grammatical flexibility of the terms make it preferable to understand them as abbreviations of the term "posted document" or the formula "to post a document" rather than errors.[13]

Posted documents included various kinds of content. Texts with legal force often occur, while others appear to be more or less simple announcements. Posted documents also promulgated edicts from the imperial government. Edicts' prominence among public documents is reflected in the number of examples that archaeologists have recovered, and most of the examples I consider are imperial government pronouncements.

Related texts attest to the functioning of the system of displayed documents, providing important evidence that these things really happened. The following order of supplies for several squads along the border is one such example:

> Linghu squad, Yanhu squad, and Guangchang squad each request writing strips and double-width strips, fifty per squad, and twenty fathoms (46.2 m.) of cord, needed for writing and sending down edicts.
>
> 淩胡隧、厭胡隧、廣昌隧, 各請輸札、兩行, 隧五十, 繩廿丈, 須寫下詔書.[14]

Another text specifies special treatment for copying the text of edicts: "Edicts must be clearly and largely written. Use double-width strips to record former edicts of imperial mercy" 詔書必明白大書. 以兩行著故恩澤詔書.[15] The emperor's clemency could not merely exist. The population had to know about it, in the border regions as elsewhere.

An Edict from 10 CE

One form imperial mercy took in Han times was the amnesty, a remission of legal punishment. Both excavated documents and received texts attest to the existence and function of amnesties in Han times.[16] Archaeologists found twelve writing strips with content relating to an amnesty among the ruins of one watchtower in the Juyan region. The twelve strips are similar in size and appearance, suggesting they were part of a single document or group of documents. The relationship between the twelve is unclear, and scholars' opinions vary about the sequence and grouping of the larger set of strips. Everyone who has written about the topic, however, agrees that four of them belong together.[17] These four strips constitute the integral text of an edict as it arrived at the watchtower. The first two strips convey the most important information, which treats recordkeeping rather than the amnesty itself:

> 2nd year of the Shijianguo period (10 CE), 11th month, *jiaxu* day,[18] [this is] sent down.

> 11th month, *renwu* day, grand administrator Liang of Zhangye; grand administrator's regional Major of Cavalry Wu, carrying out the tasks of the assistant; and armory assistant Xi carrying out the tasks of the assistant send this down to the offices and prefectures subordinate to the grand administrator.[19] Upon receiving this document, carry out the tasks, and send it down to those that should use it. Clearly post the document in obvious places in the districts, boroughs, markets, and villages, and cause the officers and people to all recite it. Assemble and submit the name-list of all[20] officers and people who received clemency and were not punished for crimes. This is due now. Separate them according to crime and send it by courier. Carry it out as in the edict document. When the document arrives, report.

> 始建國二年十一月甲戌下.

> 十一月壬午, 張掖大尹良、尹部騎司馬武行丞事、庫丞習行丞事, 下部大尹官縣: 丞 (承) 書從事, 下當用者, 明白扁書鄉、亭、市、里顯見處, 令吏民盡誦之. 具上吏民壹切蒙恩勿治其罪者名, 會今, 罪別之, 以郵行者, 如詔書=到言.[21]

At the core of this text is a brief command ordering the compilation and submission of a list of persons who had benefited from a legal amnesty. As an imperial edict, the text originated with the central government, even though the copy in front of us names only lower authorities. After the date of the edict's promulgation and subsequent forwarding come the names of the governor of the commandery and others of his staff involved in sending the information along to the local level. The opening portion of the text also contains the order to post the document and makes its contents known to the entire populace, the members of which were to recite it—just as soldiers were to do with signal guidelines.

The contents of the two subsequent strips reiterate the core command and direct it down through the lower levels of the bureau-cracy, until reaching the level of the watchtowers and squads, which is where the archaeologists found this copy. At each level, the officers and people were supposed to understand its content.[22] The command in this case was a supplement to the actual amnesty, which had pre-ceded it. Received history records an amnesty that occurred earlier the same year.[23] There is no way to be certain that specific amnesty was the one the present text supplemented, but it might be. At the very least, there is confirmation from different sources that these practices existed at the same time.

Some readers of this text treat it and the predecessor it postu-lates as actions taken as part of the military response to the Xiongnu, arguing that the amnesty was supposed to free prisoners who would become soldiers and bolster Chinese military forces.[24] That approach emphasizes the geographical context of this example and makes some sense. After all, the watchtower it came from was part of the defense system against incursions by the Xiongnu and other neighboring groups.

Despite that, there is nothing in the text itself to indicate any sort of geographical constraint. The only specific geographical terms concern the path of this particular example through the bureaucracy. They reflect one route among many possibilities, and another copy would necessarily have followed a different one. And there is no indication of a geographical limit to this edict's efficacy. As such, I read this text in a larger context, as one that worked throughout the realm. This does not mean it was unconnected to the concerns of the northwestern region, such as the conflict with the Xiongnu. But its importance is larger.

The document bears a date in 10 CE, which places it in the time of Wang Mang's Xin 新 dynasty (9–23 CE), a brief interregnum between the Western and Eastern Han periods. The very language of the document links it to its time. The text of the present document bears a date from the Xin dynasty's first reign period, Shijianguo 始建國 (9–13 CE), literally "the first establishing of the state." Reign periods were the usual forms of dating, and any edict would bear a date in a corresponding way, mutatis mutandis. Wang Mang carried out numerous systematic changes during his rule, one aspect of which concerned language.[25] Wang Mang's changes to the language went beyond this, and his language changes are visible in the text I translated (and in the section that I do not).

Wang Mang altered many official titles as part of his drive to create a government structure in line with that of an imagined and idealized past.[26] These included the title of grand administrator, which appears as *taiyin* 大(:太)尹 rather than the Han dynasty equivalent (*taishou* 太守); and the chief commandant, who is a *taiwei* 大(:太)尉 rather than *junwei*.[27] Wang Mang's changes encompassed many place-names, too, even minor locations. Indeed the very company to which this copy of the edict was directed is referred to as Jiagou 甲溝 rather than its Han name, Jiaqu 甲渠.[28]

Small changes like these can have broad communicative effects, working to establish common knowledge—a state of knowing something oneself and knowing that others know it, too—about power, which can have potent political results.[29] This text thus reflects one aspect of Wang Mang's wide-ranging efforts to create common knowledge of his new dynasty.[30] Beyond this general level of understanding, though, this edict also recalls late Warring States and early imperial actions and practices that worked to shape perceptions of the ruler. Wang Mang's initial amnesty was a sign of his power over the penal system, while the later command to compile the names of those who had benefited would have underscored the directly and specifically personal nature of the ruler's benevolence in this instance. The order to make this command known to the ordinary population would ensure the broadcast of its message.[31]

Close consideration of the command at the core of this edict suggests more specific effects. The phrase used to describe the amnesty is "to receive clemency" (*meng'en* 蒙恩), a commonplace that designated all sorts of imperial acts reflecting, however tenuously, the ruler's mercy.[32] The text immediately explains this phrase as referring to an abatement of punishment for crimes. This small point of explanation indicates larger functions. It reflects that in the context the connotation of "to receive clemency" was uncertain.

The implication is that proper understanding of the phrase mattered. If this were strictly a formal announcement, the comprehension of which by its audience was immaterial, such explanation would be unnecessary. The audience needed to apprehend both imperial mercy and the fact of the amnesty, and to be reminded or informed of it. Those persons who had benefited would also learn—if they did not already know—that the empire forgave, and did not forget, their crimes. Those who had not directly benefited would nevertheless be reminded of the emperor's beneficence, as well as of the power of the imperial government to track its subjects.[33]

Edicts as Texts to Learn From

The repetitiousness and formulaic structure of most of this edict reflect its bureaucratic nature. Although I elide the rest of this document, it goes on to relate two additional routes of distribution, in each instance repeating the central command to record the names of those who benefited from the amnesty.

For a reader seeking literary interest, this dreary monotony is bleak. But in conjunction with orders to make the content known to the broader population, the document's repetitions take on more significance. Officials were to post it, and the ordinary people were to recite it. Repetition would increase the likelihood of audience retention.[34] Its repetitiousness would turn even the bureaucratic aspects of this text's content into the subject of learning, whether or not that was the intent. Through reading aloud and being made to understand the posted content, the common populace would become aware of the governmental structures and the hierarchy of officials that created and delivered the content of the edict. Thus, an edict subject to public posting and reading became more than a message about the specific change that it conveyed. Public communication, reading, and recitation made this kind of document a medium that created common knowledge of a complex government apparatus among the populace, including but not limited to the soldiery.[35]

This text evinces a complicated relationship to power. On the one hand, this common knowledge and its political effects were part of the functioning of the central state and so worked to maintain and extend its potency. And yet the text also included the names and titles of those involved in its creation and distribution. An understanding of these structures—of the bureaucracy—was itself a kind of power, the sort of power common people in at least some cases wielded.[36]

The Edict of Monthly Ordinances from 5 CE

A few years prior to the previous edict, Wang Mang had orchestrated an edict that promulgated a set of "monthly ordinances" (*yueling* 月令) governing activities throughout the year. Archaeologists excavated the site of a Han-era post called Xuanquanzhi 懸泉置 near Dunhuang (Gansu) in the early 1990s. The heart of the site is a walled compound, roughly square and about fifty meters on each side. It once contained the offices and living quarters of officials and soldiers who were part of the border-monitoring network, hosted official travelers, and transmitted documents between local bureaucrats and higher-ups.[37]

From an interior room in the post that had once been an office, archaeologists recovered fragments of a plaster wall, upon which someone had inscribed an edict. This is the only published example of an extensive bureaucratic text copied onto a wall in Han times. Its ninety-nine lines contain a preamble, fifty statutes with accompanying commentary, and a closing section. A thick border surrounds the entire text. A separate label in two additional lines comes outside the lower left corner of the inscription that identifies the text as monthly ordinances and as edict.

Most examples of edicts that archaeologists have recovered are sets of writing strips, originally connected by cord to form a textual unit. In all but a very few exceptional cases the cord has disintegrated, leaving the grouping and arrangement of the strips to scholarly deduction. That inevitably leads of varying opinions, as in the case of the 10 CE edict commanding the compilation of name lists that I just discussed.

The edict of monthly ordinances from 5 CE presents a very different sort of problem. The plaster wall bearing the edict had broken into many pieces and archaeologists restored it by fitting together the fragments. Because of missing sections and uncertainty about the placement of text, some questions remain about some aspects, though most of the object is unambiguous. In its reassembled form this object shows us the whole of the edict defined by a thick outside border. It shows clearly the entire text as a unit, including a preface, the body, and the closing.

The first section of the edict is a preamble, putatively from the mouth of the grand empress dowager Wang Zhengjun 王政君 (71 BCE–13 CE), someone with great personal, if not exactly official, authority, whom Wang Mang used as a figurehead.[38] The preamble presents the new laws as an effort to redress an imbalance in Yin and Yang energies that had resulted in climatic disruption. In the opening section the empress dowager professes her worry about these things and names the examples of sage rulers from antiquity as the source of the edict's concrete measures. The preface weaves in quotations from the *Book of Documents*, already a text of hoary antiquity in Han times.[39]

The ordinances themselves derive from ritual rules about activities to undertake and to avoid in each month of the year. These injunctions have parallels in ritual and philosophical texts, and scholars have discussed and disagreed about their origins since Han times. The edict labels them statutes, indicating legal force, and paleographic records from other sites reflect the enforcement of those laws. The statutes' contents are diverse. They include such things as the timing for planting winter wheat, a statute with autumn function: "Now exhort them to plant wheat. Do not permit them to miss the proper season; if they miss the proper season . . ." 乃勸種麥, 毋或失=時=.[40] There are regulations for taking animals for food at particular sizes and in particular seasons that as a group form a systematic program to protect those animals from overexploitation.[41] Still other statutes concern the application of five phases cosmology and its interest in pneuma to practical activities, for instance, the prohibition of earth construction projects in the first month of summer.[42] Finally, there are a number of statutes that apply to officials, though with implications for the broader population. One such statute orders, "Do not assemble large groups" 毋聚大眾 in the first month of spring. The commentary explains that this refers to gathering commoners for work duties and excludes urgent tasks from the prohibition.[43] Other statutes designate autumn as the time for such projects.[44]

Commentary accompanies most of the statutes, clarifying their scope and application, which the terse form and classical origins of the statutes apparently left uncertain, even to contemporary readers. For example, one line of the statutes reads, "Do not kill fetuses" 毋殺胎. Its commentary explains, "This refers to wild and domestic animals that are pregnant and bearing fetuses. [Killing them] is constantly forbidden until the end of the twelfth month" 謂禽獸, 六畜懷任有孕者也, 盡十二月常禁.[45] Like other commentaries on the edict, this one does several things at once: It explains how this statute was to take effect, namely, by protecting pregnant adults; makes explicit that it applied to both domestic and nondomestic animals; and explains how long the ban was in effect.

Some commentary is less directly explanatory and connects the new laws to larger concerns—including those the grand empress dowager cited in her preface. In one such instance, the statute says, "Be careful to not open covers" 慎毋發盖 (:蓋), something that is as vague in the original as it is in translation. The commentary elucidates: "This refers to not opening things that are covered for storage, in order to concord with the pneuma of the season, and applies until the end of winter" 謂毋發所盖 (:蓋) 藏之物, 以順時氣也, 盡冬.[46] The commentary thus specifies the type of cover the statute referred to and the period of its application. The mention of pneuma links this, too, to the five phases cosmology that the preface names as the basis of the edict as a whole.

Edicts as Posted Texts and Primers

The closing section of the 5 CE edict records the verbal commitment of high officials to carry out the commands and describes the legal and bureaucratic means by which it reached the population and took effect, with provision for its distribution throughout the realm. The formula marking the text as a posted document to be read aloud comes at the end of the text.[47]

The presence of this formula and its position both tell us something. The idea that the populace needed to learn of, for instance, standard planting times for wheat, seems clear. If guidance about planting was going to benefit the realm, that information had to reach peasants, that is, persons in the lowest social levels. As such, the promulgation of the edict through display and reading aloud makes immediate sense.

This document simultaneously conveyed information about rules that applied exclusively to officials—things like when they were permitted to summon the common population for labor service. Officials would need those details in order to obey their directives. The common population would gain some understanding of bureaucratic structures through this dissemination.

The formula commanding display and reading in this example appears at the very end of the entire textual unit, indicating the preceding content was posted. The surrounding border strengthens the impression of the text as an organic whole. The nature of this text as a posted document implies not only public display but also public reading. This text put the statutes into the mouths of the officials who read it aloud and the populace who, based on parallels in other texts, recited the text. And when the preamble quoted Wang Zhengjun herself, it put her words into the mouths of both the high officials who committed themselves to carrying out the orders and the multitudes of the populace who recited along. This distributed the dynamic efficacy of legal pronouncements, so that they became not only the words of the emperor but also words in the mouths of local officials. And this text, like other examples, would have been visible to the audience as they heard it, inviting those interested in doing so to acquire familiarity with the written forms of the words they were hearing.

Elevated Language and Audience Understanding

The 5 CE edict's terse diction, and the classical phrases and paraphrases that lard it and its preamble, raise questions about the degree to which someone without extensive education would be able to comprehend it aurally or learn to do so visually. Three points are relevant to understanding what we have in front of us.

The first is that, as I have noted, the phrases marking posted documents generally stipulate not just dissemination but also comprehension. This suggests explanation was usual. The second is the presence of local officials, who could elucidate obscure passages. The commentary accompanying the statutes drives home the point that auditors were to understand it, and that they might need additional information for that, which the text provides. The final point to keep in mind is that, while they represent a small part of what we have, there are in fact other elevated texts found among the detritus of the stations. I discuss examples in chapter 7. More prosaic texts, whose content supported the function of basic systems, require and required less to understand. They put few demands upon the historian's imagination and yet fill in details about how things worked. It is to examples of those texts that I now turn.

Posted Rules for Officers

Archaeologists excavating a site in an area near the Eji'na River in 2000 found amid the ruins of a small desert watchpost a set of eight wooden writing strips, two lines of twisted cord still binding it together. Its excellent state of preservation and its copyist's clear handwriting make this document as straightforward as any extended text dating to the Wang Mang period can be. This does not mean interpretation is easy. The label that occupies the first strip is obscure, for while the characters are clear, its grammatical structure presents difficulties and scholars parse it variously. Nonetheless, it is clear that it identifies a set of rules for low-level officials with responsibility for supervising soldiers and other matters connected with border monitoring.[48]

This set of strips is so well preserved that even the loops tied on both ends of both cord bindings survive. Those loops suggest this document was hung from nails or other fasteners on the wall to be seen and read. That supposition is strengthened by the location of this object's discovery, on a stair in a small border station. This has led scholars such as Ma Yi to call it an example of a "posted document" despite the absence of the usual formulas marking those—although it does provide information about posted documents.[49] The following command is why:

- Post a document with the rewards for capturing barbarians, one posting every two watchtowers. Do not let the cords rot and break.

- 扁書胡虜請(:購)[50]賞, 二亭扁一, 毋令編幣(:弊)絕.[51]

This order tells us two important things about the system of posted documents. It gives one example of a type of text that would be posted for obvious reasons. Rewards for the capture of enemies could only motivate soldiers that knew about them, so their public display makes perfect sense. The directions furthermore specify the maintenance of the binding cords, which indicates the posting of sets of strips was intended to be a long-term matter.

The officials responsible for putting up and maintaining posted documents would seem most likely to have had interest in the preceding. Yet the position of this specific posted document along a stair in the cramped conditions of a watchtower brings the possibility of multiple audiences comprising those directly addressed and other interested parties who would also see the content due to its public position. One example command on the strips reads, "Observe and count those officers and soldiers who leave their posts" 察數去署吏卒. It continues by laying out the penalties for numbers of absences for specific ranks.[52] This is a command that addresses the official doing the observing and the counting, yet it seems inevitable that more men would read a posted document than that small group, including those men subject to observation whose absences would be counted. Its posting assured their awareness of the fact of this supervision and the consequences for violation, aiding the deterrent effect of the penalties.

Another publicly posted regulation suggests still another method of encouraging compliance: "Observe whether the company commander or company clerk, even though they have no horse, draw grain for one" 察候長、候史雖毋馬廩之.[53] The early empire had regulations for feeding horses in official service, whether they were public or private property. Taking feed for a nonexistent horse was illegal, a fact that the soldiers and bureaucrats who staffed the border defenses must have known.[54] The early imperial legal system encouraged informing on criminal behavior, and broad knowledge of this specific regulation would have enabled—and encouraged—those working in and around official feed storehouses to report infractions.

A Lost Travel Document

Another example reflects a conceptually similar situation in regard to a different type of document.[55] The Han dynasty relay system offered food, shelter, and transportation to official travelers at government stations of various sorts. Proper use of the facilities required the

traveler to carry an authorizing document called a "relay certificate"
(*zhuanxin* 傳信) bearing a date; the traveler's name, rank, and business; the types of assistance to be rendered; the name of the official
who issued the certificate and a serial number. A set of strips dating
from 39 BCE relates what happened when one relay certificate went
missing. The first strip is a copy of a relay certificate issued to one Li
Zhong 李忠, otherwise unknown, who was traveling to go oversee an
official sacrifice. After the completion of that task, as the subsequent
text relates, Li Zhong passed his relay certificate to Ze Qin 澤欽,
also otherwise unknown, who promptly lost it. The document we
have consists of notification sent out through the bureaucracy that,
if anyone presented a relay certificate with a serial number matching
that of the lost certificate, it was to be sent to the clerk's office and
the bearer arrested. The text also commands:

> When this document arrives, those at the two thousand
> bushel level shall each announce to their subordinate offi-
> cials and the officers and people of their prefectures that
> whoever gets the lost relay certificate will be rewarded, as
> in the statutes.

> 書到, 二千石各明白寺告屬官縣吏民, 有得亡傳信者, 予購如
> 律.[56]

What follows concerns the dissemination of the announcement
through the bureaucracy. It seems like this sort of loss ought to have
been rare. Zhang Defang 張德芳, however, gathers five strips representing four or five cases in which relay certificates went missing,
including remnants of two additional strips that end with phrases
like those I just quoted.[57] Given that only a very small portion of
documents that once existed are available to us now, it seems these
examples must represent a fairly frequent occurrence, otherwise we
would not have these examples.

More interesting for the discussion here is the position of the
document at the nexus of oral and written systems. For the phrasing
of the command to make Li Zhong's loss of his relay certificate known
does not explicitly stipulate the posting of a copy. The announcement's written transmission nevertheless reached its final audience,
through a combination of written and oral means.[58]

There are several assumptions underlying this announcement. One is that the audience would be familiar with the system of government rewards. Without that, this edict could have had no motivating effect. I have already in this chapter mentioned regulations for rewards for soldiers in their defensive duties. The Han statutes prescribed rewards for such things as capturing or informing on thieves.[59] All such systems relied upon knowledge about them among the common population, which is what made them motivational and which reached them through combined written and oral means.[60] There is furthermore the implicit assumption that a member of the population would either be able to recognize a relay certificate or had access to someone who would, or they would not have known that it was the object of the search and would bring a reward.

An Edict from 14 BCE

I will close this chapter with a final example document, an edict from 14 BCE. Archaeologists recovered the fifteen strips comprising it at Jianshui Jinguan.[61] This document is multilayered. It begins with the edict that is its core. The edict's text as we have it does not include a date, which would have been standard. That may indicate a copy that is incomplete due to a lacuna or the loss of one or more strips. The content of the edict takes the form of recommendations from two high officials, which they submit in response to a command from the emperor and which he at the end approves. This was a common form for this type of document. The two officials' personal names are present and both are well known from historical accounts. They are Zhai Fangjin 翟方進 (d. 57 BCE), then chancellor, and Kong Guang 孔光 (65 BCE–5 CE), chief clerk.[62]

The specific occasion of the edict is a winter with insufficient snowfall. This lack of precipitation had harmed winter wheat production and localized starvation threatened. Zhai and Kong proposed gathering statistics from throughout the realm to permit the government to shift grain stores to places in need. They also note the activities of moneylenders and corrupt officials operating in collusion to exploit needy peasants. In response, Zhai and Kong propose vacating the statutes on making loans and obliging the payment of interest to lenders. Formal indication of the emperor's approval comes after this.

The edict comprising the first section of this document (in this copy) does not contain the command to make its contents known. That is probably due to damage to the strips that order, and thus describe for us now, the distribution of the document through the bureaucracy around the seventh month of that year, equivalent to roughly early September 14 BCE. A strip from a few weeks later, in early October that same year, is present and records a statement from two otherwise unknown men of Chang'an named Li Shen 李參 and Suo Fu 索輔 concerning rents and loans. While damage to the strip interrupts the text and leaves the precise contents of their statement unknown, what follows makes it clear that Li and Suo's report concerns ongoing loansharking despite the change to the law.

The subsequent text amplifies the situation, explaining in an official voice, "We have heard that in the capital area brutal and tricky officers and people are again making loans and taking heavy collateral and not stopping. We suspect it is likewise in the commanderies and states" 聞三輔豪黠吏民復占貸受重質不止, 疑郡國亦然.[63] The following strip then repeats the change to the law, stressing that while lenders could collect loans, they were forbidden to charge interest. The tone shifts in the remainder of the text, as it traces the path of the document to Jianshui Jinguan, where it was to be posted among the watchtowers and squads. Our copy emerged at the end of this long chain of distribution.

The presence of Li Shen's and Suo Fu's names is significant in two ways for the discussion here. The document describes the two simply as "men" (nanzi 男子). That is to say, they did not hold official positions or high rank, which the text would have recorded. They were commoners. And yet they still knew about the edict, otherwise they would not have known to report violations. This makes sense: As we have seen, publicizing edicts was commonplace. It follows that the ordinary population likely knew about the edict. The timeline here is short, and these two perhaps knew before those in other localities because of living in Chang'an, the capital. The subsequent text records the official conjecture that violations were probably more widespread. Knowledge of the edict, its changes to the law and the imperial compassion that motivated it, was also likely widespread.

The document quotes Li and Suo's statement as evidence, without indicating why they made it. We do not know whether Li and Suo did this of their own volition—petitioning the government for assistance or recording a complaint—or if they were perhaps caught up in a legal proceeding. Indeed the document's phrasing at first might almost seem like ordinary diction, for it begins the statement by asserting Li and Suo "say themselves" (*ziyan* 自言) that the problems continued. In fact the phrase "say oneself" labels a formal statement, distinct from a response to police interrogation, by which various kinds of information became part of the bureaucratic record. The next chapter discusses these statements.

Chapter Four

Statements of Individuals and Groups

In the preceding chapter, I considered how soldiers and others interacted with text from the perspective of reading and oral/aural modes of access to information. In keeping with the primary focus of this book, that discussion concentrated on the ways people at the low end of the social scale accessed written material of various sorts, particularly including standardized signals and imperial edicts. In the closing section of the chapter, I talked about a statement that two commoners made, the content of which ended up as part of an imperial edict. The words of those two men were marked in the record by the phrase "to say oneself" (*ziyan* 自言).

In this chapter I consider statements through which the speech and experience of non-elites entered the documentary record. Thus, while the previous chapter concentrated on accessing textual information received from others, this one treats the reverse, the creation of documents on the basis of speech. Frank Smith tells us part of the motivation to learn to read comes from knowing the significance of text. The statements that I discuss here are potent examples of the sorts of motivation that the bureaucratic system provided.

These documents were created on the basis of spoken interactions, yet they still provide evidence of participation in the literate community. For what they represent is, in essence, a kind of dictation. As I discussed in chapter 1, dictation is a valid way to create written content. Such creation is as much a form of interaction with text as consuming it is. If information could flow in one direction—from an individual person to the written record—then it follows that it could flow in the opposite direction—from the record to the person—also.

Inevitably, there are questions about the nature of the records before us. As I will show, the statements that I consider in this chapter contain vocabulary that marks them as speech. One may wonder whether the subjects whose utterances became part of the documentary record knew what was happening. In some cases, such as those of men whose positions required them to have reading and writing ability and made statements, they certainly did. The weight of probability for others is on the affirmative as well. The soldiers lived in a text-rich environment; they knew about text in general and bureaucratic records specifically. Statements were part of the processes that accounted for actions and material goods and could form the basis of inquiries and procedures. Statements were also how conscripts and even those doing penal service began or contributed to bureaucratic processes that influenced their lives. The likelihood is thus that everyone involved knew at some level what was happening in the formulation of these documents. The formulas that mark these statements finally stress that persons named were, individually or as part of a group, themselves the speakers, suggesting directness.

These statements are examples of how an individual's utterances could become bureaucratic text. The processes of governance constrained the topics, but the statements demonstrate some aspects of the mental landscape the conscripts and other military personnel inhabited. They are distinct from the legal statements taken by officials investigating criminal matters, which were in general longer, more detailed, more varied, and produced in response to extensive questioning.[1]

One might object that the statements I consider are formalized and sanitized, and no doubt there is a degree of that at work. The statements exhibit a marked flatness of diction. The process of recording standardized the statements' forms and content, treating a variety of speakers in the same fashion. The statements simultaneously recorded and effaced the individuality of those whose utterances they rendered.

Yet formalization, sanitization, and flattening by themselves do not render the result void of personal significance or voice. A moment's consideration will show how much our own written and spoken communication consists of such utterances, everything from wishes of "happy birthday" or "mazel tov" to the salutations and valedictions that begin and end our written correspondence. (How many correspondents whom we address as "Dear" are in fact dear to us?) These things are important. And the exigencies of a difficult situation—a death or other serious loss, for example—often result in a retreat to standardized, cliché formulations that mark the presence, not the absence, of particular kinds of feeling. Formalized content is far from without meaning.

The statements I study in this chapter help illuminate the edges of the literate community. They demonstrate the openness of the documentary bureaucracy that formed the textual core around which the community took shape. As I argued in chapter 1, the literate community of the border defense area was defined by a combination of geographic proximity and interaction with bureaucratic texts.

Recorded statements furthermore demonstrate the activity of women in the literate community. Through their statements, women's participation in the community and indeed their words became part of the record in the same manner as those of male community members. Statements demonstrate the literate community's openness—an openness that extended even beyond Han subjects, whom I, for the sake of concision, refer to as Chinese. For non-Chinese persons who encountered Han systems, utterances became statements in the same way that Han subjects' words did, recorded in the same language and the same forms. A group of representatives from Kangju 康居 lodged a complaint with the Han government that shows this at work.

Participation in the literate community of the northwest did not result in a permanent state, even setting aside questions of mortality. Its geographical character meant that those who came into and left service there did the same in respect to the community; conscripts, officers, other troops, and their families arrived and departed from the community. Records of the presence of non-Chinese persons and the inclusion of their statements in the documentary bureaucracy indicates, however, that for those moments of contact at least, they were part—however provisionally and briefly—of the community that was linked by location and interaction with text.

To Say Oneself

The most easily identifiable statements that come to us in the northwestern materials are marked by the phrase "to say oneself" or "to state oneself" (ziyan). This is the same phrase that marked the two commoners' statement I talked about at the end of chapter 3. While at first appearing to be ordinary language, this phrase occurs more often in the corpus than one would expect of a commonplace phrase. Its repeated occurrence and forms of use indicate it was a label; use as a label in turn indicates it denoted a type of document recognized at the time. The available set of examples is varied, which makes determining the institutional characteristics of the type complicated. What is clear, though, is that in essence it marks the entrance of an assertion into the written record without judging its accuracy, merely attributing it to someone as an utterance and giving it a specific legal status as such.[2] One example of this sort says,

> Company soldier Yin Shang states himself (*ziyan*) that he is seeking from no. 21 squad's Xu Shengzhi money owed for a long robe in the amount of less than 2,000 cash.

> 郭卒尹賞 · 自言責(:債)第廿一隧徐勝之長襦錢少二千.[3]

Based on the sense of the label and word choice in the examples, these statements appear to have resulted from spoken interaction between the recorder and one or more other persons, whose speech in this way became part of a written record. It seems unlikely that any written mode of communication other than speech would have resulted in the statement I just quoted.

This close relationship to speech distinguishes the statement formulation from texts with other bureaucratic markers, which ostensibly refer to speech in only a pro forma fashion. For example, many bureaucratic documents began and ended with a marker that literally means "[I] dare to say this" or, better, "[I] may say this" 敢言之.[4] The bureaucrat responsible for indicting a given text would use this formula even when incorporating material from another documentary source. But "saying" was no more necessarily involved than "daring" was. The form was rather an "affirmation," a way of taking formal responsibility for a document and marking its beginning and ending. This marking also worked to prevent someone from altering a document by adding text to it.[5]

These two forms, a personal statement and a formal affirmation, sometimes appear together, representing the intermingling of types.

There was then the writing of the document, for which the bureaucrat took responsibility, and within it was the content of the statement, for which he did not. The marking of something as a spoken assertion could also be a way to embed content related to official tasks in a document that a different official affirmed.

On the *bingxu* day of the 8th month, which had *shuwu* as its first day, in the 2nd year of Ganlu (52 BCE), foreman clerk Qi of Jiaqu affirms: Squad leader Bi of the 19th [squad] states himself (*ziyan*) that he should, in accord with the edicts, perform the autumn shooting [test] and record the score of the appropriate draw weight[6] strength and that in shooting the crossbow bolt [and] crossbow stock both match the ordnance. [I,] Acting foreman clerk Qi of Hanqiang, Jiaqu company, record the number of arrows that hit the target on the tablet. The rest is as in the dossier. I affirm this.

甘露二年八月戊午朔丙戌甲渠令史齊敢言之 第十九隧長敵自言, 當以令 秋射 署 功勞 即石力發弩矢□弩臂皆應令. 甲渠候漢彊守令史齊署發□矢數于牒它如爰書敢言之.[7]

This sort of document was part of the periodic verification of abilities that Han officers underwent. Since a squad leader was required to be literate, and no deficiency of that sort is noted here, it follows that he would have had the ability to write his statement. It is thus clear that this sort of statement was not exclusive to persons who could not write. Rather it was a way for a scrivener to attribute something to someone else. There is also an example of a document that recorded the confirmation of this kind of record, and provisions for new arrivals whose scores were insufficient. Unfortunately, the details are missing.[8]

In another case, a villager's statement that he intended to engage in personal trade served as basis for the issuance of a travel document. The one who took down the statement marked it as such. The document furthermore includes the issuing official's confirmation that there were no impediments to the man's travel, such as a legal conviction or an outstanding corvée labor obligation. But labeling the villager's own statement as such separated the putative purpose of travel from those things the official himself could attest to.[9] From our perspective, it is a trace of an individual's purpose, distinct from that of the official.

Other times an individual could make a statement as part of the formalities connected with changing status. It might be because a soldier had completed the required number of days of service. Or it might be because someone whose service was due to a conviction had benefited from an imperial amnesty and wished to return home.[10]

Many statements contain standard formulations.[11] Existing examples show, however, that the form could express various things, and not only formulas. A straightforward, although damaged, instance of this reads, "Border soldier Yuan Ying states himself (*ziyan*) that company commander Li Shun sent the soldier Xie Yi and others, eight men, to gather firewood and transport hay. Upon questioning, he was unable to meet . . ." 戍卒爰應自言候長李順使卒謝乙等八人取薪運茭驗問未能會.[12] It seems unlikely that the situation this statement describes could have been a usual occurrence and thus associated with a formula.

A statement could represent what one person asserted, as when a certain Wang Bo 王博 said that he had not received his rations. It could also relate what a number of people said through a single representative. In the preceding, Yuan Ying stands for eight men who said functionally the same thing. Alternatively, a group statement could present the assertion of a large number of persons. There is, for instance, an example in which a man named Hu Zhao 胡朝 together with twenty others claimed that they had not received their salt rations. In another, two men received joint authorization for travel. The fact that they came from two different villages and had two different surnames suggests they were not related. The official who handled their request perhaps grouped them together because they had similar travel plans.[13]

Example statements exist that record group assertions, sometimes even when a given group was not of one mind. A dossier summarizing a legal case records the response of one Zhuang Qiangyou 莊彊友 and three other border soldiers to allegations they had falsified accounts and illegally sold government wares. They "all responded saying" that they had done no such thing, and "all implicated each other," and in so doing confirmed their joint culpability in the minds of the adjudicating officials.[14] This statement records a tangle of cross-accusation and finger-pointing, which it presents en masse rather than setting out each person's individual words. From the official perspective of those taking down the statement, these men formed a single set, however various their opinions. Groups constituted through the process of recording could comprise those of equal status, as in Zhuang Qiangyou and comrades' case, or include men of different statuses.[15] They could also include women.[16]

Women Interacting with Text

Indeed the presence of women is one of the most noteworthy aspects of the statements. Traditional sources give us limited information about the lives of commoner women and record their voices in only the rarest of cases. Chinese society in early imperial times was patriarchal, a fact that the body of text we have from the period reflects. While there are notable women authors in the traditional corpus, they are invariably individuals of elite status.[17]

The statements that I study in this chapter offer a radically different perspective, for they put women and men on an equal documentary footing. Except for noting that a given person was a woman, either by labeling her as such or by noting she was the wife of some man, the forms of women's statements are identical to men's. These examples are of limited number, which increases the documentary value of each. Their presence in these examples contrasts with the near absence of records of non-elite women in received sources and reflects a social situation that was different from the world of transmitted sources.

Nevertheless, these women had limited social status, which entailed exclusion from ordinary bureaucratic offices, including those of local governance.[18] As chapter 8 will show, this did not mean women were entirely excluded from the workings of the military bureaucracy. But the available sources reflect a situation in which their participation in those systems was conditioned by connections to male relatives.

In all cases I have been able to identify from the northwestern context, women's statements concern or otherwise depend upon a male

relative. Usually that is the husband, although one woman's statement refers to a younger brother.[19] The following is a well-preserved
example of an application for permission to travel, which refers to
the husband and illustrates one form such connections could take:

> The first year of the Yuankang period, 10th month, which
> had *renyin* as its first day, on the *jiachen* day (5 November
> 65 BCE), border station bailiff Guangde's auxiliary Xi
> affirms: Zhao Fuqu of Shouling village, Dunhuang, states
> herself (*ziyan*) that her husband Xin is squad leader of the
> Qianqiu squad and she is going to give him clothing to
> use. On the basis of the ordinance, allow her to pass the
> border station. I affirm this.

> 元康元年十月壬寅朔甲辰, 關嗇夫廣德佐熹敢言之: 敦煌壽陵
> 里趙負 趣自言夫訢為千秋隧長往遺衣用以令出關. 敢言之.[20]

There is no indication that Xi supports or has verified Zhao Fuqu's
assertions; he merely records them as the basis for permitting her travel.
Some examples I will discuss later mention verification of content,
as one might expect. Probably there was a process of confirmation
that the example before us does not reflect. Or perhaps Zhao Fuqu's
husband's status as a squad leader, while not elevating him out of the
working environment of the soldiers he led, imparted some privilege
or degree of added respect to his wife. It is also conceivable that his
status was merely an identifying detail, as a woman generally took
her social status from her husband in the Han.[21] Her husband's status
may have in effect been identifying information for Zhao Fuqu.

Most women's statements are, as they come to us, even shorter
than Zhao Fuqu's. In one case, a woman reports in a few words that
her husband is sick; in another, a woman relates that her husband
is dead.[22] There is also a statement in which a wife reports that her
husband's salary has not been paid, without detail.[23]

In all extant cases in which there is information about the status
of these women's husbands, only officers' wives appear. Two potential
explanations offer themselves. First, this may indicate that these wives
had privileges denied, by rule or by practice, to women whose husbands
held lower status. Since the husband's status is not always noted, it

may also be the case that such information was included only when
it made the statement somehow special—such as when the person
was of somewhat elevated status. Or it may result from other factors.

Even if we were to assume that all these women benefited from
their husbands' positions that would not diminish the value of these
statements. The women themselves had low social status; at the same
time, they still participated in the literate community by means of
statements. They were not passive bystanders. They interacted with
the bureaucracy in their own names, and their statements were taken
up into documents in the same form that men's were. This reflects
that women were part of the same literate community that men were.
Whether or not women themselves wrote is uncertain; I have found
no case of a document manifestly drafted by a woman among the
published documents from Juyan and Dunhuang. Future archaeological finds may change this.

Yet, as I argued in chapter 1, dictation is a legitimate form of
composition. Statements by women provide unambiguous evidence of
women's activity within the community, activity I return to again in
chapter 8. Recognizing this activity is an important expansion of the
social scope of interaction with text in early imperial China. And in
fact we can push the borders of the literate community even further
than this. For among the northwestern documents come records of
interaction with non-Chinese persons.

The Blurry Borders of the Literate Community

The documentary record from the northwestern border regions contains
example statements from people who were not Chinese. One such
example begins with a string of identifying information that tells us
it came from a Qiang person named Ganmang 幹芒, who had given
allegiance to the Han, and who "stated himself" (ziyan) the content
of the document.[24] Unfortunately, the fragment does not continue
much beyond that. Another, more extensive example relates a complicated incident, in which Kangju representatives made a complaint
to the Han government.

The Kangju polity was a confederation of nomads who lived
in the area of modern Kazakhstan and Uzbekistan, well beyond the

western borders of the Han empire. Modern scholars have identified them, with various degrees of certitude, as either the forerunners of the Sogdians or an early form of that group. Famous as traders, the Sogdians were speakers of a language related to Iranian and culturally far removed from China. They nonetheless played important roles in medieval Chinese history. In Han times, as part of the complex and shifting network of relations among groups in Central Asia, the Kangju held the nominal status of Han tributaries. It is likely that the motivation for the Kangju visits to Han territory was ultimately mercantile. Documents from Xuanquanzhi, a station along a road that connected the Han empire with Central Asia, include records of Han contacts with the Kangju and other Central Asian polities.[25]

Among the materials from Xuanquanzhi comes the long record of a grievance that a group of official visitors from Kangju lodged concerning the valuation of some camels. Several additional strips appended to the complaint detail the first steps of the Han authorities' subsequent investigation. The entire document consists of some three hundred characters on seven wooden strips. The content divides into four sections, three of which contain dates showing the events occurred around the year 39 BCE.[26]

The first section is the longest and represents nearly half of the record. The first part records the specifics of the grievance, which it presents in the form of a joint statement, and names the visiting emissary Yangbodao 楊伯刀, who represented the Kangju king, and Gumo 姑墨, the emissary of the Suxie 蘇薤 king, a subordinate of the Kangju ruler. They traveled with an entourage, which the document refers to only in general terms.

The substance of their complaint concerns an "offering" of camels that they brought with them. The document marks their statement with the formula I have already mentioned in connection with other statements: "they state themselves" (ziyan), with the addition of a written ritual obeisance not found in other statements I have located. This seems likely to have marked non-Han subjects' address to the imperial government.

The first part of the complaint lays out the background and precedent. The group explains that on previous trips to Han territory, the Kangju representatives entered the Han realm at Dunhuang and proceeded to Jiuquan, enjoying en route the hospitality of the imperial post relay system. Upon arrival in Jiuquan they would then meet with the grand administrator to jointly evaluate the value and physical condition of the camels they brought with them.

On this particular visit, though, things were different. The embassy did not receive its customary sustenance on the way.[27] And when the group arrived at Jiuquan, the grand administrator and his staff there appraised the camels out of the presence of the Kangju representatives. The result was the difference of opinion that occasioned the complaint. For while the administrative staff at Jiuquan judged the camels the entourage presented to be scrawny, Yangbodao and colleagues asserted they were in fact well fed. Gumo furthermore had brought three camels—one male and two females—on behalf of his king. The Kangju described all three as white, but the Jiuquan administrators recorded them as being the usual tan. Although the Kangju representatives did not allude to any sum of money, the end result of this process was obviously what they considered to be an underestimation of the camels' value. The emissaries saw that, as the statement puts it in closing, as "not in accord with reality—an injustice!" 不如實, 冤.

The remaining three sections are short. Two of them record the first few steps of the government's response to the allegations. The first indicates that the grievance reached the central court. There, an official at the bureau responsible for foreign guests wrote to the grand administrator of Dunhuang commandery, ordering him to investigate the complaints. As Hao Shusheng 郝樹聲 points out, the central events of the complaint took place in Jiuquan, which was not in Dunhuang's jurisdiction. There must have been separate communication with Jiuquan, which did not become part of this particular chain of correspondence.[28]

The point of writing to Dunhuang becomes clear in the subsequent strip. It records a command from the Dunhuang grand administrator and members of his staff to the prefectural officials, who were to report on the grain that the Kangju entourage's camels had consumed. This is obviously seeking evidence concerning the Kangju claims that they had not received the treatment to which they were accustomed—and, the implication is, entitled.[29] The final strip contains an order to the post to submit information about grain left unconsumed by relay horses. Its relationship to the other sections of the document is unclear.

The document we have does not record the result of the complaint. But it nevertheless provides telling information about the literate community. The most important point is also the most obvious: although not Han subjects, the Kangju representatives were able to become at least temporary members of the literate community in the border region. They passed through Han territory and stayed at Han government facilities before reaching the town of Jiuquan, itself a government center. In other words, they were within the space of the community. The document reflects furthermore than the Kangju interacted with text generally and with the Han bureaucracy specifically. They were responsible for the content of the complaint, and their contribution bore the same mark—namely, the designation *statement*—that any other member of the literate community's statement would have borne. The inclusion in their account of not only the events in question but also the relevant precedents as the Kangju understood them strengthens the impression that the Kangju representatives themselves were responsible for the content.

The Kangju representative's complaint drew a response from the highest levels of government. Their success in this respect suggests that they had some knowledge about Han systems and the roles of documents in them. That information was both conveyed through text and ultimately concerned with a text-based system. That their assertions were subject to verification reminds us that recording a statement was taking the named person or persons' words into the bureaucratic record, which was distinct from asserting their veracity. The content of the utterance remained the responsibility of the speaker(s).

Since this record concerns a group of non-Han persons, the matter of communication between speakers of different languages seems like it should arise. Yet the document makes no mention of translation. Indeed, in general, differences between the languages spoken by those within and outside the Chinese realm received limited attention in the time up to and including the early imperial period.[30] There was some mention, though, of course. The poet Sima Xiangru 司馬相如 (179–117 BCE), while working as a Han imperial official, once drafted a message to a regional administrator in which he referred to the Kangju specifically as bringing "offerings" to the Han court—just the sort of thing that the Kangju complaint in this case records. The descriptor "offering" is not to be taken too seriously as an assertion of fact. It is, as I have noted, much more likely that the Kangju were more interested in trade than in becoming Han subjects in any real sense. But it reflects a pattern of ongoing contact, in which the Kangju played a subordinate role.

What I would like to draw attention to in the context of the discussion here is that Sima Xiangru mentions contact with the Kangju required "repeated translation" (*chongyi* 重譯). In other words, Sima Xiangru says that not only was there no shared language between the Han and the Kangju, there was no single person who spoke both the Han and the Kangju languages and could translate between them. The Han and the Kangju hence (supposedly) needed translation of translation in order to be able to communicate. Sima Xiangru's specific phrasing was a trope—one with a long life—and not a literal description. Yet it reflects the great linguistic and cultural distance between the Kangju and the Han empire.[31]

The silence of this document about translation makes it hard to draw conclusions. The situation seems similar to the problem presented by soldiers from different parts of the Han empire, who presumably spoke dialects that varied considerably. This is something I referred to in chapter 2, where I noted that the available sources do not tell us how conscripts from various parts of the empire communicated with each other. Translation between dialects or between languages seems to have been a matter of course and not worth recording. In this case, we might imagine that perhaps the Kangju—apparently consummate traders, like the later Sogdians—mastered languages as part of the practice of trade.[32] Sima Xiangru's reference suggests, however, that the issue of translation arose in at least some contexts. Yet there is no mention of it among the documents from the northwestern border zone.[33]

In the present instance, there is no indication that this in any way affected the connection between the statement so generated and the group of Kangju who had responsibility for it. This seems unexpected, as the early bureaucracy put much weight on establishing responsibility at the stages of written transmission. Translation, whether by the Kangju themselves, by the Han, or by someone else, is in this way unlike, for instance, the requirement for copyists who wrote out duplicate bureaucratic documents to mark their work with their name.[34] Officials recorded the names of even those who carried mail from one place to another as part of the functioning of the postal system.[35] There is furthermore nothing distinctive about the language of this document to suggest the statement originated with a nonnative speaker. Nor is one person named as speaking on behalf of the group, as happened in other instances I have already mentioned. That might hint at a translator among the Kangju group. It seems most reasonable to assume that translation took place and was not recorded, whether the translator or translators were Chinese or Kangju.

However they and their bureaucratic interlocutors achieved communication across the language divide, the representatives of the Kangju addressed the Han imperial government in writing and saw a result. That is itself remarkable evidence for the ongoing and active connection between the border regions and the Han central government, and for the ability of the bureaucracy to extend its reach from the center to the periphery. It shows that these non-Han visitors—men from beyond the realm—were able to function as members—temporary members, at least—of a literate community that reached from the hinterlands to the centers of government.

The residents of these areas participated in a textual culture in other ways, as well. The Han dynasty, especially the period from the first century BCE into the early first century CE, was a time when many texts that constitute the received body of literature came into being through processes of editing, assembly, and composition. Some in the northwest border regions pursued the same kinds of projects on a modest scale. They are the subject of the next chapter.

Chapter Five

Composite Texts

The preceding two chapters treated two ways of interacting with text. One of these was consumption of text through visual or aural means, or a combination of those two. The other was the creation of text through dictation. In recent years scholars have given increasing attention to still another form of interaction with text, which was of great importance during the early imperial period: creation through assembly. Appreciation for assembly as a kind of creation, and the wide-ranging influence that early editors and compilers wielded, has come late. Yet some of the most important early Chinese texts came into being this way and I argue we can see similar practices in the context of the northwest. This was a form of interaction with text that the border region shared with the center.

In this chapter I concentrate on two examples, one of which is a set. In the first example, the creator of the subject text juxtaposed an unusual imperial pronouncement with a personal letter. Archaeologists found this text at a small site in the desert, which shows the practice of creation by assembly had reached the edges of the empire. The second example is a group of composite texts that deal with the privileges enjoyed by those who held the "king's staff" (wangzhang 王杖), which Han law granted to men of advanced age. While the latter texts come from the geographical northwest, they emerged from graves rather than the trash piles and other detritus of military installations. These texts appear to have been locally created from official source material for the use of individual commoners. In the cases of both the letter/edict text and the king's staff texts, I give attention to previous studies on them. This helps me situate them in their historical contexts and to place my own consideration in relation to broader historiography. But I begin the discussion by taking a step back to put the subjects of this chapter into a larger context still, that of the mode of composition, which functioned through piecing together textual components to make something new.

Creation by Assembly

The texts at the center of this chapter have an obvious patchwork character about them. Rather than representing organic wholes, they integrate pieces of writing from different sources. The significance of this goes further than reflecting a mode of interaction practiced at the edges of the empire. Similar processes were at work at the center of Han civilization, shaping textual culture in its contemporary and later forms.

The assembly of anthologies and other composite texts was a meaningful creative task in premodern China. Previous scholars have given poetic anthologies, in particular, a great deal of attention. While that attention is well deserved, concentrating on poetic anthologies essentially treats text creation within the confines of a traditional definition of literature, which concentrates on particular forms of belles lettres.[1] In recent years, scholars have gone beyond those boundaries to consider other composite texts, a class of texts that includes some of the most influential in Chinese history. Already in the early Han, editors gathered, selected, and ordered texts on military methods, reflecting high-level interest in this topic.[2] Michael Hunter has examined at length the development of the *Analects* (*Lunyu* 論語), the most important collection of sayings and lore associated with Confucius. Hunter shows how it came into being during the Western Han period, pieced together out of material from numerous sources.[3]

Two of the most influential intellectuals in early imperial history, Liu Xiang 劉向 (ca. 77–ca. 6 BCE) and, to a lesser degree, his son Liu Xin 劉歆 (d. 23 CE), shaped the texts that guided perceptions of preimperial antiquity. They collected, edited, and ordered texts and fragments, then promulgated the resulting compilations. Sometimes the purpose in creating these anthologies was preservation, but other times it was, tacitly or not, to convey messages to readers, to influence them. Those readers included men as elevated as the emperor but would come to include everyone acquainted with high culture and history. Scholars long failed to adequately appreciate the Liu contributions.[4]

The excavated documents I discuss in this chapter have likewise been undervalued. For they constitute similar processes of purposeful selection and assembly. Being neither poetry nor belles lettres, they fall outside the limits of literature as it was ordinarily conceived of in China. But there can be no doubt, it seems to me, that they represent a mode of interaction with text that those in the border regions shared with those in the center of the empire. This was a form of cultural production and interaction with text that those in humble social strata pursued, just as those in places of influence did.

A Western Han Composite Text

Background

In August 1977, workers taking a day off from the Jiuquan Steel Company made the chance discovery of an archaeological site. As the story goes, they were out hunting and pursued a gazelle atop what appeared to be a mound of earth in a farm field at a place called Huahai 花海 (Yumen, Gansu), some seventy kilometers from the city of Jiuquan.

There the workers found ancient wooden strips, which they reported to the local bureau for the protection of archaeological relics, and two archaeologists subsequently traveled to the site. What had seemed like a natural feature turned out to be the remnants of a Han-era beacon post on a low hillock. The post was a small one, about two meters tall, its base measuring 2.4 by 2.6 meters. All that remained of the structure upon excavation was a corner of the eastern adobe brick wall. The excavations turned up ninety-three wooden strips and fragments with writing on them and a further twelve with no remaining writing, a writing-brush handle and case made from bamboo, hempen clothing and shoes, and wooden utensils and structural elements.[5]

The most unusual find was a stick, thirty-seven centimeters long and somewhat crooked. Originally round, someone had shaped it with seven flat faces separated by distinct edges. Those seven faces contain a text just over two hundred characters in length comprising two sections, one an unusual imperial edict, the other a letter.[6] The content of the two differs in tone, style, and topic, leaving no doubt about the separation. There is, however, no difference in format or script that I can detect in the photographs. An empty space divides what appears to be the final character of the first text from the first character of the second. An imperfection in the wood there leaves it uncertain whether that was intentional. There is no other separation between them.

Most scholars who consider this document concentrate on the first section, the edict. They give little attention to the other part, often eliding it. Some have made the opposite move, concentrating on the letter and skipping the edict.[7] Yet both sections of the document are present. There is no clear demarcation between them; there is no change in script or hand. The content alone indicates that this is a composite text comprising distinct elements, rather than an organic unit. Scholars have not given this dual nature the attention it deserves. The text is worth considering in its entirety:

Edict issued to the imperial heir designate:

My body is distressed and I am now going to perish. I will join with the earth, end and not arise again. I look reverently to the oversight[8] of august heaven, which has extended my presence [on earth]. Treat the ordinary people well and tax them according to proper principles. Preserve the worthy, remain close to the sagely, and definitely gather savvy gentlemen. Exemplify proper teaching, offer to the ancestors, and exert yourself[9] in being Son of Heaven. Huhai[10] destroyed himself, ruining his name and ending his line. Look carefully into what I say. My end will not be long now. I will not long be able to look upon the azure heavens, nor long walk the mighty earth. My way ends here. Tell later generations and my descendants! I am distracted and worried and fear [I will not live to] see my hometown. Do not go against[11] heaven and earth. Sometimes there is loss, sometimes preservation. Departing like leaving a dwelling-hut, going out from a camp or a village:[12] a person is certain to meet death. Be careful—do not choose reckless or base actions.

Younger brother[13] Shi respectfully prostrates himself and bows repeatedly in greeting: May Uncle[14] Mi[15] be well and without worry. You must be suffering greatly in your observation post duties; it is just now spring and the weather is not clement. I prostrate myself and hope that you are provided with well-fitting[16] clothes and agreeable beer and food; that you are keenly watchful in your signal fire duties; that you are lenient and tolerant toward those in your charge.[17] Do not carry out . . . ;[18] I will be extremely favored, extremely favored. I prostrate myself on the ground and bow repeatedly in greeting. I prostrate myself and hope that if you, Uncle Mi, should have someone traveling [this way] that he will then grant me a message, that I may receive . . . urgently your solemn instruction.

制詔皇大(:太)子: 朕(:朕)[19]體不安, 今將絕矣. 與地合司, 眾(:終)[20]不復起. 謹視皇大(:天)之苛 (:伺), 加曾朕(:朕)在. 善愚(:遇)百姓, 賦斂以理. 存賢近聖, 必聚謂士. 表教奉先, 自致天子. 胡佑(:亥)自氾 (:圮), 滅名絕紀. 審察朕(:朕)言. 眾(:終)身毋久. 蒼=之天不可得久視, 堂=之地不可得久履, 道此絕矣. 告後世及其孫子. 忽=錫(:惕)[21]=, 恐見故里. 毋負天地. 更亡更在. 去如郘 (:舍)廬, 下敦閭里. 人固當死, 慎毋取 悇 (:妄)[22]賤. 弟(:弟)時謹伏地芧拜請翁糸足下善毋恙甚苦候望事方春不和時伏願翁糸將侍近衣便酒食, 明察蓬火事, 寬忍小人, 毋行 庶 汶, 時㠯甚=. 伏地再拜請. 時伏願翁糸有往來者便賜時記令, 時奉聞翁糸紤急叡教.[23]

The opening word "edict" marks this text as an imperial pronouncement, and immediately afterward comes the title of the recipient, "imperial heir designate" (*huangtaizi* 皇太子). This format is familiar from received texts, although this is the only example directed at the emperor's heir designate that I have located.[24] The first, imperial, section is where most scholarly attention has focused since the object's recovery. The second part is a letter from a man named Shi to another named Mi. Shi calls himself "younger brother" and refers

to Mi as "uncle." It is, of course, conceivable that the two were
relatives. But far more likely is that these terms were used not in a
literal sense but rather to reflect a personal relationship between a
subordinate writing to someone who is his superior in both age and
position. The use of fictive kinship terminology in this way is common across cultures.[25]

Previous Studies

The writing stick contains neither date nor information that identifies
its precise period. Its dating has thus been a major topic of discussion among those who study the text, in large part because scholars
would like to ascribe the edict to a specific emperor and connect it
to familiar historical events.

Most scholars who have considered the question now believe
that the object comes from the end of the reign of Emperor Wu 武
(140–87 BCE), a judgment based on the content of this edict and the
presence of another document at the same border post dated to 21
August 74 BCE.[26] The year 74 BCE was the last in which Emperor
Wu's successor, Emperor Zhao 昭 (Liu Fuling 劉弗陵, r. 86–74 BCE),
reigned and provides a general periodization for the entire site. That
same document also mentions a man named Feng Shi 馮時. The authors
of the report believe him to be the same "Younger brother Shi" who
features in the letter and who, they think, created the writing stick.[27]

According to the initial report, the 74 BCE date suggests three
likely possibilities for the edict's author: Emperor Zhao; his predecessor, Emperor Wu; or his successor, Emperor Xuan 宣 (Liu Xun
劉詢, r. 73–49 BCE). The report's authors eliminate Emperor Zhao
as potential creator because he had no son and no heir designate.
There is also no mention of Emperor Xuan having left behind any
posthumous edicts, which is how they describe this one. In contrast
to those two, Emperor Wu not only had sons, but historical accounts
record that he addressed several texts to them and left a posthumous
edict for his heir, the future Emperor Zhao.[28]

Emperor Wu composed this edict in 89 BCE, near the end
of his reign, and in it expressed regret about his extensive military
activities in the western reaches. In a discussion of the 89 BCE
edict, historian Tian Yuqing 田余慶 argues that the Huahai text has
a similar, regretful tone. Tian furthermore links the Huahai text's

mention of Huhai, the Second Emperor of Qin, to remarks Emperor Wu made in 91 BCE: "If later generations repeat what I have done, this will be following the path of the fallen Qin" 若後世又如朕所為, 是襲亡秦之跡也.[29] For Tian, the regret that Emperor Wu conveyed and his expressed fear of reprising the end of the Qin dynasty tie the Yumen Huahai text to the historical record and support identifying Emperor Wu as its author.[30] Other scholars have accepted this attribution.[31] But not all. Hu Pingsheng 胡平生 disagrees and follows a conceptually similar path to suggest instead that the Han founder, Gaozu 高祖 (Liu Bang 劉邦, r. 206/2–195 BCE), was the author and the future Emperor Hui 惠 (Liu Ying 劉盈, r. 195–188 BCE), the primary intended recipient.[32]

He Shuangquan 何雙全 also rejects the notion that Emperor Wu composed the Huahai edict. More important than that is the important distinction He makes between dating the creation of the original edict—that is, the content of the text—and the copy that the archaeologists found. As He rightly says, these need not be the same. He believes the stick was copied around 74 BCE from an early Han original. He suggests the text was perhaps Gaozu's composition, but he acknowledges that the available evidence does not support any definitive attribution. Despite the neatness of the copy we have, He sees difficulties in reading the text, making him think that the writing stick is a practice piece. He suggests that the content of the first section may have been cobbled together from multiple sources, although he adds that it retains significant research value.[33] The fact that he makes this argument referring only to the imperial edict and ignoring the obviously distinct letter demonstrates how little importance he grants the latter.

He Shuangquan is undoubtedly correct that a definitive attribution of the edict is impossible. I agree with the authors of the initial report and Tian Yuqing that Emperor Wu is the probable creator. The general dating of 74 BCE is not in doubt for the Huahai site, and Emperor Wu is the most likely possibility from around that time. The preservation of an imperial edict from Gaozu is possible but seems doubtful. Why would an edict like this one, lacking any apparent binding force to motivate its preservation, be found over 120 years later and far from any sort of major archive? The much shorter period of retention required for attribution to Emperor Wu makes it more probable.

Ultimately, the question of the edict's attribution has no definitive answer. Yet, as I have discussed, scholars often choose to focus on that question. They usually give little attention to the letter that follows, often leaving it out. This is typical of how the materials I study in this book have been treated: scholars often ignore their individual content in favor of anything that connects them to prominent historical figures and events. Any possible link to larger events becomes the focus of discussion—even when the evidence is dubious or worse. That impulse is understandable and not limited to the study of early China. Famous historical figures and influential events attract the attention of historians and other readers, and connecting a text to them lends immediate significance. In the case of this stick, scholars have concentrated on the edict that may be linked to Emperor Wu, which then becomes worthy of examination, and give little attention to the letter of an otherwise unknown man that accompanies it. The cost is overlooking the potential for better understanding the lives of less exalted people.

The Object Before Us

He Shuangquan is not the only person to deem the text on the Huahai stick a practice work. Yet I doubt it is practice, or at least that it is an ordinary practice. The most important basis for calling it a practice text is its form: scholars connect it with multisided sticks (gu 觚) that were a medium for writing practice and copying related materials, particularly lexica and proto-lexica in Han times.[34] And the Huahai object does have that general shape.

Yet the Huahai text is obviously no dictionary. Nor does it have the common characteristics of Han-era writing practice, which include repeated characters and phrases, and, usually, a general lack of order.[35] The Huahai text does not appear to be a draft version of some other piece of writing, either. The two constituent parts are distinct and yet complete, and the copy itself is neat and clean. A writing stick from another site, as counterexample, is considerably less well finished than the one from Huahai and bears a more typical practice text, complete with repetitions.[36] The Huahai stick lacks that haphazard form.

The Huahai stick's differences from recognizable student pieces leads me to believe it is something more than writing practice. I suggest instead that we have something like a sampler. I do not mean this in the sense of a collection of models for imitation, but rather as a piece of work done with special care to demonstrate mastery of a skill, with content that was itself a form of self-expression.[37] This would explain both the care of the object's preparation and the choice of its contents.

Matthias L. Richter has argued that the co-occurrence of texts at a given archaeological find or on a given piece of early writing medium alone does not prove an ideological connection between them.[38] Richter's point is a good one, and assumptions based on simple proximity or the fact that texts emerged from a single site deserve scrutiny. Yet in the narrow context of the Huahai writing stick, some relationship seems likely; why else would the two have been copied with such care onto one stick? At the very least, we can say that both texts were part of the life and memory of the copyist who created the version that we have. At the broadest level, we have a concrete example of coexistence of an imperial text—albeit an imperial text of an exceptional tenor—with evidently individual composition.

While these two texts come to us alongside each other, they function in opposition. Their modes differ, as befits individual and official expressions. Both give advice: in one a superior instructs his subordinate, in the other this is reversed. Despite this polarity, clear thematic connections exist between them. There is a general concern with the proper fulfillment of one's appointed tasks, be they those of a border guard or of the sovereign of the realm. And there is exhortation to treat those in one's charge with care, as the emperor's advice to his heir pertains to governing the population of the realm and Shi's letter to Uncle Mi expresses this as the hope that he will be generous toward his subordinates.

That an emperor would exhort his son is not surprising, and history provides examples of similar phenomena, as already noted. The content of the first part of the Huahai composite text is thus not out of keeping with expectations. It is perhaps, however, unexpected that its second part contains advice for a superior from an apparent inferior, even if the latter expresses it in the form of a wish and alongside conventional expressions of goodwill. As I will show, this is not the only case in which that happened.

Despite their apparent differences, a concern for the recipient, expressed in the form of advice, unites these two texts. Their modes of expression differ. The edict is an elegant and evocative composition, while the letter is blunt and repetitious. It is texts like the latter that occupy much of this book. In this instance, however, the two co-occur.

Most scholars who treat the Yumen Huahai text do not consider it as a whole but rather as two things, a letter and an edict, which happen to be alongside each other. They are interested in one or the other. But this is a single object and I think we should treat the text as a unit, however subdivided. Looking at some other examples can help us understand the object, how it came to be, and what it has to tell us about the literate community in which it existed. These other examples can also show the connections this object has to textual activities at the center of the empire and its culture, confirming again that the interaction with text we see in the border regions was part of broader cultural trends.

Texts concerning the King's Staff and the Privileges It Brought

A group of three texts provides a useful comparison for considering composite texts. Unlike the Huahai writing stick, they are grave texts. Archaeologists recovered them from Han dynasty graves in Wuwei Prefecture (Gansu), some five hundred miles south and east of Dunhuang and Juyan. The three examples contain closely related content concerning the privileges due to a holder of the king's staff. The king's staff was an actual wooden staff, just under two meters long (typically, 1.94 m.), with a bird figure atop it. Archaeologists have recovered numerous examples of these bird finials from Han graves and a few staves with the finials still in place.[39]

The Han government granted the king's staff to men of advanced age. The most common formulation, which occurs in traditional and excavated sources, is that men who reached the age of seventy received one. Excavated texts, however, indicate some men received the staff before or after that age. Round numbers often work in general rather than specific senses in classical Chinese and that seems likely to be the case of the received texts relevant to these practices.[40]

The Ten Strips

The first of the three texts comprises ten wooden strips that archaeologists recovered in the late 1950s from a tomb that also contained two bird-topped staves.[41] Although the strips' bindings had decayed so much over time that most of the strips had fallen away before excavation, enough remained to show that the text had originally been wrapped around one staff.[42] The sequence of these strips has provoked a great deal of discussion. A general agreement has emerged among scholars about the blocks of content, with only minor variations persisting.[43]

There is no question about the general sense of the content. The text contains material from one or two edicts detailing the privileges that staff-holders had. They were free to enter government offices and to walk normally when in those offices, rather than being required to rush—a sign of respect—as was usual for commoners. They were immune to prosecution for all but the most serious crimes, and if a criminal proceeding was to occur, it required a formal indictment before any action could be taken. They had the right to travel the side lanes of the imperial highways, instead of outside the reserved area entirely like others. And *anyone*, including an official, who beat or berated one of them was guilty of a serious crime. The text also describes the purpose of the staff as a sign of the holder's status, and it authorizes refurbishing a staff if it grows dingy.

Two brief records supplement these dicta. One concerns the legal complaint lodged by a staff-holder whom an official had ordered beaten. This was, of course, a violation of the staff-holder's privilege, hence a crime. According to the case summary, the official responsible received a sentenced of execution. The other record relates merely that a certain Youbo 幼伯—no surname—was born in 5 CE and received a king's staff in 72 CE. If correct, these dates leave Youbo a bit short of seventy years old. This is one of the pieces of evidence indicating that there was more involved in granting the staff than just age.

The Numbered Twenty-Six Strips

The second text that features here is likewise from a grave in the Mozuizi 磨咀子 tomb group. A local peasant found it and turned it in, in 1981.[44] This means that the details of its excavation are missing. Like the previous example, it consists of a set of strips without bindings. But unlike that text, the strips in this case are numbered on the back, from one to twenty-seven; strip fifteen is missing. These numbers obviate discussion about the text's sequence and integrity. That is helpful, because the text is made up of what are evidently a number of component sections. Without numbers, there would doubtless be even more questions about this text than there were concerning the first example I discussed, since its content has more divisions.

The number of components makes the exact division of this text into sections a matter of disagreement, and scholars have suggested different possibilities.[45] Hu Pingsheng divides the content broadly into two types and twelve sections. These divisions include legal texts concerning treatment afforded elderly persons, and example cases of officials and others who violated those prescriptions being punished, including the forms those punishments took. This general breakdown of content certainly holds true. The content, however, does not match this sequence, as what Hu sees as two types intermingle. I accordingly divide the content into three sections.[46]

The text begins with an undated imperial pronouncement of vague generalities about reverence for the aged and outlining privileges due to them, particularly freedom from paying rents (i.e., taxes) when selling in the market. Another command follows the first, which defines a number of groups that are outside the usual requirements to which commoners were subject. It goes on to say that elders without children to care for them were exempt from rents on their farm fields and in the markets, and were furthermore granted permission to sell beer in the marketplace.

The next section of the text contains two case summaries. One consists of a case summary the grand administrator of Ru'nan 汝南 commandery (in modern Henan and Anhui) submitted to the central government, which bears the date 71 BCE. It concerns an official who had illegally forced a holder of a king's staff to do roadwork. In the fashion of Han case dossiers generally, this one includes not only information about the crime but also the relevant legal text. The wording it gives is quite similar to, but not exactly the same as, that found in the "ten strips" version.

The subsequent example case summary consists mostly of a letter from a commoner named Guang 廣, who addressed the emperor.

Guang complained that he had been insulted and abused by an official, a contravention of his privileges he blamed on a general decline in social mores. Unfortunately, the strip missing from the set comes from this section, leaving us guessing about the result of the complaint. While it may seem fanciful for a commoner to address the emperor, addressing the government was part of early imperial practice.[47] That is not to say the emperor ever saw the document, of course. There is no indication of that. According to the document, the government's response was a request for more information and a command to effect a speedy resolution. The document's date is 10 BCE.

The third and final portion of this text begins with the privileges of the staff-holder—content similar to that I mentioned in regard to the previous texts. The wording here is different from those examples, yet it is unmistakably the same basic content. This is followed by a group of four very brief records of cases dealing with violations of king's staff-holders' privileges and the results of adjudication. In every instance, the result was the execution of the violator. A summary relating numbers of officials and commoners who had been punished for these cases follows that.

The Hantanpo Fragment

My third example text is a fragment that archaeologists recovered in 1989 from a Han grave at Hantanpo 旱滩坡, also in the Wuwei area of Gansu. Among the sixteen pine strips they found are two with content related to privileges afforded to elders. The first strip relates rights I have discussed: that of persons of advanced age to enter official structures at will and to walk normally while in them. Also listed is the stipulation that the elderly were free from being summoned and interrogated by officials in the absence of a formal indictment. The second strip is a fragmentary short summary of a case from the Chang'an region, in which an official stood accused of summoning an elder, then insulting and beating him. This strip is broken and the disposition of the case is absent. Based on parallel content in the "twenty-six strips," it seems likely that things went ill for the official. Interestingly, archaeologists found a staff with a bird finial in this tomb, and the staff shows significant wear, reflecting use over time.[48]

Explanations for the Texts concerning the King's Staff

Official Life

Scholars have put forth a number of theories about the purpose or purposes of these texts, beginning from the recovery of the "ten strips" version and continuing ever since. One opinion holds that this sort of text was buried in the tomb because it had to do with the work of the tomb occupant, whom these scholars believe to have been an official.[49] This proposition aligns these texts with known phenomena. The modern study of legal history has seen a revolution because of extensive textual finds in the tombs of early officials at Shuihudi and Zhangjiashan. In those instances, the usual working assumption is that the texts were objects the deceased used in the performance of official duties, which became part of his burial accountrements.[50]

There are reasons to question interpreting the king's staff materials in this fashion, however. In the cases of both Shuihudi and Zhang-jiashan, the grave assemblages were consistent with persons of some means and included bronzes, lacquerware, and other valuable items alongside large quantities of written material.[51] The graves from which the "ten strips" version and the Hantanpo fragment were excavated were both simple graves containing only very basic coffins. Neither bronze vessels nor other indications of wealth were present. In the former case, no written material other than the "ten strips" version of the king's staff text was found; in the latter, a single bundle of sixteen wooden strips was excavated, of which the relevant fragment was a part. If these were officials of some sort, they could only have been very lowly indeed. It seems at least equally likely that they were simply ordinary people, without special rank or wealth.

Grave Text

One theory holds that the "ten strips version" was created specifically for the purposes of burial with a holder of a king's staff. This hypothesis might then also apply to other copies, as well. There are different explanations for why this might have happened, but I do not find them convincing.

Tomiya Itaru suggests that the staff-holder enjoyed privileges in this life that he wished likewise to have in the afterlife. Tomiya proposes that the document details those privileges in order to convey them to underworld officials.[52] Momiyama Akira 籾山明 agrees with Tomiya that when archaeologists find these texts in graves, those texts were created for burial. While Momiyama does not reject Tomiya's postulation, he expresses reservations about it. For archaeologists have found texts directed to underworld officials. As Momiyama points out, examples of such texts exist and they have labels indicating their purpose, whereas not one of the texts concerning the king's staff does. Momiyama suggests instead that the king's staff texts were memorial documents commemorating the deceased.[53]

While I see some merit in Momiyama's objection to Tomiya's hypothesis, I find his own response unconvincing. If one imagines a text created to function as part of a memorial, a hodgepodge of edicts, statutes, and precedents seems an unlikely candidate. Indeed, no imagination is necessary to know what such a funerary text could look like: the composition of memorial texts for stele inscription was widespread in Eastern Han China. Those texts incorporate various kinds of information yet deal specifically and explicitly with commemorating one subject, taking the form of an integrated whole.[54] These seem much more likely to have been used during the decedents' lives, not funerary creations.[55]

Individual Use

Hu Pingsheng argues that these texts were created by or for individual persons for use during their lives and then buried with them. The purpose was to enable a holder of the staff to assert his prerogatives. This is the line of reasoning that I find strongest and most persuasive. Much of Hu's discussion is based on an important aspect of the texts that other scholars do not take into evident account, and that is the great variation among them. And there is a great deal of variety. The wording of the edicts and ordinances varies, as do the example cases that accompany them. Hu believes that because these were created through or for individual use, the exact wording of the legal stipulations did not matter.[56]

We should not look for an exact matching of written forms in the context of early Chinese manuscript culture. As I discussed in chapter 2, the documentary record is incomplete and various. Seeking perfect consistency is futile. Yet it seems only sensible that, graphic variation aside, the actual texts of legal statutes, edicts, and ordinances should more or less match. Otherwise officials would be hard-pressed to make the sort of precise and consistent decisions about the application of those texts that the early legal system required, upon pain of punishment. The early legal system had room for flexibility in application of the law, but it was a clearly defined space, not a consequence of inconsistent wording.[57]

Hu's analysis is also better supported, in that the actual presence of staves indicates the grave inhabitants held those same items in life. This contrasts with the notion that they were officials or that these texts were directed at the afterlife, neither of which has any concrete evidence supporting it. Hu's interpretation thus requires less assumption. It also accords with Alain Thote's broader assertions about the placement of shengqi 生器 ("objects from life") in tombs, which were items associated with the decedent prior to death and then made part of the grave assemblage.[58]

Although Hu does not present his argument in this way, his position has points of intersection with both of the two other hypotheses. The first position holds that because the graves' occupants were officials, these materials had relevance to their lives. Hu Pingsheng's argument also posits a relevance to their lives, but because they were holders of king's staves. (Asserting that they were officials would require a higher standard of proof.) The fact that actual examples of king's staves were found in the two tombs for which we have excavation information supports this interpretation. A similar assumption of relevance to the occupants' lives undergirds the second position, as well. In the second case, however, that relevance is supposed to be because the deceased were holders of staves who wished to extend their privileges into the afterlife. Hu argues for relevance, like the first position, and specific relevance in the form of ownership, like the second, but for relevance to an individual life in the mundane world.

Conclusion

There is general agreement among previous studies that these composite texts from the northwest were purposeful creations. That is to say, these specific texts came into being through processes of selection and arrangement. While the source material came from elsewhere, creators at the local level determined the concrete forms of these texts. These are points of agreement about the grave texts concerning the king's staff and also offer a way for us to interpret the Huahai composite as a single text unit. This analysis takes it as a whole and does not reduce it to two unrelated sections, in the manner of previous studies.

The first point is that the composite texts were most likely local creations. Indeed no one has expressed doubt about that. But I would argue that there was a shared purpose to their assembly. The king's staff texts seem to have been for personal use, in the asserting of one's legal prerogatives. The Huahai stick was personal, as well. I suggest it was a kind of sampler comprising a text its creator created by selecting and assembling source material, then copying the result onto a stick to demonstrate ability in writing. These composite texts are akin to anthologies and similar collections in terms of character, if brief and unsophisticated in form, and thus connect to modes of creation functioning at the highest levels of Han literary production. In the next chapters, I consider further forms of textual culture that the people of the northwest shared with elites. That begins in the next chapter, which takes up the border regions' version of technical texts, a genre that appeared in multiple forms across the realm.

Chapter Six

Practical Texts

Interaction with text took many forms in early China, including those that did not leave traces. Reading was one such form of interaction. The question of what might motivate someone other than an official or a literato to read is an important one. This chapter presents part of the response. Here I examine texts that were *practical*. As I discussed in chapter 1, scholars have adduced practical motives for acquiring the ability to read and write. They generally construe that practicality in a narrow fashion, however, as concerning work within the imperial bureaucracy. The texts in this chapter offer information that would have been of use in different ways.

Many Han-era texts that archaeologists have recovered from sites of various types are technical, in the sense that they convey information about how to do things. Some of this information might seem like magic or similar practices from a modern, materialist perspective. Yet those texts drew from a body of specialist knowledge and theory and count as technical, too. Hemerological texts are a well-known example. Their analyses of days as suitable or not for particular acts derived from the application of systems of knowledge in the world. And as Donald Harper has recently noted, they have also emerged from the northwest.[1] Medical and veterinary texts have emerged in large numbers from the northwest and are similarly concerned with techniques of healing, primarily through the use of medicaments of various sorts.[2]

Most of the texts in this chapter concern methods of visual examination (*xiang* 相). These texts instructed their users on making determinations about the quality of some type of item, animal, or person on the basis of informed viewing. I consider examples that treat the examination of horses and dogs, as well as a text on evaluating swords. This is an important group of texts, and not only because they concern making decisions that could have major—perhaps even mortal—consequences. Evaluation texts, including the same topics that I discuss here, were part of the broader culture of the time. The transmitted canon reflects their presence, as does their presence among Han-period tomb arrays. The people who lived in the northwestern border regions were not separate from this culture.

In this chapter I first consider evaluation texts that archaeologists found in tombs before shifting to consider examples from the northwest. I do this for two reasons. First, the tomb texts confirm the wider presence and forms of this type of text in Han times. Just as in the case of composite texts, the subject of the preceding chapter, users of evaluation texts in the northwest were part of broader textual culture. Discussion of received accounts supports this. The tomb examples furthermore provide illustrative contrasts to the material at the core of the discussion. The texts of the northwest that I focus on were written in a simple style, with few complexities of presentation or reasoning. But the tomb texts preserve a variety of presentations, including one that is complicated. Considering tomb texts confirms that the plainspoken style of the examples from the northwest was not the only one, which in turn suggests an audience of less-skilled readers.

While I treat mainly evaluation texts here, I do not title this chapter "Evaluation Texts" because of the final section. There I consider a technical text of a different sort. It offers advice concerning the brewing of beer. While the specific form of the text is ritual, the information it conveys is practical. As an example, the fragment helps bridge the gap between the utilitarian writings of this chapter and the more elevated content of the next.

Evaluation Texts as a Type

Visual evaluation in the form of examining human physiognomy was widespread in early China. It derived conclusions about a person's qualities from their facial features and other physical characteristics, sometimes with distinctly counterintuitive associations. Many early philosophical and historical texts speak of these practices. No early text on evaluation survived as part of the received body of literature from early imperial times, except as quoted in other texts. The Dunhuang corpus includes later, medieval manuscripts concerning evaluation of humans on the basis of physical features, including facial characteristics, the shape of the body and limbs, and the presence of moles and other spots.[3] The excavated examples I discuss in this chapter are the earliest texts concerning evaluation that I have been able to locate.

There is a subheading that lists evaluation texts in the first extant bibliography in China, the "Monograph on Literature" ("Yiwenzhi" 藝文志), a chapter in *Han History*. This bibliography has a heading for technical texts, "Techniques" (*shushu* 數術), under which it includes subheadings for astronomy, calendrics, and prognostication of various sorts.[4] Evaluation texts come under the subheading "Methods of Form" (*xingfa* 形法). This classification includes texts that give instruction in evaluation of various sorts, mostly by performing visual observations and drawing conclusions on that basis.

Li Ling 李零, considering the *Han History*'s monograph together with other materials, divides evaluation into four types: mountains, rivers, buildings, and cemeteries; humans and domestic animals; inanimate objects; and agriculture and husbandry, concerning such things as soil.[5] The compiler's notes concerning this subsection in the "Monograph on Literature" similarly summarize the titles as treating the suitability of topography for construction, the physiognomy of humans and animals, and considering the appearances of objects to make decisions about worth and auspiciousness. The notes explain the relationship between the exterior characteristics of these things and their attributes as a mundane one: "It is like pitch pipes, each of which, being long or short, calls forth its tone. It is not that there is a ghost or spirit in them—the calculation itself makes it so" 猶律有長短, 而各徵其聲. 非有鬼神, 數自然也.[6] Yao Minghui 姚明輝 (1881–1961) compared the conception this line represents to the physics of musical tones, in which faster and slower rates of vibration correspond to higher and lower pitches.[7] In his desire to stress its proto-scientific aspects, Yao may give the "Monograph on Literature" credit for more sophistication than it has. Yet the explanation's prosaic tenor and concrete focus are undeniable. It explicitly refutes any supernatural aspect of the relationship. While practices connected to auspiciousness or the absence thereof may strike a modern reader as intrinsically superstitious, the texts explain the mechanisms involved in a pragmatic fashion.

"Methods of Form" includes two titles that relate to the materials I consider in this chapter: "Evaluating Valuable Swords" ("Xiang bao jiandao" 相寶劍刀) and "Evaluating the Six Kinds of Beasts" ("Xiang liuchu" 相六畜).[8] There is nothing to link these two titles to the specific texts that archaeologists have recovered. This fact has not prevented modern scholars from asserting connections between them and the texts, unilluminating as those attempts have been. Yet the presence of these titles among the small number listed confirms the prominence of these specific types of evaluation—of swords and of animals—in Han times.

Its title tells us that "Evaluating the Six Kinds of Beast" treated a variety of animals, but commentators explain the specific identities of the "six beasts" variously. Even the number is uncertain, as "six" in such contexts can denote either the number *six* or a set of uncertain size about that big. The most common explanation is these were in fact six in number: horse, ox, goat, fowl, dog, and pig.[9] The seventh-century *Sui History* (*Sui shu* 隋書) contains a bibliographic monograph, which lists the "Classic on Evaluating Horses" ("Xiangma jing" 相馬經). Commentary on that entry further names the titles of works on animal evaluation, including several each on horses, oxen, and fowl of different sorts.[10] Presumably at least some of those derived from early antecedents, but none is extant and only a few fragments remain.[11] Archaeologists have in recent decades recovered three texts concerning the evaluation of horses and dogs, some of which have been published and others that await publication.[12] Veterinary materials, including treatments and records, also feature among excavated medical texts.[13] While not directly related to evaluation, they show that a body of serious texts on animals existed in Han times.

Evaluating Horses

The best-known text on animal evaluation that archaeologists have recovered concerns horses. It comes not from the northwestern military context, but from a Han-era tomb at a site called Mawangdui

馬王堆 in Hunan Province. The Mawangdui tomb is famous for the manuscripts of well-known texts it produced, including *Laozi Daodejing* 老子道德經 and *Zhouyi* 周易, along with others. But they are not all that was there. Among the Mawangdui texts comes a work on evaluating horses, written on silk and comprising seventy-seven lines and more than five thousand characters. Scholars have written a number of articles about this text since its discovery, generally referring to it as the "Classic on Evaluating Horses" ("Xiang ma jing" 相馬經).[14] That phrase, however, does not occur in the text. Zhao Kuifu 趙逵夫 points out that the text in fact begins with what seems like an obvious title: "The Chapter on the Analysis of the Great Brightness" ("Daguang po zhang" 大光破章). He suggests this is a better label for the text we have, which he believes to have been part of the "Classic on Evaluating Horses," just not the entire work.[15]

The lack of an extant "Classic on Evaluating Horses" and the absence of that title here make any connection between the two speculative and, in my view, not very useful. But Zhao is certainly correct that "The Chapter on the Analysis of the Great Brightness" is the best designation for the text we have in front of us. Given that its label suggests it is a chapter, it likely comes from a larger work. But there is nothing to indicate it was part of a "Classic on Evaluating Horses," despite scholars' assumptions to the contrary. This is a case of a phenomenon that occurs elsewhere, in which the expectation that a recovered text must necessarily relate to one mentioned or found in the received corpus leads to discussion of the new material down particular, uncertain, and often unilluminating paths.[16] Here I will examine it in its attested context.

The Content of "Great Brightness"

Zhao Kuifu examines the text of the manuscript "The Chapter on the Analysis of the Great Brightness" and deduces from its content, structure, and repetitions that the text contains three layers, which the copyist did not differentiate by paratextual means. The core content, discussing how to evaluate a horse on the basis of its eyes, comprises the first twenty-two lines of the text. The remaining lines contain two commentaries: an explanatory commentary (lines 23–43) that elucidates some—not all—aspects of the core text, and a glossing commentary (lines 44–77) that explains a number of specific terms. There is nothing in the text to mark the three segments, but Zhao's proposal so neatly explains the text's repetitions and apparent digressions that scholars now accept it as fact.[17]

The presence of commentary also makes sense because of the difficulty of the core text's content, much of which is obscure and filled with specialized vocabulary.[18] This is not the sort of vocabulary problem that occurs whenever a modern reader encounters words that are rare because they are specific to a particular context. Rather, parts of "Great Brightness" are so far removed from evaluating horses that, without the accompanying commentary, they seem more lyrical than expository.[19] The extensive use of rhyme strengthens this impression, and the repeated use of analogy further complicates matters.[20] The end result is a composition that scholars from the first have asserted resembles a rhapsody (*fu* 賦), the most recondite poetic form of Han times, or a riddle.[21] A couple of brief passages will give an impression of the text. In the interest of clarity, I have chosen example passages that are relatively straightforward.

Wang Shujin 王樹金 describes the following lines as an internal summary of the text: "Get the rabbit and the fox, the bird and the fish. If you have these four things, do not [bother to] evaluate the rest" 得兔與狐, 鳥與魚, 得此四物, 毋相其餘.[22] This brief, rhymed section uses animal analogies to communicate a set of characteristics. If a horse possesses all of these, it says, the evaluator need look no further. Yet the body of the text contains no explanation of the significance of the animals or the characteristics they might represent. The combination of obscurity and rhyme here makes earlier comparisons to rhapsody and riddle seem plausible. Only later in the text, in the section Zhao Kuifu identifies as the glossing commentary, do we find the explanation:

> "Get the rabbit and the fox, the bird and the fish" means you want to get a rabbit's head and shoulders, and you want to get a fox's eye . . .[23] and its ears and its cheekbones, you want to get a bird's eye and neck and chest, and you want to get a fish's dorsal fin (i.e., mane) and backbone.

> 得兔與狐, 鳥與魚者, 欲得[兔]之頭與其肩, 欲得狐周草與其耳與其肫, 欲得鳥目與頸膺, 欲得魚之鬐與脊.[24]

This, too, is impressionistic, but it is at least explicit in its identification of what characteristic each animal stood for. Without the commentary, the original lines have little apparent connection to horses. The following lines from the primary text work in a similar fashion:

> Next to the river, there is an abrupt mound. Behind, do not reject the high; outside, do not reject the precipitous. In the upright, do not reject the straight; in the round, do not reject the square. Then you can pursue good fortune and flee misfortune. The one who follows this way can differentiate Yin and Yang.
>
> 水之旁, 有危封, 後不厭高, 外不厭篕. 立不厭直, 團不厭方, 可以馳福, 可以逃凶, 守此道者辨陰陽.[25]

Only from the commentary does the reader learn that—in the commentary's reading, anyway—this passage instructs the reader in the evaluation of a horse's hooves.[26] The mention of Yin and Yang adds an additional layer of complexity by linking this text to cosmological thinking, and indeed content related to cosmology appears elsewhere in it, too.

The remainder of "The Chapter on the Analysis of the Great Brightness" consists of similar passages and patterns of assertion and commentary. The result is a long and complicated work that consists, at least in the copy we have, of multiple, interwoven layers. A reader who wished to use this chapter—and any larger work it might derive from—in evaluating a horse would need to comprehend not only an extended text but also its accompanying sections and the relationships between the parts. Using this text for its apparent purpose would thus have been a complicated and iterative process.

Evaluating Dogs

Horses are not the only animals whose examination was important enough to warrant written consideration in Han times. Archaeologists have also recovered text fragments from tombs that give instructions for evaluating dogs. One of these has not yet been published. According to its description, it consists of just a few damaged strips that discuss the physical form of hounds and its relationship to speed. The specific context of that text's recovery is significant: it came from the tomb of a famous Han-period nobleman, whose tomb also contained a great deal of canonical literature. This tells us that an interest in dogs was not incompatible with high culture.[27]

Archaeologists recovered another text concerning dogs from a tomb at Yinqueshan 銀雀山 in Shandong Province. The occupant of this tomb seems to have been a government official, and his burial array included a variety of texts dating to around the second century BCE. A number of these are military in nature, suggesting he had an interest in martial matters, and it is those military texts that have drawn most scholarly attention.[28] His tomb also produced a severely damaged text fragment consisting of approximately 230 legible characters on fourteen strips and bearing the title "Method for Evaluating Dogs" ("Xiang gou fang" 相狗方).[29]

By all appearances, "Evaluating Dogs" was not as long as "The Analysis of the Great Brightness" was. Although much content is missing, "Evaluating Dogs" seems to have consisted of hundreds of characters, rather than thousands. Its style is direct and the questions that exist about understanding it result from damage or problems of usage—things that would not have presented difficulties to an informed contemporary reader. This contrasts with the main text of "Great Brightness," with its difficult style and absence of clear connection to its topic. "Evaluating Dogs" has no layers to its text, and no accompanying commentary. Indeed, little commentary is necessary, as its unadorned style leaves few ambiguities, and there are no connections to expressly philosophical issues. This is not the result of inferior subject matter. The dog appears in canonical texts, early philosophical works, in accounts of emperors' activities, and slightly later in a poetic rhapsody—and as I noted already, another text on dogs was found in a nobleman's tomb.[30]

The text fragment begins, "Method for Evaluating Dogs: If there are three sections between the shoulders . . . it will catch large game; if there are two, it will catch medium game" 相狗方: 肩 □ 間參瓣者, 及大禽; 二者, 及中禽.[31] This line reflects the pragmatic focus of the entire text, which concerns predicting a dog's hunting ability on the basis of its appearance. The text presents the process of evaluation in plain language and using simple logic. The only question in the interpretation of this example line arises from a lost character that leaves its specific anatomical referent uncertain. The sense, which asserts a relationship between the width of the withers and hunting capability, is nonetheless clear.

Another line is more general: "Whenever evaluating a dog, the leg should be higher than the knee, and the rump should be higher than the shoulders" 凡相狗, 卻 (:腳)高於桼卩 (:膝), 尻高於肩.[32] This is a bit puzzling. The word I translate here as "leg" is generally used to mean "foot," which does not work in context to describe normal anatomy. Even understanding this word as "leg" leaves the sense a bit unclear, as it seems self-evident that a leg should extend above the knee. I suspect the point of this clause is to avoid short-legged dogs, with short thighs that leave their knees close to the body, and to prefer long-legged dogs, whose knees are well below the trunk. The second part, at any rate, is evident, and while modern dogs often slope downward from the withers, a preference for high hindquarters, like the one this text reflects, still exists among some breeds.[33] These questions are far removed from the interpretive difficulty of a text like "The Chapter on the Analysis of the Great Brightness."

The Texts in Comparison

Despite sharing a similar purpose, in that they guide the evaluation of animals, the texts I have discussed so far in this chapter differ in their presentations. They represent a variety of approaches to the conveyance of technical knowledge. "Great Brightness" is a complicated text that presents the task of determining a horse's quality in an elaborate and allusive fashion, complete with built-in auto-commentary. "Method for Evaluating Dogs" presents the process of judgment in a simpler way, without allusion, commentary, or real complexity. The two thus place very different demands on their readers, which in turn indicates they could reach distinct audiences. The audience for "Great Brightness" would have needed a high level of education and sophistication to comprehend that text. The reader and user of "Evaluating Dogs" would have needed far less. It would have been accessible to a larger number of people from a variety of social strata. In the next section I am going to discuss two fragments of text recovered from the Han dynasty northwestern military context. Shorter even than "Evaluating Dogs," they are more akin to it in terms of language and reasoning, suggesting accessibility to readers without the extensive education needed to make sense of an elaborate composition like "Great Brightness."

Texts on the Evaluation of Horses from the Northwest

That "Great Brightness" is difficult to understand probably reflects the existence of an elite equestrian culture. Surely, its user would have needed to be very well educated in order to make sense of its elaborate, multilayered structure and the allusive phrasings of the core text. There are references to material and texts related to the evaluation of horses throughout the received corpus from the imperial period, confirming that such writing was part of the broader literate culture of the time.[34]

Horse texts are uncommon among paleographic finds, even by the very relative standards that must apply in such a small body of material. Yet "Great Brightness" is not the only example that archaeologists have recovered. Some examples come to us embedded in other types of writing. He Runkun 賀潤坤 points to a recovered Qin period hemerological "daybook" (rishu 日書)—an example of a genre familiar from excavated texts—that names positive physical qualities of horses alongside rituals connected with horse husbandry. It is not a manual on selecting horses, but He's insight that this sort of text presages the more directly practical approach of evaluation texts seems spot on.[35]

There are two tantalizing fragments that deal directly with evaluating horses among the excavated materials from the northwest.[36] While brief, they demonstrate another register of language in evaluation texts—one far more accessible than "Great Brightness." The first of these other texts is a short and clear fragment: "When Bole checked a horse, he had his way to know: / At age fourteen or fifteen, the teeth are flat below" 伯樂相馬自有刑 (:形), 齒十四五當下平.[37] Bole is the name of a famous legendary expert on the evaluation of horses, the subject of stories that grew more marvelous over the centuries. Here his name is metonymic shorthand for someone knowledgeable about horseflesh.

I have opted for a loose rendering of this fragment that preserves what I think are its two most noteworthy characteristics.[38] The first of these is the lack of anything hard to understand. Aside from a common variation in graphic form, the text is simple and easy to comprehend, devoid of difficult vocabulary and obscure phrasing. The other thing to note about this short section is the simple rhyme, which is also present in the original. This implies something not merely meant for reading but for reciting, and in this context perhaps functioned as a mnemonic for learning how to tell the age of a horse. "Great Brightness" contains rhyme, too, but in that intricate context, the effect becomes poesis rather than simple aid to memory, as in the case of the Bole rhyme.

A second fragment of horse evaluation text from the northwest presents a middle ground between "Great Brightness" and the Bole rhyme. While the strip is apparently intact, its content is clearly part of a longer, no longer extant, text. The lack of context makes any reading tentative but I translate its core content as follows:

> "The gut small." "The gut small" means the bottom of the belly is flat. "The spleen small." "The spleen small" means it will be obedient. If the ears are matched, it will be obedient. For the ears, you want them low; for the eyes you want them high; between them should be four inches (9.2 cm.) at the base.

> 腸小, 所胃(:謂)腸小者, 腹下平. 脾小, 所胃(:謂)脾小者, 聽. 耳寓(:偶), 聽. 耳欲卑, 目欲高 閒本四寸.[39]

Nowhere does this text mention the word "horse." Yet the content of its advice closely resembles that concerning the evaluation of horses in the sixth-century agricultural handbook *Important Techniques for the Common People* (Qimin yaoshu 齊民要術). For this reason, in one of the first books to treat recovered materials, Luo Zhenyu and Wang Guowei deemed this strip to be a section of a text on equine evaluation, and everyone who has written about it since agrees.[40] While I would avoid asserting an association with a specific title, that general categorization seems correct.

The text on this excavated strip contrasts with the Bole fragment in presentation. It does not rhyme, and its phrasing is a bit more complicated. The text also has something of a commentarial appearance, in that it explains the significance of certain short phrases. This suggests it might gloss or otherwise explain a larger text. Or it may be that its own advice is truncated into very brief points, with most information in its auto-commentary. On the other hand, its diction is lucid and its explanations give the practical reasons behind expressed preferences rather than unpacking allusive language in the fashion of "Great Brightness." The cosmological thinking present in that text is not apparent here. This fragment gives advice about recognizing a good horse that is uncomplicated and easy to understand, and yet deeper than just linking tooth wear with age. Texts conveying practical advice in this mode were not limited to animals, as the next section shows.

Sword Evaluation

Archaeologists recovered a short document discussing the visual evaluation of swords from the site of a Han-era military outpost in the Juyan area, within Inner Mongolia. The text concentrates on identifying a quality sword by examining the metal of its blade. The manuscript has no label. I will refer to it, on the basis of its content, as "Evaluating Swords."[41]

We know nothing about "Evaluating Swords" aside from what its contents and the circumstances of its recovery tell us. We are completely ignorant about its source and its authorship. Some scholars have proposed it could be a selection, either from an expert's experience evaluating swords or from an earlier, sword-related text.[42] Even more readers have supposed, explicitly or implicitly, that "Evaluating Swords" has a relationship with the title "Evaluating Valuable Swords" that appears in the *Han History* "Monograph on Literature."[43] There is, however, nothing connecting "Evaluating Swords" to that title, or any other found in the "Monograph on Literature." This is another example of the phenomenon I mentioned already, in that readers sometimes forcibly relate a recovered text to a known title or event. Since "Evaluating Swords" makes sense as it is, and there is no indication that it comes from another text, treating it as an independent work is best.

"Evaluating Swords" as we have it comprises six pine strips, each containing one line of text, with a total of 209 characters. The hand that copied out the "Evaluating Swords" manuscript did so in a very legible script, and the strips are very well preserved. There are seven bullet points in the text, marking breaks of different sorts. No other punctuation occurs. There are notches on the strips for three lines of binding, one each at the top and bottom and one in the middle of the strips, but the bindings are not present and the strips are loose.[44]

The separation of the strips invites questions about the sequence and integrity of the text as we have it. Due to the flow of the text and the presence of brief summaries of content in it (see the following discussion), there is no real question about the sequence of the strips. The completeness of the text is another matter. A number of scholars have suggested that "Evaluating Swords" as we have it is incomplete.[45] But others argue on the basis of structure, textual parallels, and content that nothing significant is missing, at most only an internal summary.[46] While we cannot know with certainty whether this copy of "Evaluating Swords" is intact, the text seems whole and there are no obvious lacunae. On the other hand, some content that does not fit into any of the internal summaries is present in the text, suggesting at least one more such summary might have existed.

"Evaluating Swords" is undated, but other materials from the same pit bear dates ranging from 9 BCE to 21 CE, giving a rough idea of when this copy of the text circulated.[47] It is important to distinguish between the date of the manuscript copy and that of the text's creation, because they can differ.[48] The content of "Evaluating Swords" may date to early Western Han times, over a century earlier than the manuscript. Its descriptions apply to swords made from worked and treated steel, which became important in the early Western Han. There seems to have been a shift in the style of popular sword around the middle of the Western Han, and "Evaluating Swords" treats the earlier form.[49] On the other hand, the records I treat in the next section show by their choice of vocabulary that the shift in sword types was not complete.

An early Western Han dating would put "Evaluating Swords" at the tail end of what Ma Mingda 馬明達 has called the "Golden Age of the Sword" in China, which lasted from the eighth century BCE until the Han dynasty. Ma Mingda notes that this was a time in which there were both technological advances in metallurgy and developments in sword theory and technique. In this period, swords were both weapons and signs of social status. Along with developments in technology and practice came connoisseurship, collecting, and high prices for rarities. This, in turn, led to the potential for counterfeiting valuable swords and a need for skilled assessment. These things are part of the background of "Evaluating Swords."[50]

As Ma Mingda points out, however, "Evaluating Swords" is exclusively practical in focus. Nowhere does it show any interest in identifying famous swords, recognizing antiques, or avoiding fakes. The text is concerned only with judging a particular example as a weapon. According to "Evaluating Swords," for a sword to be old is certainly in its favor; I think this is probably because its quality is proven. But an interest in rarities as such would be different. Nor does the text refer to decorative embellishments, such as one might expect to grace an implement made or owned for show rather than for use. The descriptions in "Evaluating Swords" concern only things that indicate properties of the blade. This text is not about how to find a collector's item or an antique, but rather how to determine a sword's quality on the basis of visual examination and so as to select the good and avoid the poor.[51]

One other sort of information is noticeably absent from "Evaluating Swords" and that is explanation. The text never explains why a particular characteristic indicates good quality and merely states that it does. This suggests that the text was not created by or for a maker of swords or someone otherwise interested in the deeper aspects of the smith's art but rather for someone whose interest was solely in selecting a sword for use. That swords were a part of a soldier's circumstances would seem self-evident, and excavated records of various types confirm they were.

Swords in Recovered Documents from the Juyan Region

Manuscript texts from China's northwest show that swords were part of life in the border regions during Han times. One way the presence of swords emerges is records of their use for unauthorized interpersonal violence within the Han population. A pair of documents from 67 BCE records the convictions and arrests of two men involved in an armed altercation with each other. One document states that the border soldier Jin Gui 靳龜 was guilty of using a sword to wound a certain Han Heyang's 函何陽 hand in two places. A second says Han

Heyang was guilty of wounding Jin Gui in the thigh by means of a sword.[52] Another group of three manuscript fragments relates how an official named Xian 憲 argued with a man named Tan 譚, used a sword to wound Tan in the chest, then stole a government crossbow and some bolts and fled.[53] Other documents mention apparently similar occurrences.[54] Sometimes criminals obtained arms for illegal purposes by stealing them from an official armory.[55]

Equipment inventories are common among the military documents from Juyan and show the presence of personal and government swords. Some simply list swords, without indicating who owned them, as in the case of one strip that records swords alongside spears and shields.[56] Others tabulate specifically "official" (guan 官) swords, marking them as government property. That implies the presence of private swords: otherwise there would be nothing to distinguish the official swords from.[57] One document, an accounting of items that a particular teamster transported, provides further evidence of this because, along with other things, it itemizes "official" crossbows and "private" (si 私) swords.[58] This confirms the presence of both public and personal weapons. These records do not provide any information beyond counts. There is no indication that there was official tracking of specific government-owned weapons. That suggests a soldier would have had some level of ability to determine which sword he carried and thus an interest in identifying the quality of a blade.

Official records of individuals also mention swords, confirming the fact that soldiers would have been interested in evaluating swords. Some documents identify a person by name and village—that is, give basic identifying information—and include both physical description and the fact that the one in question had a sword. One such example enters the sword after the description of its owner, with his other property; another example inserts that man's sword among the aspects of his physical description.[59] This suggests a particularly high level of identification of swords with individuals. Other documents list personal effects, including weapons such as swords (as well as crossbows, bows, and arrows), in the possession of individuals. In at least some cases, those include government property held by individuals.[60]

While the government issued swords, which soldiers held as accoutrements of their service, that was not the only route to their possession. Written records of sales of swords on credit, and of debts owed for sword purchases, indicate that low-ranking soldiers owned those weapons personally. One from Juyan, for instance, states that a border soldier named Kong Ding 孔定 sold one Guo Jiajun 郭嬬君 a sword on credit.[61] A similar document from Dunhuang says that a Jing Dan 景黮 did the same, though that purchaser's name has been lost.[62] Still another document records that the military scribe Ji Shezhi 季赦之 owed a soldier named Ke Wannian 尅萬年 money for a sword and another for an overcoat.[63] Although their fragmentary state does not permit the reconstruction of a complete picture of the context, these documents leave no doubt that individuals owned the swords they used and would thus have motivation to interact with a text like "Evaluating Swords."

The Content of "Evaluating Swords"

"Evaluating Swords" is fairly short and the discussion here will cover it entirely. In the interest of brevity, though, I will not present the complete translation. I previously published a translation of the entire text and interested readers should look there.[64]

As noted already, the copy that archaeologists recovered from Jianshui Jinguan is apparently complete and comprises six strips and just over two hundred characters, all written in a clear hand for easy reading. Interacting with this text would have required far less knowledge, time, and effort than a long or complicated one would have. "Evaluating Swords" opens in a very direct fashion, with instructions about how to identify a quality sword:

• One who wishes to know whether a sword is good and old should stand and draw it. If you look at it and the body has no gouging, it is old equipment. One who looking at [a sword] wishes to know if it is a sharp one should definitely look to see that in its body there are paired black lines that are unbroken and that at the tip these seem to disappear. If you look and see that the white and hard ends before reaching the last third, this is a sharp and good sword of the realm. If you see also that the body has in it an appearance like millet grains and it is sharp, it is even better.

- 欲知劍利善故器者，起拔之，視之身中無推處者，故器
  也．視欲知利善者，必視之身中有黑兩桁不絕者，其逢
  (:鋒)如不見．視白堅未至逢(:鋒)三分所而絕, 此天下利善劍
  也．又視之身中生如黍粟狀, 利劍也, 加以善.[65]

This first passage makes clear that the text concerns a visual examination and strictly material traits. It sets out a group of four characteristics. The first of these, the absence of "gouging" left over from the sword's creation, establishes that it is an old weapon. This is clearly a positive characteristic, but there is no information about why it is so. It may have to do with equipment that has been in use for a while and is thus of proven quality, rather than something new and untested.

The subsequent characteristics indicate increasing quality of manufacture. "Paired black lines" were a requirement, probably because they would indicate a blade welded from ferrous metals of differing carbon content: high carbon material has a light color and is hard but brittle, while lower carbon metal is dark and softer but tougher. The lines reflect a blade that combined them into something better than either would have been alone.[66] Those lines should be visible but not run to the tip of the blade, as the hard material should not extend to the tip. This was probably because brittle, harder metal there would be subject to damage. The best swords furthermore had a spotted appearance on the main part of the blade that presumably reflected superior quality work in forging the blade from its constituent metals. The following section deals with swords to avoid:

- One who wishes to know if a sword is poor and so not to bear it, or that it is new equipment, should go into the sunlight. If, when you look carefully, the white and hard follows up the tip; or there is gouging, or the black and the hard are clearly separated; or there is no patterning, or along the length there is patterning and it is in the hard; or the [swirling patterns of] clouds and ether follow each other; then these are all swords from poor welders. Sabers and swords are of the same sort.

- 欲知幣(:弊) 劍以不報(:服)者, 及新器者, 之日中, 驛(:達)視
  白堅隨逢上者及推處、白黑堅分朋者, 及無文、縱有文而在
  堅中者, 及雲氣相遂, 皆幣(:弊)合人劍也. 刀與劍同等.[67]

This sets out a number of indications of poor swords, all of which reflect inferior processes of manufacture. As in the case of good characteristics, most of these are associated with the process of fusing different metals together to create the blade. Most of the negatives are the reverse of the positives.

These two passages hang together, and not only from the perspective of the modern reader. The creator of this text also saw them as such, a point that emerges from the close of the section. It consists of a pair of phrases saying, "The preceding are four things about good swords; the preceding are six things about bad swords" • 右善劍四事 • 右幣(:弊) 劍六事. This groups the two sets together and divides them from what follows. It also provides helpful information for a reader who might be uncertain about the structure of the text. Knowing how many points the text makes ensures the reader will know how many were there to comprehend.

After this division, "Evaluating Swords" pivots to another section, which concentrates on a blade's surface patterns. The patterns have names that are impressionistic and their precise significance is uncertain. There are four good ones, including "hanging curtains" (*xuanbo* 縣[:懸]薄). The text also throws in, "A sword that sings is sharp and good" 劍鳴(:鳴)者利善. The patterns on poor swords include "fighting cocks" (*douji* 鬥雞), and the text furthermore warns against swords that are "of coarse make" (*cu* 麤).

In the middle of this section comes the one place where "Evaluating Swords" digresses from its narrow, practical focus to offer a brief justification for its approach: "If a strong one could have a bad exterior appearance, what would a weak one be like?" 強者表惡(:惡),[68] 弱則利奈何? This seems to be speaking in the same materialist vein as the line from the *Han History* "Monograph on Literature" about pitch pipes that I cited toward the beginning of this chapter. "Evaluating Swords," here as elsewhere, presents its content in a plain and ingenuous style.

Presentation and Reasoning across the Evaluation Texts

The writing in "Evaluating Swords" is straightforward to the point of repetitiousness. Its grammar is uncomplicated and its sentences at most string together short clauses, preferring clarity over variety. Its internal summaries tell the reader how many points to look for, in case the reader was unsure, perhaps due to a lack of experience. The text has no layers, no commentary or definitions, and its advice is not in the form of metaphors requiring interpretation. Indeed, what little ambiguity there is about its sense arises from vocabulary that is unfamiliar to a modern reader. The reasoning that "Evaluating Swords" employs is at least equally elementary, and its process of deduction moves to a binary determination about whether a given sword is good or bad. In its simplicity and self-conscious transparency, "Evaluating Swords" calls to mind a bureaucratic document.

Comparing "Evaluating Swords" to the other evaluation texts I have discussed helps bring out the importance of these characteristics. The various texts have commonalities. All deal with visual evaluation, which implies practical applicability, and none departs from the material realm in making recommendations. Yet the methods of these texts and their evaluations are quite different.

The style of "Great Brightness," for instance, is difficult, its structure complicated. Whether or not those scholars who judge it to be a rhapsody or a riddle are correct, they have a point: its elaborate presentation can plausibly be construed as literary in nature. It is certainly not a blunt, utilitarian text. Making use of "Great Brightness" to reach a decision about a horse would have required a high level of reading ability.

"Great Brightness" is close in form to elevated literature; "Evaluating Swords" is more or less the opposite, eschewing elaboration and complication in favor of simplicity. So while the two reflect a shared interest in visual evaluation, they represent quite different aspects of that interest. There is another difference as well. The lives of the wealthy occupants of the Mawangdui tomb that produced "Great Brightness" would not—at least ordinarily—depend on the selection of a horse in the same way that the life of a soldier in a border region might depend on recognizing a well-made sword.

I would further bring into this discussion the excavated fragments on horse evaluation, which are more akin to "Evaluating Swords" than they are to "Great Brightness." Their simplicity, like that of "Evaluating Swords," means they would be accessible to a broad audience. I propose that this is not a coincidence. In the context of the northwestern military installations where they were found, it is precisely this sort of text that would be meaningful to readers or listeners with little or no proper education, who had a limited vocabulary. The "Method for Evaluating Dogs," a tomb text in an unadorned writing style, suggests that written diction did not exclude upward: a highly educated person could appreciate both intricate and simple writing. The accessibility of the latter, however, would make it appealing to a wider range of readers and listeners.

Coda: Ritual Brew

The texts I have looked at so far in this chapter all tell the reader how to do visual examinations of different kinds. They are *practical*, in that they are concerned with doing concrete things for concrete purposes. In this closing section I would like to shift the focus and look at a final text from the northwestern border context. It relays information about brewing beer—another kind of practical information. The fragment that we have consists of a single, damaged strip:

> . . . the one responsible for beer: the grains must be pure, the starter and malt must be at their right time, the soaking and the boiling must be clean, the water source sweet, the clay vessels must be goodly, and an evenness of fire must be achieved—all these six things. The master brewer . . .

□掌酒者, 秫稻必齋, 麴糵必時, 湛饎必絜, 水泉香, 陶器必良, 火齊必得, 兼六物. 大酉[69]

This is some good advice for making beer in the early Chinese fashion. With exception of a prepared starter, necessary for properly fermenting the available grains, these things apply, mutatis mutandis, for small-scale brewing even today.[70] As a text, this fragment has some evident commonalities with "Evaluating Swords," being similarly uncomplicated in diction and repetitive in structure. It even includes a label that provides the reader with a count of the points just covered, like "Evaluating Swords" does, giving its structure added clarity.

In the case of this fragment there is, however, a complicating factor, as the text has a parallel in the "Monthly Ordinances" ("Yue-ling" 月令) chapter of the *Record of Ritual* (*Liji* 禮記).[71] This is not the only example of text apparently derived from "Monthly Ordinances" in the northwest region. In chapter 3 I discussed another, extensive example, that of the wall inscription from Xuanquanzhi. There, an edict turned the precepts of "Monthly Ordinances" into statutes. That parallel, and indeed the overlap with text now in *Records of Ritual* generally, raises a number of questions about the nature of the fragment on brewing. It might be a ritual text, and the use of alcoholic beverage in ritual was common in early China. Or it could be a legal text that has incorporated ritual material, in the manner of the Xuanquanzhi "Monthly Ordinances."

Whatever the source of the content, the fragment concerning beer relayed useful advice about something of interest to the people of the border regions. We knew they brewed and consumed beer there.[72] And a ritual/legal nature does not rule out practical applicability. The commentary that accompanied the Xuanquanzhi inscription named practical goals of environmental protection for some of its statutes. Their ritual formulations did not obviate this any more than the lack of understanding about how best to protect animal populations did.[73] The making of beer was (and is) a practical matter, and this text was both pragmatic and part of what would become, if it was not already, the classical canon. In the next chapter, I turn to other classical and cultural texts that appear among the northwestern documents.

Chapter Seven

Cultural Texts

This book has so far concentrated on interaction with texts that conveyed information close to daily life. Some of those texts issued from the government—edicts, statements concerning commoners' lives and circumstances, and the like. The previous chapter treated practical texts that explained how to do mundane things. But people who dwelled in the Han border regions also had access to texts not so directly related to daily life and it is to these that I turn in this chapter. Literary and other texts that were part of the broader textual culture of the realm were present in the border regions, too.

I call these texts "cultural" but acknowledge the limitations of that label. After all, at some level all texts could be deemed cultural. Yet the texts of intellectual history and literature that I treat together here represent a particular type of cultivation. Other possible labels include "literary" or "classical," but those terms—at least as they usually function in the context of early China—would exclude some of the constituent materials and bring connotations that do not fit this context.

Cultural texts contrast with the more directly functional texts at the center of the preceding chapters. These texts were part of the tradition of *wen* 文 writings, which created and communicated standards of cultural quality and propriety and worked toward the interconnection of the preimperial realm in cultural and political terms before unification of the realm in 221 BCE under the Qin. They grew increasingly important during the late Western Han and into the Eastern Han and were related—some directly, some less so—to the canon that emerged during that time.[1]

Cultural texts are important in the context of this book because they show that the interactions with text in the border regions went beyond the more mundane types I have considered so far. A person in the border regions who interacted with text had possibilities that included lofty writings. The figures, narratives, and passages appearing in these fragments were part of the textual corpus in existence during the Han. Some also come to us through other means of transmission, while others do not. Both add to our understanding of Han textual culture.

These texts attest to cultural connections between the northwest and the rest of the Han empire. As I noted in chapter 1, one of the questions about the potential existence of a popular literature in early China that scholars such as David Johnson have raised was the matter of having text to read. Johnson saw this possibility as emerging later, with the development and expansion of printing technology.[2] Yet along with the various governmental texts, records, and inventories that archaeologists found in the northwest were also prose narratives, masters' literature, and some poetry. These materials have come to us because they were disposed of in and around the military facilities of the northwest. There is no indication they were hidden away or kept secured in archives. Nor were they limited to larger military installations. They come to us from trash heaps, privies, and out-of-the-way corners at sites of various sizes across the region. As objects, they were there for the finding. They were available to the community.

One recent mode of engagement with some of these texts has been to look to traditional accounts and textual histories in order to make connections there.[3] Such approaches are analogous to those that play up, or even create, links between excavated texts and high-level historical events, something I have discussed in previous chapters. These modes of research grant excavated texts meaning primarily insofar as they fit into existing historical paradigms and narratives. I look instead for ways the materials from the northwest can open up and expand the field of historical exploration.

I do not suggest that cultural texts, by their wide dispersal, brought into existence a popular written culture exactly. Johnson was right to look to later times for that. But the distribution of these

texts does show that Han textual culture extended to the northwestern reaches and was available to the local literate community there.
Cultural texts in the classical idiom were part of some of the same
edicts that I have already touched upon, and it is with them that I
will begin the discussion here.

Edict and Canon

In chapter 3, I discussed a 5 CE edict from Xuanquanzhi concerning
"monthly ordinances" (yueling), which sought to harmonize human
activities with the broader natural world. That edict is an example of
one way that cultural texts reached the border region and the people
there, because its short introductory section borrows phrases from the
Book of Documents. For example, in alleging that the peasantry was
shirking its duties, the text says, "the lazy farmers have been at ease,
not striving at their work" 降(隋:惰)農自安, 不菫(:勤)作勞. And the
summary that epitomizes the preface and bridges the content of the
new statutes commands, "Assiduously order the people's time, saying:
Sow grain, and everyone hurry to the fields" 敬授民時, 曰: 揚 穀, 咸
趨南畝. These are lines from the *Book of Documents*, in forms just
slightly different from those of the received version.[4]

Since the 5 CE edict's content was posted, its allusions were,
too. There was a thick black border around the entire wall inscription
confirming it was a single unit. Much of the wording of the statutes
recorded in the Xuanquanzhi inscription is monthly ordinances that
come also in other classical texts, especially the *Record of Ritual*. The
statutes required explanation, which the accompanying commentary
provided.[5]

While the composers of the 5 CE edict knew they were drawing from elevated source material, they did not label it as such. That
leaves open questions about recognition and understanding among
those who read or heard the edict. We cannot know if others who
encountered the more literary portions of the text recognized them
as such. It seems likely that most who heard the text read aloud
would have recognized the literary language as unusual, but without
informed assistance they probably could not understand it. And yet
the edict was a text that was supposed to be read aloud, and all who
heard it would encounter those phrasings, that diction. Commoners

who interacted with edicts probably encountered many unfamiliar terms and concepts. Given the requirements for posted documents that I discussed in chapter 3, which demanded broad reading and understanding of the documents, it follows that the explication of unfamiliar terms and grammar must have been part of that process. Explanation was surely intrinsic to the transmission of edicts, and cultural texts were part of edicts.

Another fragmentary text hints at a complicated relationship between its content and imperial edicts. The fragment is not long and I will first present it more or less as it is. Due to factors that will become clear in a moment, translating this text is a task even more complicated than usual. Here is an initial reading:

> Zigong said, "The many changes repeat and connect. Know the selecting of words. Reside in place and await the moment. His worried heart is distressed, thinking about the misuse of the state." The master said, "The one thinking about the state is distressed? Beneath the log lintel . . ."

> 子贛曰, 九變復貫, 知言之篡. 居而俟合. 憂心橾(:懆)=, 念國之虐. 子曰, 念國者橾(:懆)=呼. 衡門之下 . . .[6]

This fragment looks like a typical, if somewhat disjointed, piece of dialogue with Confucius. It contains the name Zigong 子贛 (more commonly written 子貢), a famous disciple of Confucius, conversing with a "master" (*zi* 子). While the master's name is not present, the natural (and reasonable) assumption is that the master is Confucius. Since the most famous collection of lore concerning Confucius and his followers is *Analects*, some scholars have ascribed these lines to a version of that text.[7] They could as well come from some other source recording the Sage or his associates. At any rate, the passage does not appear in the received canon. That leaves the reader to search out other connections, which are not hard to find.

The first eight characters of Zigong's utterance form a rhyming couplet, which is suggestive of poetry.[8] While these lines do not occur in the canonical *Book of Odes*, they do appear in another received text, and in a relevant context. An edict issued by Emperor Wu in 128 BCE quotes them, with only minor textual differences, labeling them an *Ode* (*Shi* 詩).[9] That demonstrates both their poetic nature and an association with *Book of Odes*.

The last segment of Zigong's statement has an obvious poetic look due to the presence of a reduuplicative binome, something common in poetry: *cancan* 槮(:懆)=, my "distressed." The segment seems to be a variant text of a line from the *Book of Odes* poem "First Month" ("Zheng yue" 正月, no. 192).[10] Han-era histories record that Emperor Wu quoted these lines in an edict, too, this time in 123 BCE.[11] "Beneath the log lintel," from the Master's riposte, is the easiest text to recognize. It is the opening line from—and gives title to—the poem "Log Lintel' ("Hengmen" 衡門, no. 138) in the *Book of Odes*.[12] Taking these sources into account produces a different punctuation:

> Zigong said, "'The many changes repeat and connect; / Know the selecting of words.' Reside in place and await the moment. 'His worried heart is distressed, thinking about the misuse of the state.'" The master said, "'The one thinking about the state' is 'distressed'? 'Beneath the log lintel . . .'"

From this we can see that rather than a tangled conversation, we are looking at an exchange phrased in terms of poetic quotations. This form is familiar: the deployment of poetry from the *Book of Odes*, including the sort of "dueling quotation" back-and-forth we see here, is a common rhetorical mode in early texts.[13]

The occurrence of this content in edicts from Emperor Wu, furthermore, invites speculation. It is, of course, possible that coincidence alone explains why these same lines appear in edicts and among excavated texts. But the *Book of Odes* and the rest of the canon form a body of literature so large, and the northwestern corpus is so lumpy, that the chance of an accident seems small. Two further possibilities, which may overlap, offer themselves. The first is that these lines may have been part of the general literate culture of the time and thus readily available to whoever wanted to use them. That was so whether we are talking about an emperor—or emperor's ghostwriter—composing an edict or an assembler of texts working in the composite mode. The different creators may have been drawing on the same, third source. A second possibility is that the appearance of these lines in imperial edicts *made* them familiar to wider audiences through the processes of public posting and reading that I have discussed. That deployment perhaps helped them achieve broad cultural currency.

Classic Quotations, by Name or Not

In the preceding example, the absence of labels on the citations complicated the interpretation of the text. But sometimes composers cited their source texts by title. An example of this came from a small post near the Eji'na River 額濟納河:

> "Without partiality or partisanship, the kingly way is vast; without partisanship or partiality, the kingly way [ordered]."[14] *Analects* says, "Worry not about lack; worry about inequity."[15] The sagely dynasty is supremely humane and pities . . .
>
> 無扁(:偏)無黨王道湯 =, 無黨無扁(:偏)王道 □ =. 論語曰, 不患寡, 患不均. 聖朝至仁, 哀閔 . . .[16]

This fragment has three sections, and the title and familiar lines in the middle make the divisions clear. The first part, concerning the "kingly way," is a quotation from the *Book of Documents*. After it comes the title *Analects* and a short quote from that text, which varies slightly from the received version. These identifiable fragments are followed by a third section, which consists of a line that is, as far as I can tell, otherwise no longer extant. It is conceivable that the *Analects* quote should include these lines, which would mean it represents an alternate form of that text. But that seems unlikely. The received *Analects* parallel proceeds in a manner completely different from what follows here.[17] The earliest extensive copy of *Analects* we have today, a manuscript from a Han tomb at Dingzhou 定州 (Hebei), dates to around 55 BCE. While that text is heavily damaged, the final graph of the text is there, and the subsequent line matches the received *Analects*.[18] The parallels suggest that what comes after this quote on the Eji'na fragment is from another text. The damaged state of the strip means we cannot know whether the quotation from *Book of Documents* originally had a label. The example of the 5 CE edict and its preface, which cite *Book of Documents* silently, and the unmarked content that follows the quotation from *Analects* here, indicates it may not have been.

This is the only instance of the title *Analects* I have located among the materials that form the core of this book. *Analects* had probably taken shape as a text only decades before.[19] Attribution of the quotation to the title *Analects*—rather than to Confucius, putative speaker of the words—may reflect the development and increasing authority of that text in the Western Han period.[20] Or perhaps the composer(s) of the text we have thought its source might be unclear to a reader.

Other fragments familiar from the received *Analects* lack that label but are easy to recognize. One example text comes in two columns on a single strip, both ends of which are missing due to damage. It reads:

> . . . What does heaven say? The four seasons move with
> it and the myriad creatures come into being in it . . .
> . . . years' mourning is already long! The gentleman
> three . . .

> . . . 天何言哉四時行焉萬物生焉 . . .
> . . . 年之喪其已久矣君子三 . . . [21]

These are famous lines from a single chapter of *Analects* as it comes to us through traditional transmission.[22] In the received text, these lines have some content in between them, and that would also have been the case in this excavated example prior to damage.[23] The format of the excavated example, with two lines on a single strip, provides an additional bit of information, as this presentation confirms these two sections were transmitted closely together and in that sequence during Han times. They suggest a form close to that of the received version.

Another strip contains an entire, if brief, section from the *Analects*, set off by bullet points. Surrounding it are recognizable fragments of the preceding and following passages in the received version:

> . . . Zhang, it is hard to practice humaneness with him.
> Zengzi said: I heard from the Master that there has never

been a person who fully exerted themselves. If there must have been one, then it would be in personally carrying out a funeral. Zengzi said: I heard it from the Master that Meng Zhuangzi's filiality was such that he could do everything else, but would not change his father's underlings or his father's . . .

. . . 乎張也, 難與並而為仁矣.・曾子曰: 吾聞諸子, 人未有自致也者, 必也親喪乎.・曾子曰: 吾聞諸子, 孟莊子之孝, 其它可能也, 其不改父之臣與父之 . . .[24]

In *Analects*, these lines appear in a chapter that concentrates on Confucius's disciples, and Zengzi 曾子 was one of the most famous of that group. There are minor textual differences between this version and the received one, some of which also appear in other sources.[25] The content is the same, and the surrounding material both before and after the complete passage confirms that this section comes from a text that was similar to *Analects* as we have it today.

The preceding examples reflect that portions, at least, of *Analects* were present in the northwest border region. The forms are familiar to us, making it likely that this text had taken on a shape not far removed from the one that would later become part of the canonical tradition. This stability is evidence of connection between the textual life of the northwest region and the broader tradition: it confirms that at least some of the texts there were part of the larger textual world, which reached from the centers of culture to the border regions.[26] The picture that emerges from consideration of prose text in the northwest is far from simple, however, as the subsequent sections will show.

Textual Flexibility and Association

In chapter 5 I discussed the assembly of composite texts during the Han period. Creators of texts often worked by selecting and assembling existing pieces of writing, joining them together, sequencing, and structuring them, changing them to make something new. Another sort of mutability comes into view if we examine masters' texts or other canonical literature. I will take Confucius as my point of entry here, then discuss fragments related to a text I have not yet touched on, the *Classic of Filial Piety* (*Xiaojing* 孝經), and finally consider still other narratives. All these fragments tell us about forms of narrative present in the northwest, attest to the region's close relationship with broader textual culture, and hint at the complexities of textual culture in the Han. The first example fragment has more interest than might be immediately evident:

> . . . granting and blaming. If bad clothing, he called it unsuitable; if good clothing, he called it improper. Among the clerisy, in their lives, are they certain not to worry about poverty? Confucius said, "Originally, you came . . ."

> 之祚責, 惡衣謂之不巨, 善衣謂之不適, 士居固有不憂貧者乎. 孔子曰: 本子來 . . .[27]

This passage does not correspond to any received text, and it is among those that some scholars have simply assigned to an alternate version of *Analects*.[28] That is unproven and, I think, sells this fragment short. For despite not matching any canonical text, it has links to them. The fragment's first point of contact with the canon is simply the name Confucius itself, although I have not been able to identify another source for the quote this text attributes to him. The second link brings an intriguing complication, as the line preceding the name of the Sage shares a phrasing with *Analects*. In a famous line Confucius asserts that a gentleman does "not worry about poverty" 不憂貧, the same phrase that occurs in this fragment. The phrase comes in the Dingzhou manuscript version of *Analects*, so we know it was in a Han-period version of the text.[29] But this fragment is the only example I have found of this exact formulation.

The appearance of the phrase "not worry about poverty" in close proximity to Confucius's name but in an unfamiliar form suggests a possibility I would like to explore further, and that is of a general-level association rather than textual filiation. In other words, I think we should treat this as showing associations of ideas and phrases in the Han, rather than trying to connect them to specific texts as we know them now. Not every mention of Confucius needs to come from *Analects*.[30] Confucius appears in *many* texts, not only that one.

Excavated texts from the northwest contain fragments that relate to another text that became part of the canon, the *Classic of Filial Piety*. These fragments show associations conceptually similar to what I just discussed. This is one example:

In "Traveling Among Reeds" ("Xing wei" 行葦, no. 246), thus: "Brothers are close to each other." Therefore we say: Lead them with universal caring and none among the people will forsake their parents. One hundred twenty-seven characters.

行葦則兄弟具尼(:昵)矣. 故曰，先之以博愛而民莫遺其親. ●
百廿七字[31]

Despite its brevity, this fragment offers three points for consideration: a poetic allusion, a textual parallel with the *Classic of Filial Piety*, and the character count at the end.

The core of the fragment is the textual parallel, which comprises the eleven characters following "Therefore, we say." It matches a line from the "Three Potentials" ("San cai" 三才) chapter of the received *Classic of Filial Piety*.[32] As the text of the fragment reflects, the short chapter there takes as its theme the potency of filial piety as a tool for governing a population.

The reference to "Traveling Among Reeds" by title is worthy of note. While citations of *Book of Odes* poems are common in early texts, they often do not give titles. Instead, a speaker will note, "The *Odes* say" 詩曰, and proceed from there with the quotation, or else simply recite the lines without indicating their source. Here the title leaves no doubt about which poem this is, despite truncation and a textual variant.[33]

The standard commentarial interpretations of the poem explain it as an expression of generosity and humaneness rather than filiality exactly.[34] The poem moreover does not appear in or around the received *Classic of Filial Piety* parallel. That parallel ends with a line from another *Book of Odes* poem, which contains some similar phrasing and better fits the sense of the chapter than the one in the recovered fragment. This case of flexibility seems to imply that the assembler or assemblers of the text perceived a need for a quote from the *Odes*, without agreement (or consistency) about which poem would best make the point. In other words, there was an association between this text's propositions and that text or type of text.

The excavated fragment ends with an explicit quantification of characters. While no few strips have sequential numbers on the reverse sides, it is less common to end with the count of a text in this fashion. Its "one hundred twenty-seven" is close to the total number of characters in the received version of "Three Potentials," which by my counting has 129 graphs. Lai Guolong 來國龍 has suggested that counts like this one may have been a means of controlling texts.[35] Its presence also calls to mind the requirement for scribes in the Han bureaucracy to have mastered five thousand characters, which I discussed in chapter 1. Perhaps texts meant for learning or testing for the purposes of official status had character counts to facilitate comparison to a standard like that one.

Another fragment from the northwest with a parallel in the *Classic of Filial Piety* also has a complicated relationship with the received version:

> One who is above yet without arrogance will be lofty and not in peril. One whose system is moderate and is cautious about measure, and is able to properly divide and dispense, will have fullness and not overflow. *Changes* says, "The lofty dragon has regret," which speaks of arrogance and overflow. "Lofty" as a word . . .

> 上而不驕者, 高而不危. 制節謹度, 而能分施者, 滿而不溢. 易曰, 亢龍有悔. 言驕溢也. 亢之為言 . . .[36]

The first section of this text, up to the title *Changes* (Yi 易, i.e., *Zhou yi* 周易 or *Yijing* 易經), matches word-for-word part of a short chapter in the *Classic of Filial Piety*.[37] At that point, this text diverges from that one. The received *Classic of Filial Piety* goes on further in the same vein, then ends with a quote from *Book of Odes*, describing an attitude of great caution in the exercise of power: "So cautious! so apprehensive! / Like overlooking a deep pool; / like walking on thin ice" 戰戰兢兢, 如臨深淵, 如履薄冰.[38] In the excavated fragment's version, a quote from the *Changes* comes next. It implies a warning against imperiousness, symbolized by the hubristic dragon, and is absent from the received *Classic of Filial Piety*.

In terms of theme, the *Classic of Filial Piety* parallel and the excavated fragment are similar, both warning against excess. They share a rhetorical approach, both deploying quotes from core classics to make the point. As in the previous example, where I suggested that the assemblers of the texts as we have them thought a quotation from the *Book of Odes* was in order, here it seems there was a need for a classical quote. But the source of that quote was not set. Thus, in this excavated version we have *Changes*, while in the received, the *Book of Odes*.

There are other examples from the northwest of prose text written in the classical mode that do not neatly mesh with received texts. There is, for instance, this brief section of dialogue, containing yet another citation of the *Book of Odes*:

> The *Odes* ("Xiaowan" 小宛, Mao no. 196) say, "Look at the wagtail! Oh it flies and it sings. / I daily journey and monthly travel far. / I rise early and go to bed in the night, / That I may not shame those who gave birth to me." Are you sick? Oh, strive at it!

> 詩曰, "題積令載鶺載鳴. / 我日斯邁而月斯延 (:征). / 蚤興夜未 (:寐), / 毋天(:忝)璽(:爾)所生" 者, 唯病乎. 其勉之.[39]

While Han-period texts cite this poem, this exact text—with what follows the quote and the variants in the poem itself—is not found elsewhere.

There is a noteworthy example of a text fragment with an unexpected connection with the received tradition. It reads, "The master said, 'To care for the self is the acme of humaneness; to respect oneself is the acme of knowledge'" 子曰, 自愛仁之至也, 自敬知之至也.[40] The interest of this line's content for intellectual history is considerable, and in context its connection to transmitted text is unexpected, for it is a very close match to a line in one of Yang Xiong's texts.[41] I wrote about Yang Xiong back in chapter 1 as an example of a writer whose works required much erudition to understand.

It is difficult to determine the significance of the parallel here. Yang Xiong lived from the late Western Han into the Xin period, so it is not impossible that this line traces to his writings. But texts were porous in those times, and it is much more likely that Yang Xiong—or an editor of the text that bears his name—picked up this bit of wisdom somewhere and incorporated it into the text. As a modern commentator on Yang Xiong's text notes, at least one other, earlier work expresses similar ideas in comparable phrases, attributing them to Confucius and his disciples.[42] And a similar pattern of phrases, including a partial match, also comes in a ritual classic.[43] There is no way to resolve the question of what relationship the texts have, and who might be quoting whom. But some sort of relationship seems certain, even if it was only that they emerged from a single intellectual milieu and thus share phrasings.

Other manuscripts also contain phrases that appear in received texts but in different contexts than those seen in the documents from the northwest. Consider this fragment:

> Now our grain is plentiful and ripe, the population numerous. This means we have encountered an opportune time. Yet Your Majesty does not make use of it! We are losing this particular time. And I have heard that an opportune time cannot be lost.

> 今吾年穀番(:蕃)孰(:熟)、百姓殷眾. 此吾逢時也, 而王弗用. 失某時矣. 臣聞時不可失.[44]

While this takes the familiar form of a minister advising the ruler, the exact text does not appear elsewhere, as far as I can tell. But pieces of it do. The four-character phrase for "the population numerous" 百姓 殷眾 used here also appears in *Guanzi* 管子— another text that took its final shape only during the Han.[45] And the final four characters, "an opportune time cannot be lost" 時不可失, form a phrase that pops up in different Han-dynasty texts and contexts.[46]

Other fragments show a similar pattern. One reads, "for three years he did not use his fields and house, awaiting rebellion. While the lord worries, the vassal works . . ." 三年不用其田宅, 須其反也, 君憂 臣勞.[47] As in the preceding case, the entire fragment does not match any received text, yet its closing thought—"While the lord worries, the vassal works" 君憂臣勞—occurs in more than one received source.[48] A last example of this type is a fragmentary explanation of terminology for the common population, which says, "The Son of Heaven says, 'the multitude of people'; the various lords say, 'the myriad people'" 天子曰兆民, 諸侯曰萬民.[49] This is perhaps not inspiring prose, but it appears in a number of early texts.[50]

These examples attest to a body of textual units below that of extensive texts, chapters, or even of sentences that present in the northwest border region during Han times. The word-for-word overlaps between recovered texts from the northwest and received texts of different sorts are too extensive to be the result of chance. Their existence demonstrates the region's connection to broader Han-dynasty textual culture, despite its remote location. As the next section will show, sometimes the names of quasi-historical figures form another type of link.

Narrative Texts, Narrative Characters

The preceding sections have concentrated on materials from the border regions related to the contents of the classical canon. Scholars have sometimes attributed the presence of figures like Confucius to the deliberate diffusion of "Confucian" philosophy from the center to the far reaches of the empire.[51] Such an analysis assumes a great deal. In the discussion here it is, I think, most important to note what such an approach does not take into account. For there are a variety of narratives and figures found among the documents from the northwest, not just those connected with Confucius and his reception. The connections with Han textual culture are broader than the deliberate dissemination of one particular ideology could account for.

Fragments of narrative texts that deal with familiar characters are present. A figure who appears more than once is Yan Ying 晏嬰 (ca. sixth c. BCE), famous as Master Yan (Yanzi 晏子). Legendary for his short stature and quick wit, Master Yan is the subject of the *Annals of Master Yan* (*Yanzi chunqiu* 晏子春秋). He is also one of the most common figures in early Chinese writings. Master Yan appears in many texts, both received and excavated. An important collection of stories about him was recovered from a Western Han tomb in eastern China, confirming his importance at the time.[52] The following fragment comes on two damaged strips from near the Eji'na River and refers to Master Yan by name:

> Lord Jing summoned Master Yan and asked him, "What happened when you first governed?" Master Yan responded, "When first governing, I repaired damage and filled in openings and depraved people detested it. I cut ditches and put through . . . lazy people detested it. I stopped assignations between men and women and lascivious people hated it. In sending off and receiving . . .

京(:景)公召晏子, 問之曰, 子先治奈何. 晏子合(:答)曰, 始治
築壞塞缺 姦人惡之, 斬渠通 . . . 隨(:惰)民惡之, 止男女之會
淫民惡之, 送迎 . . .[53]

Zhang Defang has pointed out that this appears to represent an alternate version of a narrative found in the received *Annals of Master Yan*. In the transmitted version, Lord Jing put Master Yan in charge of governing an area, but after three years, Master Yan's reputation had become so bad that Lord Jing was going to remove him. Master Yan, however, said he recognized his mistake and asked for another chance, which Lord Jing granted. After three more years, the inhabitants of the territory praised him. When the lord asked the reason for the change, Master Yan explained that when he had begun, he did the sort of unpleasant but necessary governing a state needs. This included the kind of thing that the excavated fragment names, but the only matching phrasing concerns the reactions of the undesirable social elements. In the received version, Master Yan goes on to explain that once he stopped governing properly and gave the population free rein to indulge their excesses and deficiencies, his reputation improved.[54] This was thus a rebuke to Lord Jing, who had failed to recognize quality governance when he saw it.

Another brief fragment from the northwest border area that mentions Master Yan, without connection to the received *Annals of Master Yan* or other transmitted accounts, confirms that his appearance in an unfamiliar textual context is not an anomaly.[55] In some instances, the relationship between fragmentary narrative in excavated materials and other texts is still more complicated. The following is one such example:

> . . . letter, summoned Han Peng and questioned him about it. Han Peng replied, 'I had married my wife but two days and three nights when I left her to travel. For three years I have not returned and my wife . . ."

> . . . 書, 而召幹 (:韓) 倗 (:朋) 問之. 幹 (:韓) 倗 (:朋) 對曰:
> 臣取婦二日三夜, 去之來游, 三年不歸, 婦 . . .[56]

Archaeologists found this fragment at Maquanwan, at the site of a Han-era post. Other strips from the site bear dates ranging from 71 BCE through 22 CE, dating this fragment to around the late

Western Han or Xin-Mang periods. And while this text is itself brief, the reverse of the strip is marked with the number 112. That serial number indicates it was part of a much longer sequence.[57]

Even in its damaged state, this fragment provides enough information to connect it to a story that also occurs, in different forms, in several sources.[58] The earliest transmitted version of the story comes in the *Records of Searching for Spirits* (*Soushenji* 搜神記), a fourth-century CE compilation of weird tales.[59] It tells of Han Peng (in that version Han Ping 韓憑), the courtier of a king, and his beautiful wife. The king seized Han Peng's wife, compelling her to become his consort, and imprisoned Han Peng at hard labor. Han's wife sent him a letter communicating her feelings through poetic analogy, which fell into the hands of the king. Shortly thereafter, Han Peng and his wife both committed suicide. The king refused the wife's request to bury them together, although their graves were within sight of each other. The spouses' mutual affection was such that the catalpa trees that grew atop their grave mounds stretched out, root and branch, to intertwine. Other sources allude to this story and it had a great deal of influence on the development of literary narrative.[60]

The presence of a Tang-era "Rhapsody on Han Peng" ("Han Peng fu" 韓朋賦), known from a manuscript copy in the cache of documents from Mogao Grotto, Dunhuang, makes the matter still more complicated. While recognizably relating the same story that comes in *Records of Searching for Spirits*, the "Rhapsody on Han Peng" is also quite different. It is much longer and includes additional narrative elements and much more detail.[61]

Fu Junlian 伏俊璉 and Yang Aijun 楊愛軍 have proposed that the *Records of Searching for Spirits* narrative and the "Rhapsody on Han Peng" tell the same story in two different ways that reflect different proximate sources and fundamentally different purposes. The former version is, for the most part, plain prose, which suggests primarily a reading audience and textual focus. The "Rhapsody" has a more poetic style, which includes rhyme and intermittent prosody. It conveys a more developed narrative and contains a lot of detail. These things, Fu and Yang argue, imply oral presentation.[62]

The Maquanwan fragment does not have a direct parallel in any otherwise extant rendering of Han Peng's story. Yet its style is close to that of the "Rhapsody on Han Peng," as Qiu Xigui 裘錫圭 has noted; it seems to be a text fit for spoken presentation and thus to represent the crossover between oral and written transmission.[63] It is a text that would have permitted multiple forms of interaction.

Here is another example of a text with apparent links to the received corpus, in which the connections are of a more tenuous nature:

> . . . to be a superior person?" Tian Zhang replied, "I have heard that the height of heaven is one hundred million nine thousand miles, and the width of the earth is equal to it.[64] The wind comes from ravines and valleys, the rain arises from rivers and seas, and thunder . . ."

> . . . 為君子? 田章對曰:臣聞之, 天之高萬=九千里, 地之廣亦 與之等. 風發谿(:谿)谷, 雨起江海, 震 . . .[65]

The language of this short passage is relatively straightforward and the strip that contains it is complete. The fragmentary state of the narrative is due to this being but one of many strips, not damage to this one. While there was a fair amount of disagreement about the transcription of a few of the characters after the text's discovery, Qiu Xigui's reading fits the evidence and makes sense. Like most others, I follow him.[66]

Qiu and others have written about this fragment at length, arguing for connections between it and other texts, both received and excavated. Some authors have adduced dubious arguments to support specific links, the details of which do not withstand skeptical consideration. Nevertheless, the broad connections deserve attention, for they tell us about the link between the border regions and broader written culture. I would only suggest a different approach to those connections. There are two aspects to these questions, personal names and narrative elements, and I will discuss both briefly.

Scholars have from the first recognized the name Tian Zhang 田章 in this passage.[67] This is not the only instance of that name in excavated materials. Another very short fragment from the northwest—too damaged to translate—also mentions this name in what appears to be a similar context.[68] Among received texts, the name Tian Zhang appears in *Master Han Fei* (*Han Feizi* 韓非子) and *Plots of the Warring States* (*Zhanguo ce* 戰國策).[69] But beyond a few tidbits— advice from a father, a state of origin—those accounts convey little information about Tian Zhang.

Tian Zhang also appears in the *Records of Searching for Spirits*, albeit not in the received version. A medieval manuscript copy of *Records of Searching for Spirits* among the documents from Mogao Grotto, ascribed to one Gou Daoxing 句道興, contains the story of Tian Zhang's birth to a "heavenly woman" and eventual emergence as a famous official.[70] From an early point, scholars have suggested that the name Tian Zhang has wider connections than are apparent. Based on a combination of phonetic loans, presumed copying errors, and similar content in different texts, more than one researcher has equated Tian Zhang with Master Yan.[71]

The result is a mix of possibilities, in which names vary but appear to refer to a single figure, even as the details about that figure vary. On the one hand, this sort of variety is precisely what one would expect when dealing with accounts that circulated orally and widely—especially in cases in which the tales probably had no set form to begin with, which appears to be the case here.[72] The information scholars have adduced does not support the assertion of a genetic relationship between the various accounts; still less does it provide historical support for the tales. But it leaves little doubt about the existence of a figure, called Tian Zhang or perhaps something else, who supposedly served as a minister in the preunification state of Qi. Regardless of how one imagines the chain of causation, the tantalizing fact remains that Tian Zhang and Master Yan both feature among the Han dynasty and the later materials in the Dunhuang area. This suggests both links to broader culture and a degree of persistence in local memory.[73]

The fragment on the Tian Zhang strip under consideration here is part of a larger dialogue, apparently between Tian Zhang and his ruler, concerning the dimensions of the macrocosm. These aspects of the narrative are common in the received corpus. The prevalence of dialogue as an expository form predates transmitted texts, as some oracle bone inscriptions from around 1000 BCE already have this shape.[74] Throughout the classical period, dialogue—not soliloquy—remained the prevalent expressive form for philosophy in China, as this and other fragments reflect.

The spatial dimensions of the universe were a major topic of discussion among Han-era intellectuals. This is evident, for example, in the writings of Wang Chong 王充 (27–97), who relates and disputes various contemporary understandings of space.[75] There were many highly divergent explanations for exactly how big the world was and how high the heavens were. Medieval "transformation texts" from Mogao Grotto—including one that concerns Master Yan—also address these things.[76]

While there is no exact parallel in any received text for the content of this strip, its subject and its narrative both demonstrate connections to the broader literate culture of its time and later.

Its subject, as Tian Zhang or as one of the other permutations of his name, occurs in different texts, which together reflect a body of narrative about him. Anecdotes about many figures circulated at the time, and this strip shows that this military outpost in the northwestern border area was part of that circulation. Along similar lines, in its dialogic format and interest in the size of the universe, it aligned with topoi of intellectual inquiry of the time. The strip is clear evidence of the link between the literate community of the northwest and the larger empire of the time.

The phenomenon of familiar names and unfamiliar content also occurs in connection with persons that are—whatever their status might have been during the Han period—now lesser known. Luo Zhenyu and Wang Guowei linked a couple of fragments from Dunhuang to Li Mu 力牧.[77] Li Mu is the name of an official who, according to *Historian's Records* and other early accounts, assisted the mythological Yellow Emperor.[78] The "Monograph on Literature" in *Han History* lists two books entitled *Li Mu* 力牧, both of which it labels spurious attributions.[79] Neither is extant, so it is impossible to determine whether one of them might be the source of dialogue like: ". . . is already not known. Why is that?' Li Mu replied, 'Officials . . .'" 已不聞者何也力墨對曰官.[80] Based on Li Mu's supposed position helping the Yellow Emperor, Luo and Wang also link to him another fragment from the northwest, which begins "The Yellow Emperor."[81] Such scraps of narrative are too brief and inconclusive to demonstrate much. But in the context here, they become significant, if secondary, evidence of links to the cultural center of the realm.

Poetry

If we set aside quotations from the *Book of Odes* as representing a particular engagement with verse, poetry is rare among excavated materials from the northwestern frontier region.[82] There is just one example of an apparently intact poem, along with what seem to be fragments of others. The sole complete example is untitled and reads:

> The sun is not visible to the eye: dark clouds numerous;
> The moon cannot be seen: wind stirs up the sands.
> Rushing freshets form rivers,
> Flow around, gush and run, turning, raising waves.
> Great pillars are upended, wildly piled on each other.
> Coming from Heaven's Gate, one seldom travels mud ponds,
> But with no way to rise, what can one do?
> To raise a banner and teach—it is truly difficult.[83]

日不顯目兮黑雲多
月不可視兮風非(:飛)[84]沙.
從(:縱)恣蒙水誠(:成)江河,
州(:周)[85]流灌注兮轉揚波.
辟柱槙(顛)到(:倒)忘(:妄)相加.
天門俠小(:少)路彭池.
無因以上如之何.
興章教海(:誨)兮誠難過.

These eight lines exhibit relatively regular prosody, and their rhymed character is evident even in modern Chinese. It seems to be an early example of the seven-character line that arose during the Han and later became a major poetic mode.[86] In poetic fashion, its imagery and language lend themselves to various interpretations. Some readers have given more weight to the descriptions of the natural scene that dominate the first part. Others have looked to the context and the final line to assert connections to the tribulations of official life.[87] To me, it seems that these lines use phrasing that draws from the environment of the northwest to express the difficulties of leading any sort of exemplary life.

It is the nature of literature to admit multiple interpretations and this is no exception. However one understands the preceding text, it is unambiguously verse. The few other examples of poetry that scholars have identified among the documents from the northwest are all short enough to leave questions about their nature open. One such fragment, damaged and only partly legible, says, "Three-four, parents-in-law, six-seven, younger sister / Their talk, so profuse, / Will break your heart" 三四姑公六七妹□語眾多令腸潰. This seems to be from a poem describing the plight of a wife among her husband's family; its inclusion of nonsense numbers would fit a folk song motif.[88] Another fragment uses phrasing that is reminiscent of putative folk songs and related poetry: "Springs and autumns, ten thousand years, joy never-ending, never . . . Longevity never-ending, long life . . ." 春秋萬歲樂未央未□老壽未央長壽 . . .[89]

Rhyme marks a number of kinds of writing in the Chinese tradition, not only poetry proper; philosophical and other kinds of writing employ it, too.[90] Another type of rhymed text is also not poetry in the usual sense. Among the Juyan materials are several examples of inscribed, four-sided talismans called *gangmao* 剛卯. The received accounts of these talismans and the commentaries that accompany those accounts are confused, which probably reflects widespread usage over time and the variation and development that implies. Traditional accounts describe these as made of jade, metal, or wood in the general shape of seals like those used to sign one's name. They were worn in pairs on the sash to protect against demons and sickness. Those accounts record the inscription that *gangmao* talismans bore. That text matches closely the inscription on a jade example that archaeologists recovered from an Eastern Han tomb in Anhui Province and that on two of the three examples from Juyan. The third Juyan example's inscription is damaged and only partially legible, but that part bears no resemblance to the others. The charm text as found on this Juyan example concludes, "May none of the demons of the many sicknesses and hard diseases dare to face me!" 庶役(:疫)岡(:剛)單(:癉)莫我敢當. The close match of these texts with those in received texts and those found on jade examples attests to the Juyan region's connection to broader cultural phenomena. At the same time, the presence of rhyme suggests that these were not texts for silent reading but for reading aloud.[91]

Conclusion

This chapter has explored links between the broader textual world of the Han period—its topoi, texts, and phenomena—and the context of the border regions. Whether in terms of specific figures such as Confucius; texts like the *Classic of Filial Piety*; or compositional techniques including citation, allusion, and rhyme, the excavated materials attest to a common body of method and content that the border regions shared with the center. Edicts were again an important source of evidence, for their incorporation of classical text tells us that content explicitly intended for broad distribution contained elements shared with high culture.

On the basis of the interdisciplinary body of research I discussed in chapter 1, I argue that we should expect the range of texts that were available to the literate community to have been much broader. Archaeologists have recovered cultural texts from a variety of sites in the region. Neither secured in archives nor hidden away, they were available in the literate community. And as I have argued throughout this book, we should expect that members of the community interacted with text in different ways: some read everything, some read some things, and some listened to others read. The textual culture of the community, though, was not merely documentary or bureaucratic, and it was not "Confucian." Rather it included a body of texts that show considerable overlap with Han textual culture as it comes to us in its received form. This literate community was part of the larger literate world of Han China.

Chapter Eight

Letters

In this final content chapter, I consider a type of source material different from what I treated in the preceding chapters. The texts I consider here are letters.[1] They concern, in whole or in part, matters related to the life and work of those who created and who received them. These letters are not government communications, and the characteristics of official documents are absent from most of them. But to call them just personal would give inadequate weight to the letters' contents, which reflect relationships and tasks within the realm of officialdom. They have a dual nature that interweaves both kinds of elements. The relationships they record are similarly both official and personal.

Scholars have noted the personal aspect of the letters, and often describe them as "private" (siren 私人).[2] There is good reason for this. It is not because we have the names of the individuals involved, although we often do; we have the names of those involved in the creation of many documents of other types, too. Rather, it is because these letters generally existed outside the processes for creating and circulating official records and communications. Bureaucratic documents in the early empire typically contained specific content, including dates, names and titles of the persons involved, and formulas that bracketed the content and hampered its alteration. Those markers are absent from most letters, distinguishing them from the usual official documents. Furthermore, the government's postal system provided a means for sending documents to, from, and between locations in the northeast. Letters did not travel via official post but rather moved informally, at least in general.[3]

The letters furthermore maintain a more or less unofficial tone and express elements relating to individuals' lives. Aside from the Yumen Huahai writing stick that I discussed in chapter 5, and the letter it incorporates, the documents and materials this book has treated so far have been fairly impersonal. Whether edicts or rules, practical or universal text, their significance went beyond any specific person's circumstances. This is part of how they worked to constitute the community. And while the statements that I wrote about in chapter 4 convey information dictated by specific persons, they served mainly to connect those individuals to bureaucratic systems. The letters are different. They connected people to each other.

The letters concentrate on individual-level matters and we can see personal—sometimes very personal—purposes and emotions in them. Through the social interactions they record, the letters worked to constitute the community in a manner different from other, more detached, modes of writing. At the same time, and as this chapter will show, what the letters treat, and many of the relationships they instantiate, are of an essentially official nature. The creators and addressees often knew each other due to their work and wrote about work-related matters in an unofficial mode. Thus, while aspects of the epistles are personal, their nature was hybrid.[4]

The social status of those who created the letters I discuss in this chapter varied. In many cases, we do not know what rank they held. When we do know, those involved were often officials of humble station. It has been my contention throughout this book that in order to understand what people were doing with text in the Han period, we should look beyond the groups scholars typically identify as literate—groups that can include even low-ranking officials. Thus, while persons working in official capacities have featured previously in this book, that inclusion was more or less incidental. Here I deliberately expand the scope of my consideration because of what letters show us about the literate community of the northwest.

What the letters illuminate goes beyond the creator/addressee dichotomy. They illustrate how interaction with and through text could be a way of interacting with a group of people. Letters demonstrate roles text had in facilitating and maintaining the community. A number of the letters convey requests to their recipients, calling upon them to contact different individuals. Other times they pass along information and requests from others. All of these things were forms of interaction with text. Recognizing this permits us to see that text's efficacy extended well beyond the one who wrote (or dictated) a letter's content and the one who read (or heard read) the result. This is most notable in the case of women, whose active participation in the social life of the community is reflected in letters as nowhere else.

To describe an example of a highly varied form like letters as typical feels like a bit of a misnomer. Yet the first example I consider is typical for my purposes here, in that it touches on many of this chapter's—and this book's—main themes.

Xuan to Yousun and His Wife

This text is well preserved and comes on both sides of a single strip from the Juyan region:

> Xuan prostrates himself and bows repeatedly in greeting.
>
> Your Honors, Yousun and young wife: You must be suffering greatly on the border. It is the hot season and I hope that you have enough proper clothing and can make yourselves eat. Be careful there on the border! I, having been fortunate to receive Yousun's aid, patrol the border and am without particular difficulty.[5]
>
> On the seventh day of the intercalary month, Youdu went to Juyan together with his excellency the lead scribe. He says that your parents are without particular difficulty. He departed suddenly and I do not know if he was able to see you or not.[6] The rest is not worth enumerating in a letter. On the eleventh day, I responded to the company. It is not yet decided. I respectfully have this letter delivered by messenger.
>
> I prostrate myself and bow repeatedly to Your Honors, Yousun and young wife. As for Zhu Youji's letter: He wishes that Aide Gao may favor him by delivering it to the leader of the Linqu watch squad.
>
> To the office of Liu Yousun. • The letter will be sent from the company the same day. The messenger inspecting

the troops has fortunately not yet arrived. I hope that you
will make preparations yourself—do not be last among the
various sections!

宣伏地再拜請:

幼孫、少婦足下: 甚苦塞 上. 暑時, 願幼孫、少婦足衣強食,
慎塞上. 宣幸得幼孫力, 過行邊, 毋它急. 幼都以閏月七日與
長史君俱之居延, 言丈人毋它急. 發卒(:猝), 不審得見幼孫
不. 它不足數來記. 宣以十一日對候官, 未決. 謹因使奉書. 伏
地再拜 幼孫、少婦足下. 朱幼季書, 願高掾幸為到臨渠燧長.
劉⁷幼孫治所 ● 書即日起候官. 行兵使者幸未到, 願豫自辯(:
辦), 毋為諸部殿.⁸

This letter contains a surprise already in its opening. Its sender,
Xuan, addresses himself not only to Yousun, apparently a colleague,
but also to Yousun's wife. So unexpected is this that it occasioned
differences of interpretation among readers, some of whom believed
this must be a letter from a man to his own wife—which would be
no less surprising, if differently so.⁹ Ma Yi has persuasively argued
on the basis of content and parallels with other examples that this
is addressed jointly to a man named Yousun and his wife, and I follow her. When other examples are taken into account, the phrasing
seems unambiguous.¹⁰

In this and other examples that address or otherwise refer
to women, they come alongside their husbands or, in exceptional
instances, other male relatives. Yet addressing women remains
rare among early letters as a group. Mention of Yousun's wife here
implies Xuan had sufficient familiarity with Yousun's circumstances
to know that he had a wife, and perhaps even a degree of direct
acquaintance with her, which led to her inclusion as a recipient. If
including the recipient's wife were standard practice, then addressing
wives would be common, as being married was. That is not the case.
And if it were a pro forma element, then it would be universal, or
nearly so. That is not the case, either. The implication is that Xuan
knew Yousun, knew that Yousun was married, and perhaps even
had some acquaintance with Yousun's wife. His greeting reflects this
relationship.

The middle section of the letter brings in another person, Youdu, by name, without further introduction or information. On the basis of the graph the two names share, Ma Yi suggests that Youdu may have been Yousun's brother.[11] That is certainly possible, although there is no way to confirm it. What is certain is that Yousun and Youdu knew each other—a fact underscored when Xuan relays information about Yousun's parents. Thus, the letter indicates that these four people—Yousun, his wife, Xuan, and Youdu—were part of a circle of acquaintances, and Xuan is conscious of that fact. They were interacting in various ways and degrees through this letter.

Expressing concern about the recipient's parents is common in Han letters. Part of that is formulaic, and the common occurrence of phrases like "May your parents be without worry" might lead one to assume the phrases lack emotional force. Xuan's delivery of information concerning Yousun's parents suggests otherwise. (Of course, fully conventional expressions can be emotionally consequential: consider an English phrase like "Happy birthday," to say nothing of "I love you.") Xuan did not express any wishes about Yousun's parents—he did not need to. But he clearly thought that the information he relayed about them to Yousun was important and something Yousun would wish to know.

Xuan also refers to some unspecified matter. His reference is oblique and gives no information except to note that he visited the company about it on the eleventh of the intercalary month and learned that it was undecided. This leaves the modern reader completely in the dark. Obscure as the reference is for us, it was meaningful to Yousun. Xuan's reticence itself is thus significant in several ways. It tells us both Xuan and Yousun knew about the matter in question, knew that the other knew, and that it was important enough that nothing more than what we have was necessary to indicate it.

In the last lines of the letter, Xuan notes that an impending inspection has not yet happened—"fortunately," he says, perhaps for both him and Yousun—and advises Yousun to prepare. While it is difficult to judge tone at such a great chronological distance, the final words of the letter ("do not be last among the various sections!") seem more lighthearted than fully earnest. They lend the letter a feeling of camaraderie.

These four things together—Xuan's inclusion of Yousun's wife in the opening, the reference to Youdu and Yousun's parents, the allusion to the undecided matter, and the closing section and the comradeship Xuan expresses there—suggest a personal relationship between Xuan and Yousun that extended to include the others, as well.

The letter furthermore reflects a complex context in which social relationships mingled with official duties, and where individual connections worked within and yet separate from the institutions that employed these men. The mention of the letter that Xuan included from Zhu Youji is significant in this respect. It delineates those in this circle of acquaintances who had individual connections from others who did not. When Xuan names Zhu Youji, it is by surname, suggesting a greater distance from Xuan than the others.[12] Zhu's request is that his letter be passed to a specific person, Aide Gao, also called by surname and title.[13] I suggest that referring to him by title and surname indicates Xuan thought Gao was either unknown to Yousun or of a significantly higher rank. Otherwise he would have been named only, as Zhu Youji himself was. The insertion of Zhu Youji's request thus shows the intersection of two separate circles of acquaintance and official status. The following section considers another letter, which does something similar in a still more complicated fashion.

A Silk Letter from Xuanquanzhi

Among the finds at the Xuanquanzhi site were personal letters, and the following is one of the published examples. While in many respects representative of Han letters, it is the same time, in its way, unexpected and exceptional. The text is long but worth considering in its entirety. The letter has multiple layers and mentions multiple persons, yet the writing medium means the integrity of the text is certain. Considering the whole letter helps show its structure and complexity. It reads:

> I, Yuan, prostrate myself and bow repeatedly in greeting:
> Your Honor, Zifang: May you be well and without worry. When you left Kudao,[14] I missed the time and did not attend your departure. That was a crime deserving death. May your parents, household, and children be without

worry. I prostrate myself and hope that you are without distress concerning them. I would not dare to be careless or proud toward your parents or household. I manage an armory and respectfully take commands.

It is the hot season. I prostrate myself and hope that you wear suitable clothes, are favored with proper beer and food, and are well favored in attending to official matters.

I respectfully say: It happens that I will follow my unit to take station at Dunhuang, where shoes are lacking, as you know. I am going to be familiar. I hope you will do me the favor of buying me a pair of shoes made from grogram and tanned leather, one foot and two inches (28 cm.) in length; and five writing brushes, good ones. I shall be most favored. I request to repay the money at your home when next convenient. I will not dare leave you with the burden. I hope you will favor me by keeping in mind that I want thick shoes, suitable for walking. You know I have repeatedly had trouble with this and how hard it is to get proper shoes. I shall be most favored, most favored!

As for the amanuensis you recommended, Ciru: I would like you to ask for his reply when you pass by his home. If Ciru is not there, please see his wife Rongjun and ask for the reply. I shall be most favored, most favored. I prostrate myself and bow repeatedly to you.

Those shoes you will favor me by buying—I hope you will entrust them to the first officer coming here, so I can put them to use in good time. I shall be most favored. I prostrate myself and bow again and again.

Lü Zidu wants to have a seal carved but dares not tell you. Not knowing how incapable I am, he bids me ask you. He hopes that you will favor him by having a seal carved, imperial scribe style, seven *fen* (1.6 cm.) square and with a turtle figure on top; the seal should say, "Lü An's seal."[15] He hopes you will give attention to this, and that he will be able to accomplish it with your aid. He dares not entrust it to anyone else.

The two hundred cash that camp commander Guo sends is to buy a whip. He would like one that cracks well. I hope you will pay attention to this.

I write this myself: I hope you will favor me by paying attention in making these purchases and not being
careless—different from the others!

元伏地再拜請:

子方足下善毋恙. 苦道子方發, 元失候不侍駕. 有死罪. 丈人、
家室、兒子, 毋恙. 元伏地願子方毋憂. 丈人、家室, 元不敢忽
驕. 知事在庫, 元謹奉教. 暑時, 元伏地願子方適衣, 幸酒食、
察事, 幸甚.

謹道: 會元當從屯敦煌, 乏沓(:鞈), 子方所知也. 元不自外, 願
子方幸為元買沓(:鞈)一兩, 絹韋, 長尺二寸; 筆五枚, 善者. 元
幸甚. 錢請以便屬舍, 不敢負. 願子方幸留意, 沓(:鞈)欲得其
厚, 可以步行者.子方知元數煩擾難為沓(:鞈). 幸 = 甚 =. 所
因子方進記差次孺者, 願子方發過次孺舍求報. 次孺不在, 見
次孺夫人容君, 求報. 幸甚, 伏地再拜子方足下.

所幸為買沓(:鞈)者, 願以屬先來吏, 使得及事. 幸甚. 元伏地
再 = 拜 =.

呂子都願刻印, 不敢報. 不知元不肖, 使元請子方. 願子方幸為
刻御史七分印一, 龜上, 印曰呂安之印. 唯子方留意, 得以子方
成事. 不敢復屬它人.

郭營尉所寄錢二百買鞭者, 願得其善鳴者, 願留意.

自書: 所願以市事幸留 = 意 =, 毋忽, 異於它人.[16]

This letter is out of the ordinary, though not unique, in that it was
written on a piece of silk.[17] What makes it more unusual is the excel-
lence of its preservation, which has left its content easily legible.

    The opening consists of the creator of the letter's self-identifica-
tion, Yuan, and his salutation to the recipient, Zifang. The remainder
of the first section conveys conventional expressions of concern for
Zifang and good wishes for his family. Yuan phrases his concern in
terms of the season, summer, and the need for suitable clothing,
food, and drink.

    The apparent main point of the letter is requesting a number
of small favors in the form of making specific purchases: a pair of

leather shoes and some writing brushes for Yuan, a seal and a whip for others. While doubtless important for Yuan and his colleagues, these specifics recede in significance when viewed from a distance of centuries. And Yuan's letter at first glance might appear to consist of this list of requests alone. But much more is happening.

In the letter, Yuan evokes a context that is both social and related to time, making the present communication a part of larger things. Throughout the text, Yuan places the letter and the favors he asks into a context of both individual and official concerns. Yuan begins in the first lines of the body by alluding to the past, when he apologizes for not having seen Zifang off. In this way, Yuan establishes both he and Zifang were present in the same geographical place at the same time. Yuan's request that Zifang visit Ciru and seek his response—presumably concerning an employment offer—has multiple levels of importance. For Yuan, Ciru's tardy reply was the matter of concern. That is the first level. Yuan also reminds Zifang that he had recommended Ciru, which places the request into the context of a larger relationship, even as it probably put some pressure on Zifang. Yuan's request that Zifang, if necessary, see Ciru's wife similarly evokes a larger set of relationships. So does the inclusion of the other men's names, which were presumably already familiar or otherwise meaningful to Zifang.

When Yuan refers to Ciru's wife, he does so by her name, Rongjun. This is not the only letter that refers to women, and I have already discussed another example.[18] The use of Rongjun's name, though, is unusual. Looking briefly at another example in which women's names appear will be instructive. That letter reads, "I, Quan, kowtow, and am most fortunate . . . May you, my elder, your son-in-law, and daughters Shujun and Laijun be without worry" 泉叩頭幸甚 . . . 京國丈人、壻、女舒君、來君毋恙.[19] There, the names of two of the recipient's daughters appear: Shujun and Laijun. They come after the recipient's son-in-law (or sons-in-law) in the list, an obligatory reflection of their social status. If Quan were going to specify persons whose names he knew from hearsay alone, it seems that the son-in-law's name would necessarily have appeared alongside the daughters'. But it is absent, which suggests Quan named the women because he knew them, because they were part of his circle of acquaintance in a way the son-in-law was not. Rongjun's name hints at something similar in her case. Yuan's choice to use her name seems to indicate, even more than Xuan's inclusion of Yousun's wife in his salutation, that he knew Rongjun.

In Yuan's letter, names appear in the text belonging to persons who are neither directly party to the message nor introduced and explained, including Rongjun. This shows they are part of a circle of acquaintances—a set of individuals with connections to each other extending beyond the letter's creator and recipient. The letter's content also creates links to the future, in terms of an expected answer, in terms of money that is to be repaid. At the same time, some names are absent. The sellers of shoes, seals, and whips, for example, are not mentioned at all. They were not a part of this community.

The postscript is the most intimate portion of the text. In its criticism of unnamed and unreliable "others"—surely identifiable, at least generically, perhaps specifically, to the recipient—it strikes a final, confidential note that recalls Xuan's friendly admonition to prepare for inspection. Its direct entreaty bestows a feeling of urgency on a communication that might otherwise read a bit flat. This was perhaps Yuan's purpose in adding it. He labeled the postscript as his own, indicating he dictated the rest. Indeed we do not know how many of the letters may have been dictated. While intriguing, this question is, as I argued in chapter 1, not crucial. Dictation in the premodern world did not necessarily imply a lack of power or ability to engage text.[20]

Official life and its institutions constitute the background of this letter. Without them the letter would not exist. The favors requested concern things linked to that life: brushes for writing, a seal for signing documents. Even the shoes Yuan asks for have overtones of working life, since without duties to take him to the place, he would not have been there. Despite all that, the letter's tone is more or less casual and its closing implores Zifang's assistance not out of official duty but rather by means of an individual appeal. This letter was part of two worlds and did not belong exclusively to either one. The next two letters are more official in nature and yet maintain a similar tone.

Official Tasks

The letters in this section have a manner of presentation that differs from those in the previous sections, as I will show. They deal with matters directly relating to official service and nevertheless retain a personal character. The first letter of this group comes to us damaged and not entirely legible. The main part of the message reads:

Labor service squad leader Ren kowtows and says:
Aide, may you be without worry. I have been fortunate and received your care and have been repeatedly pitied by you, who sent my statement document to Juyan. It ought not to have included the previous matter, but you wished it well examined. This causes me to kowtow for a crime worth death, a crime worth death.
I repeatedly sought to visit and was often treated harshly by the minor officers. I kowtow, this was a crime worth death. a crime worth death. If Juyan responds to my document, I hope you will communicate to the company, sending down to our section promptly and causing me to know the news early. I wish to speak myself of the matter . . . Ren bows repeatedly to state this.

給使燹長仁叩頭言

掾毋恙. 幸得奮, 見掾數哀憐, 為移自言書居延, 不宜以納前事, 欲頗案. 下使仁叩頭死=罪=.

仁數詣前, 少吏多所迫. 叩頭死=罪=.

居延即報仁書. 唯掾言候, 以時下部, 令仁蚤

知其曉. 欲自言事 . . . 謹請書□□吏□叩□. 仁再拜白.[21]

The creator of this letter, Ren, spends little time greeting the unnamed official to whom he writes, addressing him as "aide." Things we see in other letters are absent here: Ren does not mention the aide's clothing or parents, or express solicitude for imagined difficulties. Instead Ren places his request in the context of a long-standing relationship. This is what Xuan and Yuan did in their respective letters, too, just in other ways.

The contexts of time and relationship into which Ren places his letter are framed differently from the examples I have already discussed. The bureaucratic and official nature of Ren and the aide's interaction marks every aspect of the letter. The temporal context comes mainly from a previous, concrete instance of help, in which the official forwarded Ren's statement to the higher authorities at Juyan and included information about some other matter, apparently departing in this from standard practice. The favor that Ren requests in this letter seems to be nothing more than punctually forwarding any response from Juyan down through the hierarchy so that it will reach him earlier than it might otherwise. In place of the social contexts that Xuan, Yuan, and others record, the persons that surround this interaction are, in Ren's portrayal, nameless and faceless: they are the authorities at Juyan and the petty functionaries who had bullied Ren and refused to allow him access to the aide to whom he is writing.

There is still a personal tone at work in the letter. When Ren describes the previous assistance he has received from the aide, he writes of care and of pity. He does not refer to duty in the past or in the present instance. Excavated statutes governing the bureaucracy contain legal standards for processing documents, and although the statutes do not mention the specific form of document Ren refers to, there must have been rules for it, too.[22] Perhaps Ren wished to accelerate the forwarding, but even then it seems like he is asking only for the prompt performance of duty from one who had helped him before. The following letter from a man named An 安 bears a similar request.

> I prostrate myself on the ground and bow repeatedly:
> Your Equestrian Honor, Zhangqing: Relying upon . . . the watchtower officers, instructing that the name register of soldiers, scribes, wives, and children should be assembled monthly on the fifteenth day. Now the month is already over and Cigong to today . . . Now my request and desire is that Cigong do this. Yuan has no way to know the names, ages, and counts of people. I hope that Cigong will urgently seal and send the three sets of summary accounts.[23] They must now be sent to the office. . . . This matter cannot be neglected and I hope you will pay attention to it. I will be most favored . . .

安[24]伏地再拜

長卿馬足下, 因□□候官教卒史妻子集名籍會月十五日, 今月已盡, 次公至今日□今安請欲為次公為之. 元毋從知其名年人數. 願次公急封移三通, 會今須移官□事不可忽. 願留意, 幸甚 . . .[25]

An's request for assistance went to one Zhangqing, who presumably had charge of Cigong, the subordinate who was actually going to take the action. An wastes no time with blandishments or flattery. Instead he invokes a higher authority's command to submit the required information. Yet even this short letter implies a circle of acquaintances: An knows Zhangqing and Cigong and the hierarchical relationship between them, and he further refers to another by name, whose name is lost, who is actually supposed to use the data.

The closing line of this letter is reminiscent of the postscript that Yuan added when writing his letter on silk to Zifang. In this case, the handwriting of the postscript does not differ from what went before. But he does end his text exhorting that this matter cannot be neglected and hoping that Zhangqing will give attention to it. There is no need to invoke unnamed others, like Yuan did in his letter. The slacker was Cigong. Despite asking for nothing except compliance with procedure, An phrases his request as a favor and ends his letter with a personal appeal. The following letter is another example of adopting a personal mode of communication to request fulfillment of official duties.

Personal Business, Deferential Tone

Ni Shang kowtows to explain in writing:
Recently, I sent up, saying that we have long been short of food and wished to borrow one bushel of grain. When the grain arrived and was received, I ought to have appeared before you. Also the previous accounts have not yet been sent up, as I myself know well.
Aide Yang, sir, you have very often taken pity on me, and your benevolent virtue has been most generous, most generous. I also previously wanted to send someone to bring a *hu* [of grain] to the grand administrator's offices. I wished soon to leave Yangcheng, and the adjutant[26] commanded

me to return later. I was in my heart very troubled but the matter was not worth disrupting the peace.

If the grand administrator's office would pity the son of a negligible lineage and a poor man who has long resided beyond the borders, it should send out my replacement. I hope that you will in the proper time send the name list of those doing service who have fulfilled their required years, so that the grand administrator's office must on that basis arrange a replacement. Then when the replacement arrives I will be able to return. I kowtow and kowtow.

兒尚叩頭白記 ·

聞來上, 日久食盡乏, 願貸穀一斛, 穀到奉詣前, 又前計未上, 甚自知.

楊掾坐前, 數＝哀憐, 恩德甚＝厚＝. 又前欲遣持斛詣尹府, 欲且郤(:去)²⁷陽成, 士

吏令後歸, 尚意中甚不安也, 事不足亂平. 尹府哀小姓貧人子, 久居塞外, 當為發代. 唯掾以時 移 視事盈歲名, 尹府須以調代＝到得歸, 叩＝頭＝.²⁸

This letter differs from those I have already discussed in its form and its language. This is obvious in the opening of the letter, where its creator refers to himself by surname and name, Ni Shang, rather than using his courtesy name alone, as in the preceding examples.²⁹ He addresses his recipient with the phrase "explain in writing" (*baiji* 白記).

Generally speaking, correspondence marked *ji* 記 could be elegant or common in style and deal with personal or official matters, just like other letters. In the examples I have found, the phrase *baiji* most often, but not exclusively, occurs in documents in which the creator uses both his name and surname; in a couple of other cases where this phrase occurs, the creator refers to himself by title.³⁰ These things indicate an elevated degree of formality perhaps connected with the high rank of the recipient. The creator's choice to address the recipient by title and surname here strengthens the impression of formality.

The diction of this letter is also unlike that of the previous examples. The common mode of bureaucratic writing in the early empire was leaden and graceless, characterized by repetition, a limited vocabulary, and choppy sentences. These things are common to most letters from the northwest, too. Ni Shang writes a more graceful prose reminiscent of literary language. Phrases such as "to have often taken pity" and "the son of a negligible lineage and a poor man, who has long resided beyond the borders" are unlike the workaday prose of the other letters. And in referring to Aide Yang's previous assistance, Ni Shang uses a phrase (*ende* 恩德) that often—though not exclusively—denotes a ruler's generosity. These things perhaps denote a higher degree of cultivation on Ni Shang's part, even as they attempt more effective cajolery.

Despite the formality and elegance that distinguish this letter from the others I have discussed, its creator establishes a chronological context of past and future in a familiar manner. The content of Ni Shang's apologetic references to earlier lapses—to twice when he should have paid calls but did not, to his failure to submit accounts—as well as to Aide Yang's previous assistance all work to make the present request for assistance part of an ongoing relationship. In it, Ni is the humble subordinate and Yang the generous benefactor.

For Ni Shang, the future is where the weight of the letter lies, as the favor he requests is there. His hope is for the replacement that will enable him to return home, which requires action on the part of the office of the grand administrator in the commandery. Ni Shang does not request help with this directly. Rather Ni asks only that the aide punctually submit the report that will tell the higher authorities that he has completed his requisite time of service, which he hopes will bring his desired outcome.

Ni Shang's letter requests the timely performance of duty. In this case there is perhaps some irony in his hope that the recipient will act promptly when he admits he has not submitted his own accounts on time. But it is precisely this that illuminates the reason for Ni's letter. The bureaucracy did not run on time, and Ni hopes in this one specific case that it would do so without fail. The absence of date information and documentary markers confirms that this request went in the form of a personal missive.

Ni Shang invests considerable energy in evoking his personal relationship with Aide Yang in the course of making his request. The following letter manages to combine a different sort of personal subject with clear deference:

Chang kowtows to say:

    Zihui, please hear this. Your servant previously repeatedly saw you and originally did not dare to speak in front of the group. And why? I dare death to say it happens that the bottom of my trousers has torn. In the morning I would like to have Yan take them back and repair them. I hope that Zihui might favor me by having pity and lending me your . . . trousers just one or two days. I will not dare keep them long. And I hope you will give me the money. If it were not urgent, I would not dare speak of this . . .

敢叩頭言

子惠容聽. 侍前數見, 元不敢眾言, 奈何乎. 昧死言會敢綺元幣.

旦日欲使儇持歸補之, 願子惠幸哀憐且幸藉子惠□□

綺一乙二日耳, 不敢久留. 唯賜錢, 非急不敢道. 叩□[31]

The first part of this letter's content establishes a confidential tone. It refers to past interactions, putting the current communication into a larger context. But in doing so, Chang, the creator of the letter, implicitly contrasts the public context of speaking in the presence of others with the direct domain of the personal letter. A letter was not a secret medium, and the topic of this specific message is not one of real secrecy. Rather Chang evokes a feeling of intimacy, in which he can make his requests, apparently for the loan of some trousers while his own are being repaired and some money. His passing reference to Yan, without further information except he is the one to take his trousers to be repaired, emphasizes that Chang and Zihui belong to a social circle.

    Contrasting with this familiarity is the deferential language Chang employs. He refers to himself by name only once and otherwise as "your servant," which contrasts with other letter creators' consistent use of their names to denote themselves. Chang introduces the cause of his letter—the tearing of his trousers—with the phrase "dare death," a phrase that appears frequently in received sources in addressing the sovereign. And he hopes not merely for Zihui's kindness; he hopes for "pity." In this respect, Chang's composition recalls that of Ni Shang, and it seems likely that imperial texts informed his vocabulary, as they did Ni Shang's. And in a manner similar to that of Yuan, who in his letter to Zifang promised quick repayment of a debt, Chang reassures Zihui that he will not dare keep the borrowed trousers long.

Declining a Request

The preceding examples have shared a number of traits, the most prominent of which may be their evident self-interest. But not all letters that emerge from this context ask for favors. One letter declines a request. It is only a fragment, which begins, "Zhangshi and Xiaojun sent Zhangqing to come pick up Xiaojun's clothing and bring it to your place. He favored me, Guangyi, by giving me a message . . ." 長實、孝君使長卿來取孝君衣, 至長實、孝君所, 幸賜廣意記. Guangyi slightly later in the letter appears to respond to a greeting he had received, writing, "My parents are without worry" 廣意丈人毋恙也, and saying in turn, "I sincerely ask whether you, Zhangshi, and your parents are without worry" 多問長實足下、長實丈人毋恙也.[32]

The opening of Guangyi's short letter focuses on clothing, and he returns to this topic at the close of the letter and on the back of the strip, where he writes, "I, Guangyi, prostrate myself on the ground and bow repeatedly to present this letter responding to Your Honor, Zhangshi . . . Xiaojun's clothing is not sent" 廣意伏地再拜 / 進書 / 覆長實足下 . . . / 孝君衣不行. In this way, Guangyi mingles the personal elements of exchanged greetings with a businesslike approach to declining the requested dispatch of clothing. It is possible that Guangyi's attention to the antiphonal niceties of greeting was purposeful and his response to a question meant only as a greeting was intended simply to diminish the recipient's irritation. But even that interpretation would require that Guangyi perceived the possibility of achieving something by this means, that these words had the potential for efficacy.

Guangyi's letter gives attention to these greetings and contains little other content. The exchange of courtesies that takes its place hints at some degree of connection, in that questions asked in greeting are responded to with every appearance of sincerity. The letter's core business content appears as a passing mention alone.

Accompanying Gifts

The following example letter is complex. It was written on silk and consists of several sections, the first of which has suffered damage that leaves it hard to understand. The readable text fragments on that section include personal names and things such as meat, rice, and money. These are presumably gifts that the letter accompanied, and the names those of the givers. The document's second section comprises a prose passage, which is relatively well preserved. It reads:

> Xin prostrates himself on the ground and bows repeatedly to ask sincerely:
>   Your Honors Cijun and Junping: You generously gave me gifts that I cannot match.[33] I am most fortunate. It is the cold season. I hope that you have properly fitting clothing and work hard at getting sufficient beer and food. In carrying out your duties do not become lax. Then I will be most fortunate! Though it is insufficient as ritual . . . coarse silk, one, which I, Xin, bow repeatedly to present to Junping. In the future repeatedly send letters, permitting me, Xin, to learn that Cijun and Junping are without worry. I am most fortunate, and prostrate myself on the ground and bow over and over.
>
> Your Honors, Cijun and Junping. • Chu kowtows and asks sincerely:
>   My elders, it is the cold season. I kowtow and hope that you have properly fitting clothing and are sure to make yourselves . . . beer and food. I will be most favored, most favored. I send . . . giving socks, two pairs. May you, my elders, repeatedly send letters, letting me know that you are without worry. I kowtow, and will be most favored, most favored. The gloves you sent have already arrived.

信伏地再拜多問

次君＝平足下, 厚遺信, 非自二, 信幸甚. 寒時, 信願次君＝平近衣強酒食, 察事毋自易. 信幸甚. 薄禮□絮一, 信再拜進君平. 來者數寄書使信奉聞次君＝平毋恙, 信幸甚, 伏地再＝拜＝

次君＝平足下 • 初[34]叩頭多問

丈人, 寒時. 初叩頭願丈人近衣強 □ 酒食. 初叩頭幸＝甚＝. 初寄□贛(:袜/襪)[35]布二兩□□者 丈人數寄書使初聞丈人毋恙. 初叩頭幸＝甚＝ 丈人遺初手衣已到.[36]

This text combines related letters from two men, Xin and Chu, which a bullet point on the manuscript sets apart. Both messages address the same two recipients, Cijun and Junping. Both speak of gifts previously received and of gifts given then, and of the hope for future correspondence. Both ignore the list of names and gifts that precede them on the silk.

There are distinctions that reinforce the separation of the two texts. There are small differences in the wording of their greetings, and the use of bowing in one case and kowtowing in the other. The terms of address the two employ are also different, presumably reflecting differences in status: Xin uses "Your Honor" (*zuxia* 足下), which typically occurs in correspondence between those of similar status, while Chu's "my elders" (*zhangren* 丈人) implies deference to someone of higher rank. Xin reinforces this impression, in that he advises against laxity in the performance of job duties and Chu does not. This suggests that perhaps giving such advice was the province of superiors. These things together emphasize that Xin and Chu, although writing on a single piece of silk, created distinct letters that constituted different kinds of social interaction.

Finally, this document reflects relationships that extended beyond these four persons. The initial section, which I leave untranslated due to its damaged state, names still more people, by name or by title, and refers to travel to the Han capital, Chang'an, a journey of many weeks, if not months.[37] Thus, and in a manner familiar from previous examples, we can see that what appear at first to be simple sets of greetings and lists of gifts in fact do more: they testify to the existence of groups of men who were acquainted with each other, who cooperated and communicated with each other, and who had secondhand links to the centers of power.

Interaction with Text and with Others

Taken as a group, the letters I have discussed in this chapter represent a spectrum of relationships, from men who appear to have known each other well to those who did not. Yet relationships were always part of the circumstances. Requests for aid were presented as favors, neither as appeals to duty nor as demands, even when it was one.

Text mediated those relationships, and interaction with text was corollary to this form of interpersonal interaction. The relationships extended beyond the creator and recipient, who might seem the chain of communication's logical end points. By means of their forms of address and because they ask help of the recipient and of others, the letters implicate others and give us an idea of the scope of the social circles the letters circulated within. These included groups of relatives, colleagues, and friends. Women were part of this interaction, something that conventional historical sources do not adequately record. This is yet another instance in which excavated materials provide us crucial information about life in early imperial times.

Conclusion

A *little learning* is a dang'rous thing;
Drink deep, or taste not the Pierian spring:
There shallow draughts intoxicate the brain,
And drinking largely sobers us again.

—Alexander Pope

According to *Latter Han History* (*Hou Han shu* 後漢書), the first-century CE philosopher Wang Chong was, when young, an orphan and poor. His resources remained limited even after he moved to the capital, where he studied at the Imperial Academy (Taixue 太學), and he did not have texts to read at home. Instead Wang Chong wandered the market and read the texts for sale there. Such was the power of this great skeptic's intellect that "at first sight he was always able to read aloud and remember them" 一見輒能誦憶.[1]

An account like this one invites incredulity. Yet it brings together several of the main strands of this book. We have Wang Chong: someone with interest in texts, who had access to texts that were available in his environment; someone who used those texts to learn. And we have his method for learning, namely, reading aloud and remembering.

Wang Chong's case is extraordinary, as the fact that we read his book nearly two thousand years after his death confirms—to say nothing of that book's content. But the tools of reading aloud and remembering were available to many people in the realm. Still more would see text and hear others read aloud, and remember what they heard. Research suggests that, with tools like these, people can acquire the ability to read. Even those who did not, or whose ability was marginal, would still interact with text by listening to others read. That was meaningful interaction, just as dictation was. Text and interaction with text were widespread in the early imperial period. It is possible that Wang Chong really did become familiar with the texts of the masters in the market. Others encountered and interacted with the works of lesser—even far lesser—writers in analogous ways.

It is important to avoid exaggeration, of course. Simple visual exposure to a script does not engender comprehension of its language. Archaeologists have recovered Eastern Han silks bearing textual decorations from graves in Mongolia, Siberia, and even at ancient Palmyra, in modern Syria; the texts convey wishes for long life, descendants, and other things familiar from Chinese contexts. Lothar von Falkenhausen has noted that there is no reason to think anyone at Palmyra, for instance, could read the words that decorated the silks. That does not mean the graphs were without meaning. As Falkenhausen observes, people in Palmyra may not have understood the characters as language, but the characters were still consequential, as signals of the silks' far-distant origins. They worked, together with the extraordinary fabric, "additionally to mark the object as exotic, mysterious and thus more valuable."[2]

Nor did even informed use of Chinese language by non-Chinese persons necessarily indicate they assigned it the same significance that Chinese people did. Alice Yao considers how rulers of polities on the southern periphery of the Han empire employed Chinese writing. She points out that those indigenous groups' selective deployment of the Chinese language was not a token of obedience or allegiance. It was part of a complex relationship, in which local interests and decisions interacted with the power and purposes of the Han imperium and its culture.[3]

The ability to interact with text exists on a spectrum, which in early China ranged from people who could read and write everything to those who depended on others for all reading and all writing. Most people were somewhere in between those extremes. Likewise, there was surely a spectrum in the potential significance of writing. It may have sometimes been divorced from the linguistic content, as Falkenhausen proposes for the Chinese text on silks from Palmyra. This way of thinking is not absent from scholarship in the context of the Han empire. Tomiya Itaru, for instance, proposes that the distinctive brushstrokes and aspect that Han official copyists employed created a "visual effect." This effect marked the text as part of the imperial bureaucracy, without regard to specific content.[4] Such an indication could communicate that the text was connected with governance and thus noteworthy, even if its contents were not directly available to someone.

Tomiya's observation is an astute one. It makes sense that a distinctive mode of presentation would distinguish Han official content, and that many people would recognize those characteristics and what they meant. Yet our default assumption should not be that the visual effect of a government text was the *only* level of understanding for most members of Han society.

In the context of border region military installations, for instance, we have the codes that soldiers used to communicate over distance. They existed as both official texts and as content that soldiers needed to know: the content was posted in written form, read aloud, and in fact learned. We have example edicts, too, which contain formulas that commanded their public posting and reading aloud. The edicts often conveyed things like changes to the legal system, but we also have other sorts of examples.

Some edicts had prefatory sections that cited elevated texts and high classical language. Many bore an order to make their contents known to all. I talked about these things in chapter 3. I take the commands concerning dissemination seriously. For edicts, that includes not only legal content but also other aspects, including even the high classical language of some edicts' prefaces, as the format of the Xuanquanzhi inscription indicates.

Historians sometimes minimize the possibility of reading aloud and communicating that content to the population. And, of course, life is messy, and I do not imagine exceptionless correspondence between document and reality. But on the whole, and absent reasons to think otherwise, we should take the texts to mean what they say. Naturally, one must understand the texts correctly, which can present problems. But there is little question about the general sense of the formulas, or about the general purpose of the codes. We even know that there was verification of the soldiers' knowledge of the codes.

The situation is thus that the two types of content—the codes and the edicts—were required knowledge for the soldiers in the border region. Written texts bearing the edicts and the codes were available to the soldiers, and thus offered something conceptually akin to the books on sale that Wang Chong learned from. They were texts for the reading, if one chose to do so or to learn to do so. Not everyone in the capital visited the market to avail themselves of the texts displayed there as an opportunity to learn, like Wang Chong did. Likewise we ought not expect that every soldier developed a level of literacy that we can measure from our vantage point—two thousand years away—before we can admit the conclusion that they had access to reading material and that a meaningful portion of them would have taken advantage of the opportunity that presented.

In chapters 1 and 7, I mentioned David Johnson, who connects the presence of text with expanding literacy.[5] And I think he is right about the connection. Johnson and I differ, however, in when we think text became pervasive in China. He saw widespread availability of text only coming to be in the medieval period, while my analysis suggests it existed already in early imperial times—in some contexts, at least, including the military installations of the northwestern border region.

The presence of text is one of Frank Smith's preconditions for learning to read, which I also talked about in chapter 1. Equal in importance is Smith's point, which researchers in other disciplines echo, that learning is natural. When exposed to something new, the default human reaction is to learn about it, and that includes text. When the other conditions Smith identifies as necessary for learning to read are also present—namely, an understanding of text as meaningful and important, and someone to answer questions about text—the burden of proof shifts. The question is no longer whether people would begin to learn to read. Rather, it becomes whether and why they would not.[6]

Text was important throughout early Chinese society, and we know that men and women who were not officials interacted with it and its documents. We have, for instance, many example statements from the northwest, and they were the subject of chapter 4. The officials created them on the basis of applicants' oral assertions, marked them as such (ziyan), and in effect took dictation. The statements record multiple examples of a particular form of interaction with text, a process that went from oral to written to the real world. Many of the statements we have were the basis for granting permission to travel, and travelers carried passes reflecting that process. Just as copies of signal codes and imperial edicts could work as reading primers,

making text and its function known, statements were an obligatory
form of dictation that made the creation of text familiar to all. Not
everyone whose statement came into being this way was unable to
write, but most probably had limited or no writing skills. That is not
decisive for the purposes of the discussion here. Dictation, after all, is
another way to create text, as valid as any other, and it functioned
throughout the premodern world.[7] (My phone keeps trying to push
dictation on me, even now.)

In the Han period, there was yet another way to create text,
which was to assemble content from other sources into something
new. People did it at the center of Han power, and they did it in
the border regions, too. Chapter 5 treats an example from the border
regions, created by someone who copied a section of an imperial
pronouncement alongside a personal letter. This enigmatic object
was, I suggest, something like a sampler assembled by a person who
thereby demonstrated mastery of writing and, in the process, engaged
in the same sort of creative activity that occupied intellectuals at the
center of the empire. Other examples of this sort of composite text,
which come to us from graves, indicate that this kind of creation
could have personal significance and utility.

Chapter 6 considers texts concerning visual examination. These,
too, could be of personal interest. A text on the visual evaluation
of swords is at the center of the discussion, and it is easy to imagine
why someone doing military service in the border regions would
want to know how to decide whether a sword is a good one. Anyone
acquainted with members of modern armed forces knows also that a
general interest in weaponry is far from rare among them. It seems
reasonable to think it existed in the past, too.

Whatever reasons a reader had for approaching the text on
sword evaluation, its author seems to have made allowances for an
audience of inexpert readers: the text's structure is transparent and
explicit, its presentation is straightforward, its reasoning is elementary. I discuss some other evaluation texts, too, in particular one
concerning horses, by way of comparison. The horse evaluation text
is recondite and includes an internal commentary, without which its
very subject is more or less unidentifiable. Chapter 6 ends with a text
conveying some good advice concerning the brewing of beer, a task
of interest to military personnel in the border areas. It happens that
this specific text appears also in a ritual classic, suggesting an origin

there. But classical provenance does not rule out practical use, and a dual nature seems likely.

That text is far from the only classic that we find attested among the northwestern documents. Chapter 7 discusses a number of examples, including the *Book of Documents*, *Analects*, and *Book of Odes*. The chapter ends with a piece of lyric poetry, also from the region. I refer to the subject of this chapter as cultural texts, which are more than just classics. The chapter also looks at scraps of narratives that are not part of the canon, some of which have links to previously known accounts. These texts held significance that went far beyond the local environs, and they linked the area to Han literate culture generally.

Chapter 8 examines letters that officers, including very low-ranking officers, in the region exchanged. Neither wholly personal nor fully official, these letters provide examples of how text worked to bring community into being. The letters record how people interacted with and through them as part of relationships that were both official and personal. Those relationships extended beyond the creator-recipient pair to encompass others in the community, a group that explicitly included women.

Wider Connections

This book concentrates on a particular literate community. The northwestern border region of the Han period offers a text-rich case to study. Only with recent discoveries, such as the Qin documents from Liye, have other places in the early imperial period become available for study through a comparable density of paleographic material.[8] Even so, each site offers differing types of documents, those sites' publications emerge slowly, and such places remain very few in number. The northwest desert region presents a rare opportunity.

In this book I have restricted myself to speaking about this specific area because the relative richness of text in this case made it amenable to my approach. I suspect its conclusions apply elsewhere, too. But the documents that would support the sort of work I attempt no longer exist for other places, if they ever did. Archaeological discoveries may yet change this. But for now, that is the situation.

It is nevertheless possible to think about broader connections, and that is what I would like to do in these final pages.

In chapter 1 I wrote about work by Hsing, Miyake, and Yates concerning the role of military service in disseminating literacy during the Han period.[9] One of the most important implications of that work is the idea that conscription, theoretically universal during much of the Western Han period, would help spread the ability to interact with text throughout society. In this context, it is useful to recall Smith's preconditions for learning to read and to remember how access to text, an understanding of text's importance, and the presence of someone to answer questions enable acquisition of reading ability. I have talked about these things repeatedly over the course of the book, acknowledging always that not everyone will learn to read, even if those preconditions are present.

Provided that the bureaucracy of the northwest is at all representative of how the system of Han governance worked elsewhere, Smith's preconditions take on greater significance. As I discussed in chapter 2, over much of the Western Han, every male owed two years of service. Only some conscripts went to the northwestern border region. But everyone who served in the Han military experienced a situation that met Smith's preconditions, which would change their perspective on text. The workings of the military bureaucracy meant that everyone involved in it necessarily learned about the importance of text through the personnel records that governed service life. One of the statements I discussed in chapter 4, which recorded an ordinary soldier's request to return home as his allotted time of service had run out, is a poignant example showing that soldiers knew what text could mean for their lives.

In that text-rich environment—one in which information, including things each soldier needed to know, was routinely transmitted in writing; one in which documents were so ubiquitous that they became literal bumf;[10] one in which written records of many sorts were standard—every soldier had at least some access to text. The presence of squad leaders and scribes, both required to have reading and writing ability, meant there was always someone who could answer questions about reading.

It seems to me likely that under those circumstances many soldiers would have acquired *some* degree of reading ability, including those whose service did not take them to the northwest. In all likelihood it was, for most, not a high level, but it was more than they had at the start. When they returned home, they took that ability with them. They need not have developed extensive abilities for this to affect society broadly. Alexander Pope warned against "a little learning" precisely because of its potential for disproportionate influence.[11] Walter Ong expressed a similar idea about literacy: "it takes only a moderate degree of literacy to make a tremendous difference in thought processes."[12] Since broad conscription was in place during the early imperial period, many men experienced that big change and came under the influence of "a little learning."

We can extend this line of thinking further to consider how its effects worked across society. As broad a segment of society as conscription implies, the impact of official text was still broader. For military service was not the first time a person would have encountered this sort of situation. In the early imperial period, *all* Han subjects were required to remain registered as part of a household. Registration required an official to register each person in the realm by name, as part of a household, and verify that registration annually. All registrants in turn needed to update their registration if they moved their place of residence. Registration was a means of tracking people as they moved through the realm, to ensure that duties—and *everyone* had duties—and debts owed to the government were met.[13] *Everyone* owed annual labor service unless an exemption was received. And *everyone* was answerable to the law. Each of these things entailed interaction with text. In chapter 1 I quoted Yates, who made a similar point.[14] The line of reasoning I have pursued in this book is different from his, and my claim is differently formulated. Interaction with text is a broader and more flexible conception than the usual understanding of literacy—that is, mastery of reading and writing—and I do not speak in terms of compulsion. Yet Yates and I end up in similar places.

There was text available widely to learn from in Han China. Edicts like those I talked about in chapter 3 were not only for posting in military installations. They were supposed to be everywhere. Similarly, other sorts of governmental texts, such as legal texts, were supposed to be posted, too, and evidence confirms people read them.[15] The general presence of officials meant there was someone who could answer questions about those texts. Widespread military service suggests there were others who could, as well, including those former soldiers who brought some reading ability home from their time in service.

As a result, it seems likely that most Han subjects had meaningful interaction with text. I do not suggest everyone learned to read. But there is every reason to expect that the social effects of that interaction were still pervasive. All this brings me back to something I suggested in chapter 1, and that is the crucial position of the early Chinese bureaucracy in disseminating written culture. The document bureaucracy contributed to creating a broad textual culture to a degree unlike any other discrete element of early Chinese society. This was not the highly literate culture of Yang Xiong and others. It was not the textual culture of the poets and prose writers whose works readers have encountered in all subsequent centuries. But it was a textual culture. It was a *literate culture*. And insofar as there was a community in the northwest border region—and I argued in chapter 1 that there was—it was a *literate community*.

Michael Puett has written about Wang Chong as someone who marks a shift in attitude about the creation of text. The prevailing attitude in his time and before placed the days of creating texts in the past. As Wang Chong saw it, that time had not passed. But the situation was in fact shifting. The masters were dead, but writing continued, and text's position in society was changing. It was around the time Wang Chong lived that "The age of writing as a more common activity began; the age of the great sagely book was over." Puett makes his argument from the perspective of intellectual history, and he echoes those who point to the spread of paper soon after Wang Chong's life as a conditioning factor for the expansion of writing that followed.[16] My consideration of the bureaucracy's broad impact supports this conclusion, even as it suggests another aspect of the cause. In Chinese society during the Han period, everyone knew that sages were not the only ones who created text. Interaction with text in different forms was common throughout society. Not everyone wrote, but everyone knew writing. They had felt its effects themselves, in the literate communities where they lived.

Notes

Introduction

1. These were major topics and themes of my *Communication and Cooperation in Early Imperial China: Publicizing the Qin Dynasty* (Albany: State University of New York Press, 2014).

2. M. T. Clanchy, *From Memory to Written Record: England 1066–1307*, third edition (Chichester: Wiley-Blackwell, 2013), 196, 334–35, and passim.

3. Ori Tavor, "Religious Thought," in *Routledge Handbook of Early Chinese History*, ed. Paul R. Goldin (London: Routledge, 2018), 261, and the discussion of the Qin-Han period, 273–76; see also Charles Sanft, "Paleographic Evidence of Qin Religious Practice from Liye and Zhoujiatai," *Early China* 37 (2014): 327–58; and Filippo Marsili, *Heaven Is Empty* (Albany: State University of New York Press, 2018).

4. See, for example, Sanft, "Paleographic Evidence."

5. Wilt L. Idema, "Elite versus Popular Literature," in *The Oxford Handbook of Classical Chinese Literature (1000 BCE–900 CE)*, ed. Wiebke Denecke, Wai-yee Li, and Xiaofei Tian (Oxford: Oxford University Press, 2017), 265–66; Victor H. Mair, "Buddhism and the Rise of the Written Vernacular in East Asia: The Making of National Languages," *Journal of Asian Studies* 53.3 (1994): 707–51.

6. See Jens Østergård Petersen, "Which Books Did the First Emperor of Ch'in Burn? On the Meaning of *Pai Chia* in Early Chinese Sources," *Monumenta Serica* 43 (1995): 1–52; and Michael Nylan, *The Five "Confucian" Classics* (New Haven: Yale University Press, 2001), 29–31.

7. See Yang Hongnian 楊鴻年, *Han-Wei zhidu congkao* 漢魏制度叢考, second edition (Wuhan: Wuhan daxue chubanshe, 2005), 191–203.

8. Stephen Durrant, "Histories (*shi* 史)," in *The Oxford Handbook of Classical Chinese Literature (1000 BCE–900 CE)*, ed. Wiebke Denecke, Wai-yee Li, and Xiaofei Tian (Oxford: Oxford University Press, 2017), 192–94; David

Schaberg, *A Patterned Past: Form and Thought in Early Chinese Historiography* (Cambridge: Harvard University Asia Center, 2001), 172.

9. On these things, see, for example, Denis Twitchett, "Chinese Social History from the Seventh to the Tenth Centuries: The Tunhuang Documents and Their Implications," *Past and Present* 35 (1966): 29–30, and passim.

10. Ruth Finnegan, *Literacy and Orality: Studies in the Technology of Communication* (Oxford: Basil Blackwell, 1988), 20.

11. Alice Yao, *The Ancient Highlands of Southwest China: From the Bronze Age to the Han Empire* (Oxford: Oxford University Press, 2016), 17.

12. See, for example, Michael Loewe, *Records of Han Administration* (Cambridge: Cambridge University Press, 1967).

13. Susan N. Erickson, "Han Dynasty Tomb Structures and Contents," in *China's Early Empires: A Re-appraisal*, ed. Michael Nylan and Michael Loewe (Cambridge: Cambridge University Press, 2010), 13.

14. Alain Thote, "Daybooks in Archaeological Context," in *Books of Fate and Popular Culture in Early China: The Daybook Manuscripts of the Warring States, Qin, and Han*, ed. Donald Harper and Marc Kalinowski (Leiden: Brill, 2017), 13–15.

15. See the descriptions of the sites in Xue Yingqun 薛英群, *Juyan Han jian tonglun* 居延漢簡通論 (Lanzhou: Gansu jiaoyu chubanshe, 1991), 49–95.

16. For an eponymously brief discussion of the distinction between descriptive and historiographical approaches to history, see John H. Arnold, *History: A Very Short Introduction* (Oxford: Oxford University Press, 2000), 35–57. Note that Arnold uses the term "antiquarian" exclusively, which may seem uncomplimentary. Those negative implications would not reflect my respect and appreciation for scholars who work in the mode so described, which I thus refer to instead as "descriptive."

17. Twitchett, "Chinese Social History from the Seventh to the Tenth Centuries," 31–32 and passim.

18. Personal email communication (6 November 2017).

19. Lothar von Falkenhausen, *Chinese Society in the Age of Confucius (1000–250 BC): The Archaeological Evidence* (Los Angeles: Cotsen Institute, University of California Press, 2006), 3.

20. See related discussion in David R. Knechtges, "Introduction," in Knechtges, trans., *Wen xuan or Selections of Refined Literature, Volume 1: Rhapsodies on Metropolises and Capitals* (Princeton: Princeton University Press, 1982), 1–4, 21–26.

21. In this description, I draw inspiration from Alexander Beecroft, *Authorship and Cultural Identity in Early Greece and China: Patterns of Literary Circulation* (Cambridge: Cambridge University Press, 2009), 8–9, 188, 205–16, 280–81. See also chapter 7 of this book.

Chapter One. Interacting with Text in
Early Imperial China and Beyond

1. J. D. Salinger, *The Catcher in the Rye* (Boston: Little, Brown, 1951), 24.

2. Twitchett, "Chinese Social History from the Seventh to the Tenth Centuries," 29 and passim.

3. Roger S. Bagnall and Raffaella Cribiore, *Women's Letters from Ancient Egypt, 300 BC–AD 800* (Ann Arbor: University of Michigan Press, 2006), 25–27; quote 25.

4. Wang Haicheng, *Writing and the Ancient State: Early China in Comparative Perspective* (Cambridge: Cambridge University Press, 2014).

5. Michael Nylan, *Yang Xiong and the Pleasures of Reading and Classical Learning in China* (New Haven: American Oriental Society, 2011); quote 54.

6. Miyake Kiyoshi 宮宅潔, "Shin-Kan jidai no moji to shikiji—chikukan, mokkan kara mita" 秦漢時代の文字と識字—竹簡、木簡からみた, in *Kanji no Chūgoku bunka* 漢字の中国文化, ed. Tomiya Itaru (Kyoto: Showado, 2009), 201–5; see also Tomiya Itaru, *Monjo gyōsei no Kan teikoku: mokkan, chikukan no jidai* 文書行政の漢帝國: 木簡, 竹簡の時代 (Nagoya: Nagoya Daigaku Shuppansha, 2010), 110–11.

7. Jerry Norman, *Chinese* (Cambridge: Cambridge University Press, 1988), 73, 257.

8. Anthony J. Barbieri-Low and Robin D. S. Yates, *Law, State, and Society in Early Imperial China: A Study with Critical Edition and Translation of the Legal Texts from Zhangjiashan Tomb no. 247* (Leiden: Brill, 2015), 1093; K. E. Brashier, *Public Memory in Early China* (Cambridge: Harvard University Asia Center, 2014), 388–89; Robin D. S. Yates, "Soldiers, Scribes, and Women: Literacy among the Lower Orders in Early China," in *Writing and Literacy in Early China: Studies from the Columbia Early China Seminar*, ed. Li Feng and David Prager Branner (Seattle: University of Washington Press, 2011), 351–53. Yates, "Soldiers, Scribes, and Women," 352–53, proposes that determining the sense of this precept would require counting how many different graphs appear in the texts from the northwest, subtracting toponyms and other characters "that would necessarily be used only occasionally" (353). On that basis, he arrives at a general figure of "approximately 2,500 to 3,500 different graphs" (353) as the requisite vocabulary. I would argue for a different picture. This book describes a situation in which many more people interacted with text than has been believed in the past. In such a situation, it is precisely the less common characters that would distinguish professionals from amateurs. Furthermore, writing toponyms was an important part of scribes' work, including handling written correspondence and

records of persons and their hometowns. It seems like knowing these and other less-common words should have been part of a scribe's qualifications.

9. Brashier, *Public Memory*, 11–14; see also Eno Gīre エノ・ギーレ (Enno Giele), "Kodai no shikiji nōryoku o ikani hantei suru no ka–Kandai gyōsei monjo no jirei kenkyū –" 古代の識字能力を如何に判定するのか–漢代行政文書の事例研究 –," in *Kanji bunka sanzennen* 漢字文化三千年, ed. Takata Tokio 高田時雄 (Kyoto: Rinsen Shoten, 2009), 138.

10. Evelyn Sakakida Rawski, *Education and Popular Literacy in Ch'ing China* (Ann Arbor: University of Michigan Press, 1979), 1.

11. Yates, "Soldiers, Scribes," 340.

12. See Eno Gīre (Enno Giele), "Kodai no shikiji nōryoku," 134–37.

13. Tomiya Itaru, *Monjo gyōsei*, 107; M. C. A. Macdonald, "Literacy in an Oral Environment," in *Writing and Near East Society*, ed. E. A. Slater, Piotr Bienkowski, and C. B. Mee (New York: T & T Clark International, 2005), 52, 54–56.

14. For example, Hsing I-t'ien 邢義田, "Qin-Han pingmin de duxie nengli–shiliao jiedu pian zhi yi" 秦漢平民的讀寫能力—史料解讀篇之一, *Gudai shumin shehui: Disijie guoji Hanxue huiyi lunwenji* 古代庶民社會: 第四屆國際漢學會議論文集・古代庶民社會, ed. Hsing I-t'ien and Liu Zenggui 劉增貴 (Taipei: Zhongyang yanjiuyuan, 2013), 242 and passim, refers to literacy as "the ability to read and write" (*duxie nengli* 讀寫能力) and sometimes as "recognizing characters" (*shizi* 識字).

15. Wang Haicheng, *Writing and the Ancient State*, 279.

16. Yates, "Soldiers, Scribes," 340–41.

17. Yates, "Soldiers, Scribes," 367.

18. *Oxford English Dictionary*, online ed., s.v. "literacy," accessed 23 May 2016.

19. Peng Hao 彭浩, Chen Wei 陳偉, and Kudo Mutoo 工藤元男, eds., *Ernian lüling yu Zouyanshu: Zhangjiashan ersiqihao Han mu chutu falü wenxian shidu* 二年律令與奏讞書: 張家山二四七號漢墓出土法律文獻釋讀 (Shanghai: Shanghai guji, 2007), 297 (no. 475).

20. Tomiya, *Monjo gyōsei*, 112–16.

21. Hsing I-t'ien, "Qin-Han pingmin de duxie nengli," 241–46.

22. Miyake, "Shin-Kan jidai no moji to shikiji," 201–8; Tsang Wing Ma, "Scribes, Assistants, and the Materiality of Administrative Documents in Qin-Early Han China: Excavated Evidence from Liye, Shuihudi, and Zhangjiashan," *T'oung-Pao* 103-104-105 (2017): 297–333.

23. Konrad Hirschler, *The Written Word in the Medieval Arabic Lands* (Edinburgh: Edinburgh University Press, 2012).

24. Stanislas Dehaene, *Reading in the Brain: The New Science of How We Read* (New York: Penguin, 2009); see also later in this chapter.

25. Jean-Pierre Drège "La lecture et l'écriture en Chine et la xylographie," *Études chinoises* 10.1–2 (1991): 78–85; Insup Taylor and Martin M. Taylor, *Writing and Literacy in Chinese, Korean and Japanese* (Amsterdam: John Benjamins, 1995), 58–61.

26. Writers from the second and third centuries CE dated the development of calligraphy and the emergence of a distinct cursive script, pursued for aesthetics rather than utility, to the first and second centuries CE; see André Kneib, 'Le *Sitishu shi* de Wei Heng (252–291): Première traité chinois de calligraphie," *Cahiers d'Extrême-Asie* 9 (1996): 103–4, 116–28; Zhao Yi 趙壹 (d. ca. 185), "Fei caoshu" 非草書, in *Quan Shanggu Sandai Qin Han Sanguo Liuchao wen* 全上古三代秦漢三國六朝, ed. Yan Kejun 嚴可均 (1762–1843) (Beijing: Zhonghua shuju, 1958), 82.916–17; Vincent S. Leung, "Bad Writing: Cursive Calligraphy and the Ethics of Orthography in the Eastern Han Dynasty," in *Behaving Badly in Early and Medieval China*, ed. N. Harry Rothschild and Leslie V. Wallace (Honolulu: University of Hawai'i Press, 2017), 106–21.

27. Clanchy, *From Memory to Written Record*, 49–50.

28. Anthony J. Barbieri-Low, "Craftsman's Literacy: Uses of Writing by Male and Female Artisans in Qin and Han China," in *Writing and Literacy in Early China: Studies from the Columbia Early China Seminar*, ed. Li Feng and David Prager Branner (Seattle: University of Washington Press, 2012), 370–99.

29. For example, Zhang Jinguang, *Qin zhi yanjiu* 秦制研究 (Shanghai: Shanghai guji chubanshe, 2004), 711, 716–17.

30. Florian Coulmas, *Writing and Society: An Introduction* (Cambridge: Cambridge University Press, 2013), 8.

31. Macdonald, "Literacy in an Oral Environment," 58–64, 78–82; quote 81–82.

32. Varuni Bhatia, "Six Blind Men and the Elephant: *Bhagavata Purana* in Colonial Bengal," in *Founts of Knowledge: Book History in India*, ed. Adhijit Gupta and Swapan Chakravorty (New Delhi: Orient Blackswan, 2016), 113.

33. Mark Edward Lewis, *Writing and Authority in Early China* (Albany: State University of New York Press, 1999), 73–83.

34. For examples of this approach, see Walter J. Ong, *Orality and Literacy: The Technologizing of the Word*, revised edition (London: Routledge, 2002); Maryanne Wolf, *Proust and the Squid: The Story and Science of the Reading Brain* (New York: Harper Perennial, 2007).

35. Cf. Coulmas, *Writing and Society*, 98 and passim.

36. Dehaene, *Reading in the Brain*, 122–42 and passim. See also Drège, "La lecture et l'écriture en Chine," 80, who makes a similar point about the essential similarity of reading in Chinese and in alphabetic scripts.

37. Frank Smith, *Understanding Reading: A Psycholinguistic Analysis of Reading and Learning to Read*, sixth edition (Mahwah: Lawrence Erlbaum Associates, 2004), 2–4, 55–71, 212–232.

38. See also Dehaene, *Reading in the Brain*, 142–44; James J. Gould and Peter Marler, "Learning by Instinct," *Scientific American* 256.1 (1987): 74–85.

39. Bhatia, "Six Blind Men and the Elephant," 113.

40. Smith, *Understanding Reading*, 2–4, 55–71, 212–232.

41. Martin Kern, "The Performance of Writing in Western Zhou China," in *Poetics of Grammar and the Metaphysics of Sound and Sign*, ed. Sergio La Porta and David Shulman (Leiden: Brill, 2007), 109–112, quote 109.

42. Ong, *Orality and Literacy*, 77–135; both quotes 117.

43. This is an important theme in Clanchy, *From Memory to Written Record*.

44. Gregor Schoeler, *The Genesis of Literature in Islam: From the Aural to the Read*, revised edition, in collaboration with and translated by Shawkat M. Toorawa (Edinburgh: Edinburgh University Press, 2009).

45. Kern, "The Performance of Writing," 140–159; quote 150.

46. Li Feng, "Literacy and Social Contexts of Writing in the Western Zhou," in *Writing and Literacy in Early China: Studies from the Columbia Early China Seminar*, ed. Li Feng and David Prager Branner (Seattle: University of Washington Press, 2012), 273–279.

47. Ong, *Orality and Literacy*, 117.

48. Bu Xianqun 卜憲群, "Cong jianbo kan Qin Han xiangli de wenshu wenti" 從簡帛看秦漢鄉里的文書問題, *Wen shi zhe* 文史哲 6 (2007): 48–53; Eno Gīre (Enno Giele), "Kodai no shikiji nōryoku," 133–34.

49. Guo Qingfan 郭慶藩 (1844–ca. 1896), ed., *Zhuangzi jishi* 莊子集釋 (Beijing: Zhonghua shuju, 1961), 5B.488; translation follows Chen Guying 陳鼓應, *Zhuangzi jinzhu jinyi* 莊子今注今譯 (Beijing: Zhonghua shuju, 1983), 356–57.

50. Chen Qiyou 陳奇猷, ed., *Han Feizi xin jiaozhu* 韓非子新校注 (Shanghai: Shanghai guji chubanshe, 2000), 449.

51. Jack W. Chen, "On the Act and Representation of Reading in Medieval China," *Journal of the American Oriental Society* 129.1 (2009): 59; also Drège, "La lecture et l'écriture en Chine," and Macdonald, "Literacy in an Oral Environment," 99.

52. See *Ciyuan* 辭源, s.vv. *du* 讀 and *song* 誦; see also Wolfgang Behr and Bernhard Führer, "Einführende Notizen zum Lesen in China mit besonderer Berücksichtigung der Frühzeit," in *Aspekte des Lesens in China in Vergangenheit und Gegenwart*, ed. Bernhard Führer (Bochum: Projekt Verlag, 2005), 1–42; Chen, "On the Act," 59; Drège, "La lecture et l'écriture," 79. Some understand *du* invariably to mean other kinds of vocal communication, but that does not affect my argument here. As Ruth Finnegan writes,

" 'Spoken' in this context is to be taken as *including* (rather than contrasting with) sung or chanted verbal communication. The contrast is with *written* forms." Ruth Finnegan, *Literacy and Orality: Studies in the Technology of Communication* (Oxford: Basil Blackwell, 1988), 17n2.

53. Drège, "La lecture et l'écriture," 87–88; cf. Chen, "On the Act," 58–59.

54. Hirschler, *The Written Word*, 12–13.

55. Tomiya, *Monjo gyōsei*, 121–31; phrase from 121 and passim.

56. See Wu Shuping 吳樹平, ed., *Dongguan Han ji jiaozhu* 東觀漢記校注 (Zhengzhou: Zhongzhou guji chubanshe, 1987), 18.832; Yu Shinan 虞世南 (558–638), ed., *Beitang shuchao* 北堂書鈔 (Taipei: Wenhai chubanshe, 1978), 97.4b; *Hou Han shu* 後漢書, by Fan Ye 范曄 (398–445) (Beijing: Zhonghua shuju, 1965), 64.2101.

57. Huang Hui 黃暉, ed., *Lunheng jiaoshi* 論衡校釋 (Beijing: Zhonghua shuju, 1990), 2.73.

58. For example, Stephen Owen, *Readings in Chinese Literary Thought* (Cambridge: Harvard University Press, 1996), 35–36; Chen, "On the Act."

59. See Guo Qingfan, *Zhuangzi jishi*, 5B.490–91. The *Zhuangzi* narrative is cited and discussed in Chen, "On the Act," 59; for translation and discussion, see Owen, *Readings*, 35–36. For the later versions, see He Ning 何寧, ed., *Huainanzi jishi* 淮南子集釋 (Beijing: Zhonghua shuju, 1998), 12.851–53; and Xu Weiyu 許維遹, ed., *Hanshi waizhuan jishi* 韓詩外傳集釋 (Beijing: Zhonghua shuju, 1980), 5.174–75.

60. See, for example, *Hou Han shu*, 26.902.

61. Tomiya, *Monjo gyōsei*, 117; Shen Songjin 沈頌金, *Ershi shiji jianboxue yanjiu* 二十世紀簡帛學研究 (Beijing: Xueyuan chubanshe, 2003), 258.

62. Clanchy, *From Memory to Written Record*, 8, 127–34, 272–73; quote 8.

63. Bagnall and Cribiore, *Women's Letters from Ancient Egypt*, 6–8, 42–43.

64. Yates, "Soldiers, Scribes."

65. David Johnson, "Chinese Popular Literature and Its Contexts," *Chinese Literature: Essays, Articles, Reviews* 3.2 (1981): 225–33; quote 232.

66. Donald Harper, "Daybooks in the Context of Manuscript Culture and Popular Culture Studies," in *Books of Fate and Popular Culture in Early China*, ed. Donald Harper and Marc Kalinowski (Leiden: Brill, 2017), 100–1.

67. See chapter 2.

68. See earlier in this chapter.

69. Wang Zhenya 王震亞 and Zhang Xiaofeng 張小鋒, "Han jian zhong de shuzu shenghuo" 漢簡中的戍卒生活, in *Jianduxue yanjiu* 簡牘學研究, no. 2, ed. Gansusheng wenwu kaogu yanjiusuo 甘肅省文物考古研究所 et al. (Lanzhou: Gansu renmin chubanshe, 1998), 112; Zhao Chongliang 趙寵亮, *Xingyi shubei: Hexi Han sai lizu de tunshu shenghuo* 行役戍備–河西漢塞

吏卒的屯戍生活 (Beijing: Kexue chubanshe, 2012), 319–28; Shen Songjin, *Ershi shiji jianboxue yanjiu*, 265–76.

70. Sun Wenbo 孫聞博, "Hexi Han sai junren de shenghuo shijianbiao" 河西漢塞軍人的生活時間表, in *Jianbo yanjiu. 2015. Chunxia juan* 簡帛研究. 2015. 春夏卷, ed. Yang Zhenhong 楊振紅 and Wu Wenling 鄔文玲 (Guilin: Guangxi shifan daxue chubanshe, 2015), 182–83; Kadota Akira 門田明, "Henkyō bōei no naka de no seikatsu" 辺境のなかでの生活, in *Mokkan–kodai kara no messēji* 木簡—古代からのメッセージ, ed. Ōba Osamu 大庭脩 (Tokyo: Taishūkan Shoten, 1998), 142–49; Zhao Chongliang, *Xingyi shubei*, 94–100.

71. Tomiya, *Monjo gyōsei*, 107, proposes five distinct levels of literacy, an idea that is similar to my own, though I suggest that any gradation must be still fuzzier if it is to reflect reality. In this respect I am closer to Rawski, *Education and Popular Literacy*, 2, who writes, "If literacy can be defined as the acquisition of some functional level of reading and writing abilities, there was a continuum of such skills in Ch'ing [Qing] China." See also Twitchett, "Chinese Social History," 17, who describes something like the spectrum I refer to and notes the importance of the interaction with text that those at various points on it had. It is not a coincidence that Twitchett, too, makes this point in the context of manuscript materials, although much later than those I deal with. Coulmas, *Writing and Society*, 50, proposes something conceptually similar concerning the oral/written dichotomy: "In literate societies, the range of linguistic behavior is far too multifarious to be described adequately by means of a unilinear continuum between two opposites, oral and written."

72. Ong, *Orality and Literacy*, 50, 52–53.

73. Nicholas Orme, *Medieval Children* (New Haven: Yale University Press, 2001); quote 240.

74. Erica Brindley, *Individualism in Early China: Human Agency and the Self in Thought and Politics* (Honolulu: University of Hawai'i Press, 2010).

75. Lewis, *Writing and Authority*, 56.

76. Eno Gīre (Enno Giele), "Kodai no shikiji nōryoku," 135–38, also refers to "group literacy."

77. Roger S. Bagnall, *Everyday Writing in the Graeco-Roman East* (Berkeley: University of California Press, 2011), 2–3.

78. Yates, "Soldiers, Scribes," 344.

79. Alan K. Bowman, *Life and Letters on the Roman Frontier* (New York: Routledge, 1998), 82.

80. Macdonald, "Literacy in an Oral Environment," 49.

81. Bagnall, *Everyday Writing*, 2.

82. Both of these concepts are of course complicated and the subject of much dispute. See the discussions in Graham Crow, "Community," in *The Blackwell Encyclopedia of Sociology*, ed. George Ritzer (Malden: Blackwell,

2007), 617–20; and Larry Ray, "Society," in *The Blackwell Encyclopedia of Sociology*, 4581–83.

83. See Brian Stock, *The Implications of Literacy: Written Language and Models of Interpretation in the Eleventh and Twelfth Centuries* (Princeton: Princeton University Press, 1983), 3–9, and 88–240, especially 90–92 and 235–40; for his terminology, see 6–9 and 12–87.

84. See, for example, Schoeler, *The Genesis of Literature in Islam*.

85. Clanchy, *From Memory to Written Record*, 334–35.

86. Robert W. Bagley, "Anyang Writing and the Origin of the Chinese Writing System," in *The First Writing: Script Invention as History and Process*, ed. Stephen D. Houston (Cambridge: Cambridge University Press, 2004), 235; see also Wang Haicheng, *Writing and the Ancient State*, 5.

87. Benedict Anderson, *Imagined Communities: Reflections on the Origin and Spread of Nationalism*, revised edition (London: Verso, 1991), 1–7, especially 6.

88. Enno Giele, "The Geographical Origins of the Han Time Northwestern Border Society According to Excavated Documents," in *International Conference: Military Control on Multi-Ethnic Society in Early China*, ed. Kim Byung-Joon and Miyake Kiyoshi (Seoul: Seoul National University, 2015), 61–105; Zhao Chongliang, *Xingyi shubei*, 46–48; Mark Edward Lewis, *The Early Chinese Empires: Qin and Han* (Cambridge: Belknap Press, 2007), 138–39.

89. Kadota Akira, "Henkyō bōei no naka de no seikatsu," 154–57.

90. Hsing I-t'ien 邢義田, "Handai biansai lizu de junzhong jiaoyu–du 'Juyan xinjian' zhaji zhi san" 漢代邊塞吏卒的軍中教育–讀 "居延新簡" 札記之三, in *Jianbo yanjiu* 簡帛研究, no. 2, ed. Li Xueqin 李學勤 (Beijing: Falü chubanshe, 1996), 273–78; see also discussion in Miyake Kiyoshi, "Shin-Kan jidai no moji to shikiji," 215–17 and passim; and Yates, "Soldiers, Scribes."

91. Miyake, "Shin-Kan jidai no moji to shikiji."

92. Yates, "Soldiers, Scribes," 60–63 and passim.

93. Christopher Foster, "Study of the *Cang Jie pian*: Past and Present" (PhD dissertation, Harvard University, 2017); see also discussion in Miyake, "Shin-Kan jidai no moji to shikiji," 215–17.

94. Yates, "Soldiers, Scribes," 344.

95. Macdonald, "Literacy in an Oral Environment," 64.

96. See Anthony Barbieri-Low, *Artisans in Early Imperial China* (Seattle: University of Washington Press, 2007); and Sanft, *Communication and Cooperation*.

97. Other examples include documents in the trove discovered at Liye; for a summary of that find, see Robin D. S. Yates, "The Qin Slips and Boards from Well No. 1, Liye, Hunan: A Brief Introduction to the Qin Qianling County Archives," *Early China* 35–36 (2012–2013): 291–329.

98. On the difficulties of generalization, see Loewe, *Records of Han Administration*, 1:9.

Chapter Two. Contexts and Sources

1. For that information, the best work in English remains that of Michael Loewe, whose seminal *Records of Han Administration* was truly ahead of its time.

2. See, for example, the discussion in Zhang Defang 張德芳, "Cong Xuanquan Hanjian kan Xi-Han Wu-Zhao shiqi he Xuan-Yuan shiqi jingying xiyu de butong zhanlüe" 從懸泉漢簡看西漢武昭時期和宣元時期經營西域的不同戰略, in *Han diguo de zhidu yu shehui zhixu* 漢帝國的制度與社會秩序, ed. Lai Ming-chiu 黎明釗 (Hong Kong: Oxford University Press, 2012), 277–316.

3. The summary discussion of the historical context in this section synthesizes from Wu Rengxiang 吳礽驤, *Hexi Han sai diaocha yu yanjiu* 河西漢塞調查與研究 (Beijing: Wenwu chubanshe, 2005), 11–20; Nicola Di Cosmo, "Han Frontiers: Toward an Integrated View," *Journal of the American Oriental Society* 129.2 (2009): 199–214; Di Cosmo, *Ancient China and Its Enemies: The Rise of Nomadic Power in East Asian History* (Cambridge: Cambridge University Press, 2002); Paul R. Goldin, "Steppe Nomads as a Philosophical Problem in Classical China," in *Mapping Mongolia: Situating Mongolia in the World from Geologic Time to the Present*, ed. Paula L. W. Sabloff (Philadelphia: University of Pennsylvania Museum of Archaeology and Anthropology, 2011), 220–46; Arnaud Bertrand, "La formation de le commanderie impériale de Dunhuang (Gansu) des Han antérieurs: l'apport des sources archéologiques," *Arts Asiatiques* 70 (2015): 63–76; Qian Mu 錢穆 (1895–1990), *Qin-Han shi* 秦漢史 (Taipei: Dongda tushu gongsi, 2001), 122–47; and Lewis, *The Early Chinese Empires*, 128–51.

4. Di Cosmo, *Ancient China and Its Enemies*, 174–90.

5. Hans Bielenstein, *The Bureaucracy of Han Times* (Cambridge: Cambridge University Press, 1980), 93–94; Zhou Zhenhe 周振鶴, "Qindai Dongting, Cangwu liangjun xuanxiang" 秦代洞庭、蒼梧兩郡懸想, *Fudan xuebao (shehui kexue ban)* 復旦學報 (社會科學版) 5 (2005): 63–67; for an account of Han governing structures as reflected in traditional sources, see Qian Mu, *Qin-Han shi*, 229–68.

6. Bielenstein, *Bureaucracy*, 93–94; Zhou Zhenhe, "Qindai Dongting, Cangwu liangjun xuanxiang," 63–67; Qian Mu, *Qin-Han shi*, 229–68.

7. Tomiya Itaru, "Gaisetsu" 概説, in *Kankan goi kōshō* 漢簡語彙考証, ed. Tomiya Itaru (Tokyo: Iwanami Shoten, 2015), 31; Michael Loewe, "The Western Han Army: Organization, Leadership, and Operation," in *Military Culture in Imperial China*, ed. Nicola Di Cosmo (Cambridge: Harvard University Press, 2009), 80–81.

8. Yu Zhenbo 于振波, "Juyan Han jian zhong de suizhang he houzhang" 居延漢簡中的燧長和候長, *Shixue jikan* 史學集刊 2 (2000): 9–16; Wang Zijin 王子今, *Hanjian Hexi shehui shiliao yanjiu* 漢簡河西社會史料研究

(Beijing: Shangwu yinshuguan, 2017), 34–36; Tomiya, *Monjo gyōsei*, 117; Loewe, "The Western Han Army," 79–82. Note that Bielenstein translates *bu* in this sense as "regiment," which does not seem to represent the scale functioning in this context.

9. Rafe de Crespigny, "The Military Culture of Later Han," in *Military Culture in Imperial China*, ed. Nicola Di Cosmo (Cambridge: Harvard University Press, 1990), 90–111; Mark Edward Lewis, "The Han Abolition of Universal Military Service," in *Warfare in Chinese History*, ed. Hans van den Ven (Leiden: Brill, 2000), 33–76; Lewis, *The Early Chinese Empires*, 138; Bielenstein, *Bureaucracy*, 114.

10. Charles Sanft, "Population Records from Liye: Ideology in Practice," in *Ideology of Power and Power of Ideology in Early China*, ed. Yuri Pines, Paul R. Goldin, and Martin Kern (Leiden: Brill, 2015), 249–69.

11. Wang Zijin, *Hanjian Hexi shehui*, 107–21; He Shuangquan 何雙全, "Handai shubian shibing jiguan kaoshu" 漢代戍邊士兵籍貫考述, *Xibei shidi* 西北史地 2 (1989): 31–38; Shen Songjin 沈頌金, *Ershi shiji jianboxue yanjiu* 二十世紀簡帛學研究 (Beijing: Xueyuan chubanshe, 2003), 254; Chen Zhi 陳直 (1901–1980), *Juyan Han jian yanjiu* 居延漢簡研究 (Beijing: Zhonghua shuju, 2009), 17, 133–34; He Shuangquan 何雙全, " 'Han jian–xiangli zhi' ji qi yanjiu" 《漢簡‧鄉里志》 及其研究, in *Qin-Han jiandu lunwenji* 秦漢簡牘論文集, ed. Gansu wenwu kaogu yanjiusuo 甘肅文物考古研究所 (Lanzhou: Gansu renmin chubanshe, 1989), 148; Giele, "Geographical Origins"; Zhao Chongliang, *Xingyi shubei*, 25–42.

12. Miyake, "Shin-Kan jidai no moji to shikiji," 217–19.

13. Wang Zhenya and Zhang Xiaofeng, "Han jian zhong de shuzu shenghuo," 101–3; cf. He Shuangquan, "Handai shubian shibing," 37. Ages in these sources seem to all represent *sui* 歲, that is, they treat a person as age 1 during the first year of life.

14. Jia Liying 賈麗英, "Cong Juyan Han jian kan Handai suijun xiaceng funü shenghuo" 從居延漢簡漢代隨軍下層婦女生活, *Shijiazhuang shifan zhuanke xuexiao xuebao* 石家莊師範專科學校學報 6.1 (2004): 56–60; Kadota, "Henkyō bōei no naka de no seikatsu," 154–57.

15. Bielenstein, *Bureaucracy*, 114.

16. Chen Zhi, *Juyan Han jian*, 17–18; Hsing I-t'ien, "Qin-Han pingmin de duxie nengli," 261–62; Zhao Chongliang, *Xingyi shubei*, 48–74; Harper, "Daybooks," 100–1.

17. For example, *Juyan xin jian shijiao* 居延新簡釋校, ed. Ma Yi and Zhang Rongqiang 張榮強 (Tianjin: Tianjin guji chubanshe, 2013), 274 (E.P.T. 51:52); *Juyan Han jian jiayi bian* 居延漢簡甲乙編, ed. Zhongguo shehui kexue yuan kaogu yanjiusuo 中國社會科學院考古研究所 (Beijing: Zhonghua shuju, 1980), 8 (12.1a); *Dunhuang Han jian* 敦煌漢簡, ed. Gansusheng wenwu kaogu yanjiusuo 甘肅省文物考古研究所 (Beijing: Zhonghua shuju, 1991), 290 (no.

1817); *Eji'na Han jian shiwen jiaoben*, 76 (2000ES9SF3:1); among others; see also Sima Qian 司馬遷 (ca. 145–ca. 86 BCE), *Shiji* 史記 (Beijing: Zhonghua shuju, 1959), 2249.

18. Ma Manli 馬曼麗, "Cong Han jian kan Handai xibei biansai shouyu zhidu" 從漢簡看漢代西北邊塞守御制度, *Zhongguo bianjiang shidi yanjiu* 中國邊疆史地研究 1 (1992): 68–74; Wang Zhenya and Zhang Xiaofeng, "Han jian zhong de shuzu shenghuo," 112–18; Tomiya, "Gaisetsu," 32–33; Loewe, "The Western Han Army," 81; Zhao Chongliang, *Xingyi shubei*, 79–94; Shen Songjin, *Ershi shiji jianboxue yanjiu*, 253–56.

19. Tomiya, "Gaisetsu," 34.

20. Bagnall, *Everyday Writing*, 35–36 and passim; see also Bagnall and Cribiore, *Women's Letters*, 22–23.

21. Luo Zhenyu 羅振玉 and Wang Guowei 王國維, *Liusha zhuijian* 流沙墜簡 (1914; reprinted Beijing: Zhonghua shuju, 1993); Tomiya, "Gaisetsu," 34.

22. *Dunhuang Han jian shiwen*, 308–320; quote 308, "ledgers" discussed 310–17.

23. Tomiya, "Gaisetsu," 34–36.

24. Linda Brodkey, *Academic Writing as Social Practice* (Philadelphia: Temple University Press, 1987), 64–67, discusses typologies of literary texts that treat their subjects in terms of objective characteristics, noting that such approaches can threaten to divorce creation from context.

25. While the term "slip" is not incorrect, I prefer "strip." If one visits a store that sells wood, such as Home Depot, it is not difficult to find pieces of wood similar in shape to the Han period writing medium. They are called strips, not "slips"—at least not in the United States. Cf. also the *Oxford English Dictionary*, online version, s.vv. "strip" and "slip," in which the former is used to define the latter and not vice versa, reflecting its broader sense.

26. For an overview of bamboo and wood as writing media, see the classic study Tsuen-Hsü Tsien, *Written on Bamboo and Silk*, second edition (Chicago: University of Chicago Press, 2004), 96–125.

27. Hou Pixun 侯丕勛, "Xibei suo chutu jiandu de tedian" 西北所出土簡牘的特點, in *Jianduxue yanjiu* 簡牘學研究, no. 1, ed. Xibei shifan daxue lishixi 西北師範大學歷史系 et al. (Lanzhou: Gansu renmin chubanshe, 1996), 98–99; Tomiya, "Gaisetsu," 22–23; Li Baotong 李寶通 and Huang Zhaohong 黃兆宏, *Jianduxue jiaocheng* 簡牘學教成 (Lanzhou: Gansu renmin chubanshe, 2011), 25–26; Charles Sanft, "Edict of Monthly Ordinances for the Four Seasons in Fifty Articles from 5 C.E.: Introduction to the Wall Inscription Discovered at Xuanquanzhi, with Annotated Translation," *Early China* 32 (2008–2009): 133.

28. Tomiya, "Gaisetsu," 15–23; Li and Huang, *Jianduxue jiaocheng*, 7–26; Hou Pixun, "Xibei suo chutu," 99–101. For an extensive and detailed discussion, including a chart listing many examples from Juyan, see Xue

Yingqun 薛英群, *Juyan Han jian tonglun* 居延漢簡通論 (Lanzhou: Gansu jiaoyu chubanshe, 1991), 100–58. Enno Giele, "Private Letter Manuscripts from Early Imperial China," in *A History of Chinese Letters and Epistolary Culture*, ed. Antje Richter (Leiden: Brill, 2015), 407–12, discusses the physical characteristics of letters specifically.

29. Wu Rengxiang, *Hexi Han sai*, 183.

30. Li Fang 李昉 (925–996) et al., eds., *Taiping guangji* 太平廣記 (Beijing: Zhonghua shuju, 1961), 368.2928–2929; Xue Yingqun, *Juyan Han jian tonglun*, 97.

31. Xue Yingqun, *Juyan Han jian tonglun*, 97; see, for example, Huang Bosi 黃伯思 (1079–1118), *Dongguan yulun* 東觀餘論 (*Skqs* ed.), 1.40b–41a.

32. For a summary of Stein's journeys, see M. Aurel Stein, *On Ancient Central-Asian Tracks: Brief Narrative of Three Expeditions in Innermost Asia and North-Western China* (London: Macmillan and Col, 1933), 177–93. For more detail concerning his first trip to the Dunhuang region, see Stein, *Ruins of Desert Cathay: Personal Narrative of Explorations in Central Asia and Westernmost China*, 2 vols. (1912; reprinted New York: Benjamin Blom, 1968), particularly 2:44–158. Stein described his second visit in a two-part article; see Stein, "A Third Journey of Exploration in Central Asia, 1913–16," *The Geographical Journal* 48.2 (August 1916): 97–130, and Stein, "A Third Journey of Exploration in Central Asia, 1913–16," *The Geographical Journal* 48.3 (September 1916): 193–225. For the brief description of the portion relevant to my work here, see 194–96 and perhaps 208–9 in the second part. Since the 1913–1916 trip was Stein's third to Central Asia, it is referred to that way in reference to the Dunhuang materials, for example in the publication of the paleographic finds. For the documents Stein recovered, see Édouard Chavannes, ed. and trans., *Les documents chinois découverts par Aurel Stein dans les sables du Turkestan oriental* (Oxford: Oxford University, 1913); and Henri Maspero, ed. and trans., *Les documents chinois de la troisième expédition de Sir Aurel Stein en Asie centrale* (London: Trustees of the British Museum, 1953). See also Zhao Huacheng 趙化成 and Gao Chongwen 高崇文, et al., *Qin-Han kaogu* 秦漢考古 (Beijing: Wenwu chubanshe, 2002), 205–7; for an overall discussion, including consideration of Chinese perspectives, see Justin Jacobs, "Confronting Indiana Jones: Chinese Nationalism, Historical Imperialism, and the Criminalization of Aurel Stein and the Raiders of Dunhuang, 1899–1944," in *China on the Margins*, ed. Sherman Cochran and Paul G. Pickowicz (Ithaca: Cornell University Press, 2010), 65–90.

33. Folke Bergman, "Travels and Archaeological Field-work in Mongolia and Sin-kiang: A Diary of the Years 1927–1934," in *History of the Expedition in Asia 1927–1935, Part IV General Reports of Travels and Field-work*, by Folke Bergman, Gerhard Bexell, Birger Bohlin, and Gösta Montell (Göteborg: Elanders Boktryckeri Aktiebolag, 1945), particularly 146–48;

Bo Sommarström, *Archaeological Researches in the Edsen-gol Region Inner Mongolia: Together with the Catalogue Prepared by Folke Bergman* (Stockholm: Statens Etnografiska Museum, 1956), particularly 44–83; see also Zhao and Gao, *Qin-Han kaogu*, 208–9. On criticisms of the European archaeologists, see Jacobs, "Confronting Indiana Jones"; and, for example, Li and Huang, *Jianduxue jiaocheng*, 53–55.

34. Zhao and Gao, *Qin-Han kaogu*, 210–12.

35. See, for example, the list in the preface to Wu Rengxiang, Li Yongliang 李永良, and Ma Jianhua 馬建華, eds., *Dunhuang Han jian shiwen* 敦煌漢簡釋文 (Lanzhou: Gansu renmin chubanshe, 1991), i–iv; and *Eji'na Han jian shiwen jiaoben* 額濟納漢簡釋文校本, ed. Sun Jiazhou 孫家洲 (Beijing: Wenwu chubanshe, 2007).

36. Gansu jiandu baohu yanjiu zhongxin 甘肅簡牘保護研究中心, et al., eds., *Jianshui Jinguan Han jian* 肩水金關漢簡, five vols. (Shanghai: Zhongxi shuju, 2011–2016).

Chapter Three. Posted Texts

1. Hsing, "Handai biansai lizu de junzhong jiaoyu."

2. Miyake, "Shin-Kan jidai no moji to shikiji."

3. Xu Pingfang 徐苹芳, "Juyan, Dunhuang faxian de 'Saishang fenghuo pinyue'–jian shi Handai de fenghuo zhidu" 居延、敦煌發現的 "塞上蓬火品約"–兼釋漢代的蓬火制度, *Kaogu* 考古 5 (1979): 445–54; Xue Yingqun 薛英群, "Juyan 'Saishang fenghuo pinyue'" 居延 "塞上烽火品約"冊, *Kaogu* 考古 4 (1979): 361–64; Shangguan Xuzhi 上官續智 and Huang Jinyan 黃今言, "Handai fengsui zhong de xinxi qiju yu fenghuo pinyue zhiyong kaolun" 漢代烽燧中的信息器具與烽火品約置用考論, *Shehui kexue jikan* 社會科學輯刊 5 (2004): 93–98. Enno Giele, "Evidence for the Xiongnu in Chinese Wooden Documents from the Han Period," in *Xiongnu Archaeology: Multidisciplinary Perspectives of the First Steppe Empire in Inner Asia*, ed. Ursula Brosseder and Bryan K. Miller (Bonn: Rheinische Friedrich-Wilhelms-Universität Bonn, 2011), 49–75, gathers, translates, and discusses a number of excavated documents related to these systems.

4. *Dunhuang Han jian*, 307–8 (no. 2257).

5. See Xu Pingfang, "Juyan, Dunhuang," 446–47. Cf. the translation of a set of similar regulations referring to the Xiongnu, specifically, in Giele, "Evidence for the Xiongnu," 66–69.

6. *Dunhuang Han jian*, 239 (no. 521).

7. *Juyan xin jian shijiao*, 593; *Juyan xin jian* 居延新簡, ed. Gansusheng wenwu kaogu yanjiusuo, et al. (Beijing: Zhonghua shuju, 1994), 165 (E.P.T59:274).

8. *Juyan Han jian jiayi bian* 居延漢簡甲乙編, ed. Zhongguo shehui kexueyuan kaogu yanjiusuo 中國社會科學研究院考古研究所 (Beijing: Zhonghua shuju, 1980), 33 (46.9A); see also Xu Pingfang, "Juyan, Dunhuang," 449; and Li Zhenhong 李振宏, "Handai Juyan tunshu lizu de jingshen wenhua shenghuo" 漢代居延屯戍吏卒的精神文化生活, in *Jianduxue yanjiu* 簡牘學研究, no. 3, ed. Xibei shifan daxue wenxueyuan lishixi 西北師範大學文學院歷史系, et al., eds. (Lanzhou: Gansu renmin chubanshe, 2002), 241.

9. *Juyan Han jian jiayi bian*, 222 (332.21); see also He Shuangquan, "Saishang fenghuo," 847.

10. See my previous discussion in Sanft, *Communication and Cooperation*, 143–45, and the citations I give in the notes to that discussion.

11. *Dunhuang Han jian*, 271 (no. 1365); photo plate on 123.

12. Xu Shen 許慎 (fl. ca. 100 CE), *Shuowen jiezi* 說文解字 (Beijing: Zhonghua shuju, 1963), 48; see also Tang Kejing 湯可敬, *Shuowen jiezi jinshi* 說文解字今釋 (Changsha: Yuelun shushe, 1997), 304.

13. Cf. Satō Tatsurō 佐藤達郎, "Kandai no hensho, kabegaki—toku ni chihō teki kyōrei to no kakei de—" 漢代の扁書・壁書—特に地方的教令との関係で—, *Kansai gakuin shigaku* 関西學院史學 35 (2008): 87.

14. *Dunhuang Han jian*, 284 (no. 1684A); with reference to Ma Yi 馬怡, "Bianshu shi tan" 扁書試探, in *Jian bo (di yi ji)* 簡帛(第一輯), ed. Wuhan daxue jian bo yanjiu zhongxin 武漢大學簡帛研究中心 (Shanghai: Shanghai guji chubanshe, 2005), 423.

15. *Dunhuang Xuanquan Han jian shicui* 敦煌懸泉漢簡釋粹, ed. Hu Pingsheng 胡平生 and Zhang Defang 張德芳 (Shanghai: Shanghai guji chubanshe, 2001), 2–3 (II 0114 3: 404).

16. Tomiya, *Shin-Kan keibatsu seido no kenkyū* 秦漢刑罰制度の研究 (Kyoto: Dōhōsha, 1998), 171–79; Brian McKnight, *The Quality of Mercy: Amnesties and Traditional Chinese Justice* (Honolulu: University of Hawai'i Press, 1981).

17. For transcription of the strips in question, see *Eji'na Han jian shiwen jiaoben*, 82–83 (nos. 2000ES9SF4:4, 2000ES9SF4:3, 2000ES9SF4:1, 2000ES9SF4:2). In sequence and approach I most closely follow Ma Yi, "'Shijianguo ernian zhaoshu' ce suojian zhaoshu zhi xiaxing" "始建國二年詔書"冊所見詔書之下行, *Lishi yanjiu* 歷史研究 5 (2006): 166–71; and Li Junming 李均明, "Eji'na Han jian fazhi shiliao kao" 額濟納漢簡法制史料考, in *Eji'na Han jian* 額濟納漢簡, ed. Wei Jian 魏堅 (Guilin: Guangxi shifan daxue chubanshe, 2005), 54–70, especially 57–58; see also Shen Gang 沈剛, "'Eji'na Han jian' Wang Mang zhaoshu lingce pailie cixu xinjie" "額濟納漢簡"王莽詔書令冊排列次序新解, *Beifang wenwu* 北方文物 2 (2007): 75–77; and Terigele 特日格樂, "Jiandu suojian Wang Mang dui Xiongnu caiqu de zhengce" 簡牘所見王莽對匈奴採取的政策, *Zhongyang minzu daxue xuebao (zhexue shehui kexueban)* 中央民族大學學報(哲學社會科學版) 6 (2006): 66–70.

18. According to the conversation chart in Wang Shuanghuai 王雙懷, ed., *Zhonghua rili tongdian* 中華日曆通典 (Jilin: Jilin wenshi chubanshe, 2006), 1411, there is a problem with this date and others in this edict. As Wang reckons it, there was an intercalary month inserted between the tenth and eleventh months of the second year of the Shijianguo period. The date in this edict (*jiaxu* 甲戌), however, does not appear in Wang's eleventh month; it does appear, however, in what he calls the intercalary month. That date corresponds to 7 November 10 CE and it is the one I accept. Similarly, the next date that appears in this text (*renwu* 壬午) does not fall in Wang's eleventh month, either, even though it is so labeled in the text; instead it comes in Wang's intercalary month, where it is equivalent to 20 November 10 CE, the date I use to convert *renwu*. Two further dates appear in this edict, although I do not discuss that part of the text. The first is the *dinghai* 丁亥 day of the eleventh month, which like the two preceding days comes in what Wang deems the intercalary month; it corresponds to 15 November 10 CE. The final date is given in the edict text as the *bingshen* 丙申 day of the intercalary month; Wang's chart has no *bingshen* day in his intercalary month but does have that date in his eleventh month, where it corresponds to 29 November 10 CE. The calendar represented in this edict text and that in Wang Shuanghuai's book apparently have reverse sequences of the eleventh and intercalary months. I suspect the copy of the edict is in error.

19. The title here is *yin* 尹, in context an abbreviation for *dayin* 大尹, which appears just above, the Wang Mang period term for grand administrator (usually *taishou* 太守); see *Kankan goi*, s.v. *yin*.

20. Following Wu Wenling, "Ejian Shijianguo ernian zhaoshuce 'yi gong' shijie" 額簡始建國二年詔書冊 "壹功" 試解, in *Eji'na Han jian shiwen jiaoben* 額濟納漢簡釋文校本, ed. Sun Jiazhou 孫家洲 (Beijing: Wenwu chubanshe, 2007), 137–39; cf., for example, *Han shu* 漢書, by Ban Gu 班固 (32–92) (Beijing: Zhonghua shuju, 1962), 10.305, where *yiqie* 一切 appears in that sense in an edict.

21. *Eji'na Han jian shiwen jiaoben*, 82–83 (nos. 2000ES9SF4:4, 2000ES9SF4:3, 2000ES9SF4:1, 2000ES9SF4:2); cf. Giele, "Evidence for the Xiongnu," 58.

22. *Eji'na Han jian shiwen jiaoben*, 82–83 (nos. 2000ES9SF4:1, 2000ES9SF4:2).

23. Sima Guang 司馬光 (1019–1086), *Zizhi tongjian* 資治通鑑 (Beijing: Zhonghua shuju, 1956), 37.1178.

24. Wu Wenling, "Shijianguo ernian Xin-Mang yu Xiongnu guanxi shishi kaobian" 始建國二年新莽與匈奴關係史事考辨, *Lishi yanjiu* 歷史研究 2 (2006): 177–81.

25. See, for example, examples and discussion in Li Junming, "Xin-Mang jian shidai tezheng suoyi" 新莽簡時代特徵瑣議, *Wenwu chunqiu* 文物春秋 4 (1989): 1–3; Ji Shimei 吉仕梅, "Wang Mang gai zhi zai Juyan Dun-

huang Han jian cihui zhong de fanying" 王莽改制在居延敦煌漢簡詞匯中的反應, *Xueshu jiaoliu* 學術交流 4 (2008): 129–32; among others.

26. Nylan, *The Five "Confucian" Classics*, 182–85; Michael Puett, "Centering the Realm: Wang Mang, the *Zhouli*, and Early Chinese Statecraft," in *Statecraft and Classical Learning: The Rituals of Zhou in East Asian History*, ed. Benjamin Elman and Martin Kern (Leiden: Brill, 2010), 129–54.

27. *Han shu*, 99B.4103.

28. Neither of these toponyms is attested in received sources; see *Kankan goi*, s.vv. "Jiaqu" and "Jiagou."

29. See Michael Suk-young Chwe, *Rational Ritual: Culture, Coordination, and Common Knowledge* (Princeton: Princeton University Press, 2001); Sanft, *Communication and Cooperation*.

30. For consideration of Wang Mang's actions in terms of "propaganda," including the role of "display" in those processes, see Michael Loewe, "Wang Mang and His Forebears: The Making of the Myth," *T'oung Pao* 80.4–5 (1994): 197–222.

31. Sanft, *Communication and Cooperation*.

32. See, for example, the description of the restoration of the Han ruling house by Liu Xiu 劉秀, Emperor Guangwu 光武 (25–57), in a prayer recorded in *Hou Han shu*, 1A.22: "He pacified the realm and all within the seas received his clemency" 平定天下，海內蒙恩.

33. Cf. Sanft, "Population Records from Liye," 249–69.

34. No less an authority than Confucius alludes to this in a famous line concerning the joys of study and repetition; see *Lunyu zhushu*, 5. See also Alexander James Kirkham, Julian Michael Breeze, and Paloma Marí-Beffa, "The Impact of Verbal Instructions on Goal-Directed Behaviour," *Acta Psychologica* 139 (2012): 212–19.

35. Sanft, *Communication and Cooperation*.

36. See Sanft, *Communication and Cooperation*.

37. This and the following draws from the translation and discussion in Sanft, "Edict of Monthly Ordinances for the Four Seasons," 125–208, with additional references as necessary.

38. Sanft, "Edict of Monthly Ordinances," 144 and passim.

39. This and following references to the edict refer to line numbers within the text as found in Sanft, "Edict of Monthly Ordinances," 178–88; here, see lines 1–4. Note that I do not include nonstandard graphs here; please see the article version for those.

40. Line 60. On emendations to this line, see Sanft, "Edict of Monthly Ordinances," 195n113.

41. Sanft, "Environment and Law in Early Imperial China (3rd c. BCE–1st c. CE): Qin and Han Statutes Concerning Natural Resources," *Environmental History* 15.4 (2010): 701–21.

42. Line 37.

43. Line 16.

44. For example, lines 56, 58, 68, 71.

45. Line 12.

46. Line 73.

47. Lines 98–99. Damage to the text has left only part of the formula intact but it was surely there originally; see discussion in Sanft, "Edict of Monthly Ordinances," 140–41.

48. Ma Yi, "Bianshu shi tan," especially 421–28; Wang Zijin 王子今, "Eji'na 'Zhuan bu shili dian quzhe' jiance shiming" 額濟納 "專部士吏典趣輒"簡冊釋名, in Eji'na Han jian shiwen jiaoben, 165–69; Lai Ming-chiu 黎明釗, "Shili de zhize yu gongzuo" Eji'na Han jian duji" 士吏的職責與工作: 額濟納漢簡讀記, Zhongguo wenhua yanjiusuo xuebao 中國文化研究所學報 48 (2008): 15–33.

49. Ma Yi, "Bianshu shi tan," especially 421–28; see also Lai Ming-chiu, "Shili de zhize yu gongzuo," 19, who thinks this possibly could be a bianshu.

50. The transcription has jiang 講, which is definitely correct; Xu reads gou 購 and I follow; see also Gao Heng 高亨, Guzi tongjia huidian 古字通假會典 (Ji'nan: Qi-Lu shushe, 1989), 340.

51. Eji'na Han jian shiwen jiaoben, 5 (99ES16ST1:4).

52. Eji'na Han jian shiwen jiaoben, 5 (99ES16ST1:5).

53. Eji'na Han jian shiwen jiaoben, 5 (99ES16ST1:8).

54. Barbieri-Low and Yates, Law, State, and Society, 684–85.

55. The following summarizes from Zhang Defang, "Xuanquan Han jian zhong de 'zhuanxin jian' kaoshu" 懸泉漢簡中的 "傳信簡"考述, in Chutu wenxian yanjiu 出土文獻研究, no. 7, ed. Zhongguo wenwu yanjiusuo (Shanghai: Shanghai guji chubanshe, 2005), 65–81; Ma Yi, "Xuanquan Han jian 'Shiwang zhuanxin ce' bukao" 懸泉漢簡 "失亡傳信冊"補考, in Chutu wenxian yanjiu 出土文獻研究, no. 8, ed. Zhongguo wenwu yanjiusuo 中國文物研究所 (Shanghai: Shanghai guji chubanshe, 2007), 111–16; and Dunhuang Xuanquan Han jian shicui, 29–34 (II 0216 2: 866–69).

56. Transcription in Hu Pingsheng and Zhang Defang, Dunhuang Xuanquan Han jian shicui, 29 (II 0216 2: 866–69).

57. Zhang Defang, "Xuanquan Han jian zhong," 80.

58. The phrasing used is bu gao 布告, "to announce widely"; the relationship between the bugao and bianshu systems is discussed, for example, in Huang Chunping 黃春平, "Cong chutu jiandu kan Han diguo zhongyang de xinxi fabu—jian ping Zhang Tao xiansheng de 'fubao' shuo" 從出土簡牘看漢帝國中央的信息發布—兼評張濤先生的 "府報" 說, Xinwen yu chuanbo yanjiu 新聞與傳播研究 4 (2006): 2–11.

59. See, for example, Barbieri-Low and Yates, Law, State, and Society, 464–65, 468–69.

60. See discussion in Sanft, Communication and Cooperation.

61. My transcription, translation, and discussion draw from *Jianshui jinguan Han jian*, 4:140–41; Gansusheng bowuguan Han jian zhenglizu 甘肅省博物館漢簡整理組, "'Yongshi sannian zhaoshu' jiance shiwen" "永始三年詔書" 簡冊釋文, *Xibei shiyuan xuebao (shehui kexueban)* 西北師院學報(社會科學版) 4 (1983): 61; Gansusheng wenwu gongzuodui Juyan jian zhenglizu 甘肅省文物工作隊居延簡整理組, "Juyan jian 'Yongshi sannian zhaoshu' ce shiwen" 居延簡 《永始三年詔書》 冊釋文, *Dunhuangxue jikan* 敦煌學輯刊 2 (1984): 171–73; Ma Yi, "Handai zhaoshu zhi sanpin," 73; Ōba Osamu 大庭脩, "Lun Jianshui Jinguan chutu de 'Yongshi sannian zhaoshu' jiance" 論肩水金關出土的 "永始三年詔書" 簡冊, trans. Jiang Zhenqing 姜鎮慶, *Dunhuangxue jikan* 敦煌學輯刊 2 (1984): 174–84; Wu Dexu 伍德煦, "Xin faxian de yifen Xihan zhaoshu—'Yongshi sannian zhaoshu jiance' kaoshi he youguan wenti" 新發現的一份西漢詔書—《永始三年詔書簡冊》考釋和有關問題, *Xibei shiyuan xuebao (shehui kexue ban)* 西北師院學報(社會科學版) 4 (1983): 63–66; Xue Yingqun 薛英群, He Shuangquan 何雙全, Li Yongliang 李永良, et al., *Juyan xinjian shicui* 居延新簡釋粹 (Lanzhou: Lanzhou daxue chubanshe, 1988), 102–8; Yang Jiping 楊際平, "Xi Changsha Zoumalou Sanguo Wujian zhong de 'tiao'—jian tan hutiaozhi de qiyuan" 析長沙走馬樓三國吳簡中的 "調"—兼談戶調制的起源, *Lishi yanjiu* 歷史研究 3 (2006): 41–42.

62. For Zhai and Kong's biographies, see *Han shu*, 84.3411–41 and 81.3352–65, respectively.

63. *Jianshui jinguan Han jian*, 4:140 (73EJF1:10).

Chapter Four. Statements of Individuals and Groups

1. On legal statements (*ci* 辭) and *ziyan* statements in a legal context, see Barbieri-Low and Yates, *Law, State, and Society*, 152–57, 489n93, and passim.

2. Bu Xianqun and Liu Yang 劉楊, "Qin-Han richang zhixu zhong de shehui yu xingzheng guanxi chutan–guanyu 'ziyan' yici de jiedu" 秦漢日常秩序中的社會與行政關係初探–關於 "自言" 一詞的解讀, *Wenshizhe* 文史哲 4 (2013): 81–92; for an example of use of the phrase *ziyan* as a label for documents, see *Juyan xinjian shijiao*, 259 (EPT 50:199).

3. *Juyan xinjian shijiao*, 268 (EPT 51:8); for *zhangzu* 鄣卒, "company soldier," see *Kankan goi*, s.v. *zhangzu*.

4. According to *Hanyu dacidian*, s.v. *gan* 敢, *gan* can mean not only "dare" but also "may." The latter is perhaps the sense most often at work in legal texts.

5. Chen Zhiguo 陳治國, "Cong Liye Qin jian kan Qin de gongwen zhidu" 從里耶秦簡看秦的公文制度, *Zhongguo lishi wen* 中國歷史文物 1 (2007): 64; Li Xueqin 李學勤, "Chudu Liye Qin jian" 初讀里耶秦簡, *Wenwu* 文物 1

(2003): 74–76. Note also that *gan* 敢, "to dare," can also simply indicate the permissibility of doing something, which related to its use in this formula; see *Hanyu dacidian*, s.v. *gan* 敢.

6. *Shi* (or *dun*) 石, a unit of weight, is used here in an extended sense to measure pull weight of a bow; see, for example, *Juyan xinjian shijiao*, 246 (EPT 50:95).

7. *Juyan xinjian shijiao*, 454 (EPT 53:138).

8. *Jianshui Jinguan Han jian*, 3:137 (73EJT 31:163).

9. *Juyan Han jian jiayi bian*, 10 (15.19), photo plate *yi*–12.

10. See *Jianshui Jinguan Han jian*, 1:9 (73EJT 1:126), 1:33 (73EJT 3:55), 2:78 (73EJT 23:298), 3:137 (73EJT 31:163).

11. See, for example, *Juyan Han jian jiayi bian*, 4 (6.13) and 25 (37.29), photo plates *yi*–4 and *yi*–31.

12. *Juyan Han jian jiyi bian*, 21 (33.19), photo plate *jia*–29.

13. *Juyan xinjian shijiao*, 128 (EPT 40:25); *Juyan Han jian jiayi bian*, 97 (136.44), photo plate 65; *Jianshui Jinguan Han jian*, 3:32 (73EJT 25:15A).

14. Hu Pingsheng and Zhang Defang, *Dunhuang Xuanquan Han jian shicui*, 26–27 (II 0314 2: 302).

15. *Juyan xinjian shijiao*, 299 (EPT 51:228).

16. *Juyan Han jian jiayi bian*, 42 (58.15A), photo plate *jia*–46.

17. See Bret Hinsch, *Women in Imperial China* (Lanham: Rowman & Littlefield, 2016), 50–53.

18. For a discussion of the positions women held and the contexts in which they did so, see Olivia Milburn, "Palace Women in the Former Han Dynasty (202 BCE–CE 23): Gender and Administrational History in the Early Imperial Era," *Nan Nü* 18 (2016): 195–223.

19. *Juyan Han jian jiayi bian*, 182 (257.30), photo plate *yi*–190.

20. *Dunhuang Han jian*, 250 (796). I have corrected the transcription to the tenth month from the seventh. The numerals 7 and 10 were very similar in Han handwriting and are easily confused. The seventh month did not begin with a *renyin* day this year and the tenth did, and the tenth contained a *jiachen* day while the seventh did not.

21. Barbieri-Low and Yates, *Law, State, and Society*, 214.

22. *Juyan xinjian shijiao*, 511 (EPT 56:261); *Juyan Han jian jiayi bian*, 112 (160.14), photo plate *jia*–74.

23. *Juyan Han jian jiayi bian*, 86 (123.49), photo plate *yi*–92.

24. Zhang Defang and Hu Pingsheng, *Dunhuang Xuanquan Han jian shicui*, 168 (II 0214 2: 195).

25. For a summary of received source information about Kangju, with reference to some more recent archaeological discoveries, including both Kangju sites and the Han document I discuss here, see Hao Shusheng 郝樹聲, "Jianlun Dunhuang Xuanquan Han jian 'Kangju wang shizhe ce' ji

Xi-Han yu Kangju de guanxi" 簡論敦煌懸泉漢簡 "康居王使者冊"及西漢與康居的關係, *Dunhuang yanjiu* 敦煌研究 1 (2009): 53–58. For brief accounts, see Y. A. Zadneprovskiy, "The Nomads of Northern Central Asia after the Invasion of Alexander," in *History of Civilizations of Central Asia, Volume 2, The Development of Sedentary and Nomadic Civilizations: 700 B.C. to A.D. 250*, ed. János Harmatta (Paris: United Nations Educational, Scientific and Cultural Organization, 1994), 463–64; and A. K. Narain, "Indo-Europeans in Inner Asia," in *The Cambridge History of Early Inner Asia* (Cambridge: Cambridge University Press, 1990), 174–75. There are some 120 example documents recording contact with non-Chinese persons in Zhang Defang and Hu Pingsheng, *Dunhuang Xuanquan Han jian shicui*, 103–74; for discussion of some related materials from Xuanquanzhi, including the document I treat, see Yang Jidong, "Transportation, Boarding, Lodging, and Trade along the Early Silk Road: A Preliminary Study of the Xuanquan Manuscripts," *Journal of the American Oriental Society* 135.3 (2015): 421–32.

26. The document is transcribed with commentary in Hu Pingsheng and Zhang Defang, *Dunhuang Xuanquan Han jian shicui*, 118–20 (II 0216 2: 877–83); it is described and discussed, with further details that Hu and Zhang do not provide, in Hao Shusheng 郝樹聲, "Jianlun Dunhuang Xuanquan Han jian 'Kangju wang shizhe ce' ji Xi-Han yu Kangju de guanxi" 簡論敦煌懸泉漢簡 "康居王使者冊"及西漢與康居的關係, *Dunhuang yanjiu* 敦煌研究 1 (2009): 53–58, particularly 55–57; my discussion draws primarily from these sources, with additional specific references as necessary. See also the discussion and partial translation in Yang Jidong, "Transportation, Boarding, Lodging, and Trade along the Early Silk Road," 429–31.

27. Here I am following the transcription and explanation of Hao Shusheng, "Jianlun," 55–56, which seems to fit the content and sense of the document well. The transcription in Hu Pingsheng and Zhang Defang, *Dunhuang Xuanquan Han jian shicui*, 118, presents a somewhat different take that in my view is a bit less convincing than Hao's reading. Since no photographs of this document have been published, I cannot reach an independent conclusion about how to read the text.

28. Hao Shusheng, "Jianlun," 55–57.

29. Hao Shusheng, "Jianlun," 56.

30. Wolfgang Behr, " 'To Translate' Is 'To Exchange' 譯者言易也: Linguistic Diversity and the Terms for Translation in Ancient China," in *Mapping Meanings: The Field of New Learning in Late Qing China*, ed. Michael Lackner and Natascha Vittinghoff (Leiden: Brill, 2004), 180–85.

31. *Han shu*, 57A.2577; Wang Xianqian 王先謙 (1842–1918), *Han shu bu zhu* 漢書補注 (1900 woodblock edition; reprinted Yangzhou: Guangling shushe, 2006), 1159; Loewe, *Dong Zhongshu, a 'Confucian' Heritage and the Chunqiu Fanlu* (Leiden: Brill, 2011), 78; cf. related mention in Behr, "To

Translate," 18; for other examples of the trope, see *Hanyu dacidian*, s.v. *chongyi* 重譯.

32. As Lothar von Falkenhausen suggested to me.

33. Cf. the consideration of translators in Wang Zijin, *Qin-Han chengwei yanjiu* 秦漢稱謂研究 (Beijing: Zhongguo shehui kexue chubanshe, 2014), 395–406; Wang, while certainly familiar with paleographic sources, writes in this connection only about received accounts (including that of Sima Xiangru, which I discuss).

34. Enno Giele, "Signatures of 'Scribes' in Early Imperial China," *Asiatischen Studien* 59.1 (2005): 353–87.

35. See examples and related discussion in Yu Zhenbo 于振波, "Qin-Han shiqi de youren" 秦漢時期的郵人, in *Jianduxue yanjiu* 簡牘學研究, no. 4, ed. Gansusheng kaogu yanjiusuo 甘肅省考古研究所 and Xibei shifan daxue wenxueyuan lishixi 西北師範大學文學院歷史系 (Lanzhou: Gansu renmin chubanshe, 2004), 28–33.

Chapter Five. Composite Texts

1. See David R. Knechtges, "The Problem with Anthologies: The Case of the 'Bai yi' Poems of Ying Qu (190–252)," *Asia Major* (third series) 23.1 (2010): 173–99; François Martin, "Les anthologies dans la Chine antique et médiévale: De la genèse au déploiement," *Extrême-Orient, Extrême-Occident* 25 (2003): 13–38; David R. Knechtges, "Culling the Weeds and Selecting Prime Blossoms: The Anthology in Early Medieval China," in *Culture and Power in the Reconstitution of the Chinese Realm, 200–600*, ed. Scott Pearce et al. (Cambridge: Harvard University Asia Center, 2001), 200–41.

2. *Hanshu*, "Yiwenzhi," 30.1762–63.

3. Michael Hunter, *Confucius Beyond the* Analects (Leiden: Brill, 2017).

4. Michael Nylan, *Yang Xiong and the Pleasures of Reading*, 43–45; Michael Loewe, "Liu Xiang and Liu Xin," in *Chang'an in 26 BCE: An Augustan Age in China*, ed. Michael Nylan and Griet Vankeerberghen (Seattle: University of Washington Press, 2015), 369–89; Charles Sanft, "The Moment of Dying: Representations in Liu Xiang's Anthologies *Xin xu* and *Shuo yuan*," *Asia Major* (third series) 24.1 (2011): 127–58; see also discussion in Christian Schwermann, "Anecdote Collections as Argumentative Texts: The Composition of the *Shuoyuan*," in *Between History and Philosophy: Anecdotes in Early China*, ed. Paul van Els and Sarah Queen (Albany: State University of New York Press, 2017), 147–92.

5. The preceding is from Jiayuguanshi wenwu baoguansuo 嘉峪關市文物保管所, "Yumen Huahai Han dai fengsui yizhi chutu de jiandu" 玉門花海漢代烽燧遺址出土的簡牘, in *Han jian yanjiu wenji* 漢簡研究文集, ed. Gansusheng

wenwu gongzuodui 甘肅省文物工作隊 and Gansusheng bowuguan 甘肅省博物館 (Lanzhou: Gansu renmin chubanshe, 1984), 15–16; and He Shuangquan, *Jiandu* 簡牘 (Lanzhou: Dunhuang wenyi chubanshe, 2003), 162.

6. The initial report on the stick says it contains 212 characters, 133 of which are the imperial edict and seventy-nine the letter; see Jiayuguanshi wenwu baoguansuo "Yumen Huahai," 16. Ōba Osamu 大庭脩, *Tonkō Kan kan: Tai Ei toshokan zō* 敦煌漢簡: 大英図書館蔵 (Kyoto: Dōhōsha, 1990), 145, repeats all three of those figures, while Tomiya, *Monjo gyōsei*, 96, and He Shuangquan, *Jiandu*, 163 mention only the total count of 212. Zhang Xiaofeng 張小鋒, *Xi-Han houqi zhengju yanbian tanwei* 西漢後期政局演變探微 (Tianjin: Tianjin guji chubanshe, 2007), 23, says there are "200 plus" characters. According to my examination of the published photographs, which are clear, there are 209 characters and five pieces of punctuation, all of the latter being ditto marks. Of the 209 total characters, five are clearly present but illegible in the photograph and four others are very faint and cannot be read; all of these come in the second text. In those nine cases, I follow others' transcriptions.

7. Jiayuguanshi wenwu baoguansuo, "Yumen Huahai," 16, passes over the letter as "other content," although the authors give a complete transcription that includes the letter when they transcribe all materials from the site; see Jiayuguanshi wenwu baoguansuo, "Yumen Huahai," 28. Zhang Xiaofeng, *Xi-Han houqi zhengju*, 24; He Shuangquan, *Jiandu*, 163–64; and Hu Pingsheng, "Xie zai mugu shang de Xi-Han yizhao" 寫在木觚上的西漢遺詔, *Wenwu tiandi* 文物天地 6 (1987): 30, all skip the letter. See also Fang Shiming 方詩銘, "Xihan Wudi wanqi de 'wugu zhi huo' ji qi qianhou—jianlun Yumen Han jian 'Han Wudi yizhao'" 西漢武帝晚期的 "巫蠱之禍" 及其前後—兼論玉門漢簡 "漢武帝遺詔," *Guankan* 館刊 4 (1987): 367. Ōba, *Tonkō Kan kan*, 145–56, transcribes both parts of the texts, then says that the edict comprising the first half of this text is very valuable while pointedly skipping over the letter. Contrariwise, Giele, "Private Letter Manuscripts," 411–12, 445–47, acknowledges the presence of the edict but translates only the letter section.

8. The text has *si* 笥 here, which is difficult to understand and has given rise to varying interpretations. The *Online Dictionary of Character Variants* (http://140.111.1.40/yitib/frb/frb03178.htm) lists it as a variant of *si* 笥, "square basket," which does not apparently fit the sense of the sentence. I suggest that *si* here is an alternate for *si* 伺, "to watch, to observe," here used as a noun, "oversight"; see Wang Hui, *Gu wenzi tongjia shili*, 48. In the context of this edict, I understand *si* 伺 not as a detached observation but with the implication of a watchful observation and protection against danger, which fits with the subsequent text. The other alternate readings that have been offered are Jiayuguanshi wenwu baoguasuo, "Yumen Huahai," 17, which transcribes the graph in question as *si* 笥 and explains it as a loan

for *si* 嗣, "posterity, successor"; and Ōba Osamu, *Tonkō Kan kan*, 146, and Hu Pingsheng, "Xie zai mugu shang de Xi-Han yizhao," 30, who read *si* 笥 and deem it a borrowing for *ci* 祠, "sacrificial offering."

9. *Zizhi* 自致, literally, "to cause oneself to arrive," is a lexicalized phrase meaning "to give one's utmost" in pursuit of some worthy goal. It occurs for instance in *Lunyu*, which has the line "There is none among men that does his utmost (*zizhi*)" 人未有自致者也; *Lunyu zhushu*, 19.172; translated with reference to Yang Bojun 楊伯峻, *Lunyu yizhu* 論語譯注 (Beijing: Zhonghua shuju, 1980), 202.

10. Huhai 胡亥 (r. 210–207 BCE), better known as the Second Emperor of Qin 秦二世, ruled the Qin dynasty after the death of his father, the First Emperor.

11. I understand *fu* 負, often "to bear; to carry on the back," as "to turn one's back" on something, in this case heaven. The phrase *fu tian* 負天 occurs in the received literature in the sense of "to go against heaven's will." See, for example, *Hou Han shu*, 58.1880; see also *Hanyu dacidian*, s.v. *fu tian*. Tomiya reads the graph as *er* 貳, "two," in context meaning "be disloyal to" heaven, which in essence matches my understanding.

12. This line is difficult to understand and my reading remains tentative. The character *she* 郤 is attested only as a toponym in Xu Shen 許慎, *Shuowen jiezi* 說文解字 (Beijing: Zhonghua shuju, 1963), 136; here I read it as *she* 舍, "dwelling." Following Zhang Xiaofeng, *Xihan houqi zhengju*, 24, I take *shelu* 舍廬 as "dwelling-hut." I understand *xia* 下 as "to go out, leave"; see *Hanyu dacidian*, s.v. *xia*. In this case, my understanding of *xia* is influenced by its position, which is parallel to *qu* 去, "to leave." *Dun* 敦 is also difficult to understand as written and I believe it is a loan for *tun* 屯, "camp." A number of examples of this borrowing are listed in Bai Yulan 白於藍, *Jiandu boshu tongjiazi zidian* 簡牘帛書通假字字典 (Fuzhou: Fujian renmin chubanshe, 2008), 341; Wang Hui, *Guwenzi tongjia shili*, 781; and Gao Heng, *Guzi tongjia huidian*, 128–29.

13. Tomiya transcribes the graph that I translate "younger brother" as 弟, which *Hanyu dazidian* calls an alternate form of *ti* 黃 and of *di* 第; *Dunhuang Han jian shiwen* has *di* 第 and Ōba Osamu has *di* 弟. The was phonetic alternation between *di* 第 and *di* 弟, "younger brother," is attested in received texts; see Gao Heng, *Guzi tongjia huidian*, 534.

Looking at the image, I believe the character resembles *di* 弟 with an additional upper horizontal stroke. Such an addition or embellishment would not be unknown among handwritten early texts. Richter, *The Embodied Text*, 39–40, discusses this phenomenon in Chu manuscripts. Despite the differences among the structural analyses of the graph, all readings take the word to be *di* 弟, "younger brother." In context this is likely not meant literally but rather as a term indicating subservience and closeness to the recipient.

14. *Weng* 翁, "father; uncle; old man," in this context is a term of address for a senior male. There are other instances of this use among letters in the documents from northwestern China.

15. While the *Dunhuang Han jian shiwen* and other transcriptions have *xi* 系 here, the structure of the graph in the inscription appears to be *mi* 糸, as Tomiya has it. Since it is a personal name, the difference has no semantic significance.

16. Xu Shen, *Shuowen jiezi*, 41, defines *jin* 近 as *fu* 附, "close," which also has the sense of "to fit properly," which is how I understand it in contexts like the present one.

17. In addition to the well-known sense of "petty man," *xiaoren* 小人 can also refer to the "little people," those under the control of others, which is how I understand it here; see *Hanyu dacidian* and *Ci yuan* 辭源, s.v. *xiaoren*. *Xiaoren* can also function as a self-deprecatory first-person pronoun. However, in the context of the preceding phrases, and in a letter where the writer refers to himself by his personal name, that understanding seems less likely than the one I follow.

18. The text here is 庶浚, which is, while clearly negative, obscure in its specific sense.

19. Here and throughout, the text writes *quan* 睠, which all readers agree is in context a graphic variation of *zhen* 朕, the monarch's first-person pronoun. Jiayuguanshi wenwu baoguansuo, "Yumen Huahai," 18, suggests the copyist avoided writing *zhen* in observance of a taboo.

20. On reading *zhong* 衆, "many; the many [people]," as *zhong* 終, "to end," see Wang Hui, *Guwenzi tongjia shili*, 566–67.

21. Following Zhang Xiaofeng, *Xihan houqi zhengju*, 24, to read *xi* 錫 as *ti* 惕. This alternation is attested in received texts; see Gao Heng, *Guzi tongjia huidian*, 468.

22. The graph 悷 is as far as I can determine not otherwise attested. It appears to be a graphic variant of *wang* 妄, "careless(ly), reckless(ly)," and I follow other readers to take it thus in this sentence.

23. *Yanjiao* 嚴教, literally, "strict teaching," is a respectful term for teaching or instruction. *Mozi* 墨子 contains the phrase "to receive the Son of Heaven's instruction" 受天子之嚴教; see Sun Yirang 孫詒讓 (1848–1908), *Mozi jiangu* 墨子閒詁 (Beijing: Zhonghua shuju, 2001), 3.89.

The primary sources of my transcription are Jiayuguanshi wenwu baoguansuo, "Yumen Huahai," 16, 28; Tomiya, *Monjo gyōsei*, 96–98; and Ōba Osamu, *Tonkō Kan kan*, 145–46; with other references as indicated. In translating I referred to the rendering in Tomiya, *Monjo gyōsei*, 98; cf. also the translation of the letter section in Giele, "Private Letters," 445–47.

24. See, for example, Emperor Wen's 文 command upon his accession to the throne in 179 BCE and the one he issued in 167 BCE; see *Han shu*,

4.108, 23.1098. See also the reference to the practice of addressing edicts this way in Wang Xianqian 王先謙 (1842–1918), *Hou Han shu jijie* 後漢書集解 (1915 woodblock ed.; reprinted Yanzhou: Guangling shushe, 2006), 1B.16b.

25. Friederike Braun, *Terms of Address: Problems of Patterns and Usage in Various Languages and Cultures* (Berlin: Mouton de Gruyter, 1988), 35–36 and passim.

26. Jiayuguanshi wenwu baoguansuo, "Yumen Huahai," 28 (no. 77.J.H.S.:2). The date is given as "first year of the Yuanping era, seventh month, *gengzi* day" 元平元年七月庚子, and I convert to Western dating following Wang Shuanghuai 王雙懷 et al., *Zhonghua rili tongdian* 中華日曆通典 (Changchun: Jilin wenshi chubanshe, 2006), 1328.

27. Jiayuguanshi wenwu baoguansuo, "Yumen Huahai," 18.

28. The preceding summarizes from Jiayuguanshi wenwu baoguansuo, "Yumen Huahai," 18–21. See also *Shiji*, 111.2932, and *Han shu*, 68.2933.

29. Sima Guang, *Zizhi tongjian*, 22.726.

30. Tian Yuqing, *Qin-Han Wei-Jin shi tanwei* 秦漢魏晉史探微 (Beijing: Zhonghua shuju, 2008), 61–62.

31. Zhang Xiaofeng 張小鋒, *Xihan houqi zhengju yanbian tanwei* 西漢後期政局演變探微 (Tianjin: Tianjin guji chubanshe, 2007), 25–26; Zheng Youguo 鄭有國, *Zhongguo jianduxue zonglun* 中國簡牘學綜論 (Shanghai: Huadong shifan daxue chubanshe, 1989), 199.

32. Hu Pingsheng, "Xie zai mugu shang de Xihan yizhao," 31–33.

33. NB: He Shuangquan, *Jiandu*, 162–64; He says that the original report says the writing stick was copied in 74 BCE, the same time as the dated document; Jiayuguanshi wenwu baoguansuo, "Yumen Huahai," 18, names 74 BCE as the terminus ante quem for the document, not its date of creation.

34. He Shuangquan, *Jiandu*, 162–64; see also, for example, Hu Pingsheng, "Xie zai mugu shang," 30; and Giele, "Private Letters," 411–12.

35. See Wang Lunxin 王倫信, "'Gu' yu jiandu shidai de xizi cailiao" "觚"與簡牘時代的習字材料, *Jichu jiaoyu* 基礎教育 8.6 (2011): 120–24; Shen Gang 沈剛, "Juyan Han jian zhong de xizijian shulüe" 居延漢簡中的習字簡述略, *Guji zhengli yanjiu xuekan* 古籍整理研究學刊 1 (2006): 29–31.

36. *Juyan xin jian shijiao*, 204–5 (EPT 48.55A–E); *Juyan xin jian*, 57 and photo plate 110; *Xin-Mang jian*, 56 (no. 357).

37. Aimee E. Newell, *A Stitch in Time: The Needlework of Aging Women in Antebellum America* (Athens: Ohio University Press, 2014), 40; Sophia Frances Anne Caulfeild and Blanche C. Saward, *The Dictionary of Needlework: An Encyclopaedia of Artistic, Plain and Fancy Needlework* (1882; reprinted New York: Arno Press, 1972), 435.

38. Richter, *The Embodied Text*, 11–12, 175.

39. For sources discussing the general characteristics of the staff and the privileges it brought, see A. F. P. Hulsewé, "Han China: A Proto

'Welfare State'? Fragments of Han Law Discovered in North-West China,"
T'oung Pao 73.4/5 (1987): 265–85, and subsequent references here. I owe
the observation about the slaves' frequency in archaeological finds to Yang
Xiaoneng, formerly curator of Asian art at the Iris and B. Gerald Cantor
Center for Visual Arts, Stanford University. During conversation on 22
April 2016, I commented on a nice example of a Han-period bird finial
in the Cantor Center's collection. Yang Xiaoneng politely noted that such
objects are far from rare.

40. Wang Guihai, *Qin-Han jiandu tanyan*, 221–24; Wei Yanli 魏燕利,
" 'Wang zhang' kaobian" "王杖"考辨, *Jianduxue yanjiu* 簡牘學研究, no. 4, ed.
Xibei shifan daxue wenxueyuan lishixi 西北師範大學文學院歷史系, et al.
(Lanzhou: Gansu renmin chubanshe, 2004), 150.

41. The excavation report treats the grave that produced this text,
no. 18 of the Mozuizi 磨咀子 Han tomb group, with minimal detail as part
of the group; see Gansusheng bowuguan 甘肅省博物館, "Gansusheng Wuwei
Mozuizi Han mu fajue" 甘肅省武威磨咀子漢墓發掘, *Kaogu* 9 (1960): 15–28.
The text I discuss here is the only one that report mentions. It is also the
subject of a focused article in the same issue of *Kaogu*, which presents a
transcription and annotations; see Kaogu yanjiusuo bianjishi 考古研究所編輯
室, "Wuwei Mozuizi Han mu chutu wangzhang shijian shiwen" 武威磨咀子漢
墓出土王杖十簡釋文, *Kaogu* 9 (1960): 29–30; this site and text are discussed
and translated in Michael Loewe, "The Wooden and Bamboo Strips Found at
Mo-chü-tzu (Kansu)," *Journal of the Royal Asiatic Society* 1/2 (1965): 13–26;
see also Enno Giele, "Excavated Manuscripts: Context and Methodology,"
in *China's Early Empires: A Re-appraisal*, ed. Michael Nylan and Michael
Loewe (Cambridge: Cambridge University Press, 2010), 114–15. The following paragraphs summarize these sources, with additional sources as cited.

42. This detail is included in the initial report and widely mentioned;
see Gansusheng bowuguan, "Gansusheng Wuwei Mozuizi Han mu fajue," 19;
it features prominently in Tomiya's hypothesis about the strips' sequence; see
Tomiya Itaru, "Ōjō jukkan" 王杖一簡, *Tōhō gakuhō* 東方學報 64 (1992): 66–71.

43. Gansusheng bowuguan 甘肅省博物館, et al., eds., *Wuwei Han jian*
武威漢簡 (Beijing: Zhonghua shuju, 2005), 140; photos of strips on plate 22.
For discussion of questions about sequence specifically, see, for example, Hao
Shusheng, "Wuwei 'Wang zhang' jian xinkao" 武威 "王杖"簡新考, in *Jianduxue
yanjiu* 簡牘學研究, no. 4, ed. Xibei shifan daxue wenxueyuan lishixi 西北師
範大學文學院歷史系, et al. (Lanzhou: Gansu renmin chubanshe, 2004), 133,
who summarize six different sequences that scholars had offered; Tomiya,
"Ōjō jukkan," 66–71; and Loewe, "The Wooden and Bamboo Strips," 21–23;
among others.

44. *Wuwei Han jian* 武威漢簡, ed. Gansusheng bowuguan 甘肅省博物館
and Zhongguo kexueyuan kaogu yanjiusuo 中國科學院考古研究所 (Beijing:

Zhonghua shuju, 2005), 140–47; Wuweixian bowuguan 武威縣博物館, "Wuwei xinchu Wang zhang zhaoling ce" 武威新出王杖詔令冊, in *Hanjian yanjiu wenji* 漢簡研究文集, ed. Gansusheng wenwu gongzuodui 甘肅省文物工作隊 et al. (Lanzhou: Gansu renmin chubanshe, 1984), 35–37; Hulsewé, "Han China: A Proto 'Welfare State'? Fragments of Han Law Discovered in North-West China," discusses and translates this document.

45. For example, Hu Pingsheng, "Yumen, Wuwei xin huo jiandu," 220–25; Hao Shusheng, "Wuwei 'Wang zhan' jian xinkao," 137.

46. Hu Pingsheng, "Yumen, Wuwei xin huo jiandu," 220–25; cf. *Wuwei Han jian*, 141, which divides the text into four sections.

47. See Sanft, *Communication and Cooperation*, 140–43 and 202n64.

48. Wuwei diqu bowuguan 武威地區博物館, "Gansu Wuwei Hantanpo Donghan mu" 甘肅武威旱灘坡東漢墓, *Wenwu* 10 (1993): 28–33; the texts are discussed there and in the accompanying article: Li Junming 李均明 and Liu Jun 劉軍, "Wuwei Hantanpo chutu Han jian kaoshu" 武威漢灘坡出土漢簡考述, *Wenwu* 10 (1993): 34–39; this article is reprinted in traditional characters in Li Junming, *Chuxuelu* 初學錄 (Taipei: Lantai chubanshe, 1999), 196–209.

49. For example, Loewe, "The Wooden and Bamboo Strips," 18.

50. Questioning this assumption in at least some contexts is a major theme in Enno Giele, "Using Early Chinese Manuscripts as Historical Source Materials," *Monumenta Serica* 51 (2003): 409–38; see also discussion in Thote, "Daybooks in Archaeological Context," 40–47; and Barbieri-Low and Yates, *Law, State, and Society*, 105–9.

51. Xiaogan diqu dierqi yigong yinong wenwu kaogu xunlianban 孝感地區第二期亦工亦農文物考古訓練班, "Hubei Yunmeng Shuihudi shiyi hao Qin mu fajue jianbao" 湖北雲夢睡虎地十一號秦墓發掘簡報, *Wenwu* 文物 6 (1976): 1–10; Barbieri-Low and Yates, *Law, State, and Society*, 7–8.

52. Tomiya, "Ōjō jukkan," 86–88.

53. Momiyama Akira 籾山明, "Ōjō mokkan saikō" 王杖木簡再考, *Tōhōshi kenkyū* 東方史研究 65 (2006): 1–36, discusses these texts throughout, with repeated reference to Tomiya's analysis; for these points particularly, see 31 and 36n19.

54. See, for example, Miranda Brown and Zhang Zhongwei, "A Tale of Two Stones: Social Memory in Roman Greece and Han China," in *Citizens and Commoners*, ed. Hans Beck and Griet Vankeerberghen (Cambridge: Cambridge University Press, forthcoming).

55. See also the discussion of the distinction between *mingqi* 明器, funerary objects, and *shengqi* 生器, objects from a deceased person's life, in Thote, "Daybooks in Archaeological Context," 39–47.

56. Hu Pingsheng, "Yumen, Wuwei xin huo jiandu," 224–25.

57. See Miranda Brown and Charles Sanft, "Categories and Legal Reasoning in Early Imperial China: The Meaning of *Fa* in Recovered Texts," *Oriens Extremus* 49 (2010): 283–306.

58. Thote, "Daybooks in Archaeological Context," 39–47 and passim; quote 44.

Chapter Six. Practical Texts

1. Donald Harper and Marc Kalinowski, "Introduction," in *Books of Fate and Popular Culture in Early China: The Daybook Manuscripts of the Warring States, Qin, and Han*, ed. Donald Harper and Marc Kalinowski (Leiden: Brill, 2017), 4–5; Harper, "Daybooks in the Context of Manuscript Culture and Popular Culture Studies," 99–101 and passim; Marc Kalinowski, "Hémérologie," in *Divination et société dans la Chine médiévale: Étude des manuscrits de Dunhuang de la Bibliothèque nationale de France et de la British Library*, ed. Marc Kalinowski (Paris: Bibliothèque nationale de France, 2003), 213–16; Marc Kalinowski, "Diviners and Astrologers under the Eastern Zhou: Transmitted Texts and Recent Archaeological Discoveries," in *Early Chinese Religion, Part One: Shang through Han (1250 BC–220 AD)*, ed. John Lagerwey and Marc Kalinowski (Leiden: Brill, 2009), 387–89.

2. See Miranda Brown, "'Medicine' in Early China," in *The Routledge Handbook of Early Chinese History*, ed. Paul R. Goldin (London: Routledge, 2018), 459–72; Xie Guihua, "Han Bamboo and Wooden Medical Records Discovered in Military Sites from the Northwestern Frontier Region," in *Medieval Chinese Medicine: The Dunhuang Medical Manuscripts*, ed. Vivienne Lo and Christopher Cullen (London: Routledge Curzon, 2005), 78–106.

3. See Cordula Gumbrecht, "Die Physiognomie von vier Kaiserinnen im China der späten Han-Zeit (25–220)," *Monumenta Serica* 50 (2002): 177–82; Mark Pitner, "Disability in Early China" (unpublished paper, 2015); Rune Svarvarud, "Body and Character: Physiognomical Descriptions in Han Dynasty Literature," in *Minds and Mentalities in Traditional Chinese Literature*, ed. Halvor Elfring (Beijing: Culture and Art Publishing House, 1999), 120–46; Catherine Despeux, "Physiognomonie," in *Divination et société dans le Chine médiéval: Étude des manuscrits de Dunhuang de la Bibliothèque nationale de France et de la British Library*, ed. Marc Kalinowski (Paris: Bibliothèque nationale de France, 2003), 513–38.

4. *Han shu*, 30.1774–75. While his focus is on religion, Marc Kalinowski, "Technical Traditions in Ancient China and *Shushu* Culture in Chinese Religion," in *Religion and Chinese Society: A Centennial Conference of the École française d'Extrême-Orient*, ed. John Lagerwey (Paris: École française d'Extrême-Orient, 2004), 223–52, gives a general overview of techniques and the texts about them, including the *Han History* "Monograph on Literature."

5. Li Ling, *Zhongguo fangshu kao* 中國方術考, revised edition (Beijing: Dongfang chubanshe, 2001), 84–85; see also discussion and translation in Gumbrecht, "Die Physiognomie von vier Kaiserinnen," 177–82.

6. *Han shu*, 30.1774–75, quote 1775; see also Chen Guoqing 陳國慶, *Han shu Yiwenzhi zhushi huibian* 漢書藝文志注釋彙編 (Beijing: Zhonghua shuju, 1983), 200–35; quote 223.

7. Quoted in Chen Guoqing, *Han shu Yiwenzhi zhushi huibian*, 223.

8. *Han shu*, 30.1775; Chen Guoqing, *Han shu Yiwen zhi zhushi huibian*, 222–23.

9. *Hanyu dacidian*, s.v. *liuchu* 六畜.

10. Zhangsun Wuji 長孫無忌 (d. 659), *Sui shu* (Beijing: Zhonghua shuju, 1973), 34.1039.

11. Yao Zhenzong 姚振宗 (1843–1906), *Sui shu jingji zhi kaozheng* 隋書經籍志考證, *Xuxiu Siku quanshu* 續修四庫全書 ed. (Shanghai: Shanghai guji chubanshe, 2002), 591–93, gathers information about listings of those texts in other bibliographies as well as fragments cited elsewhere.

12. Li Ling, *Zhongguo fangshu kao*, 85–87.

13. Zhou Zuliang 周祖亮, "Han jian shouyi ziliao ji qi jiazhi kaolun" 漢簡獸醫資料及其價值考論, *Nongye kaogu* 農業考古 4 (2011): 457–60.

14. See the transcription in *Changsha Mawangdui Han mu jianbo jicheng* 長沙馬王堆漢墓簡帛集成, ed. Qiu Xigui 裘錫圭 (Beijing: Zhonghua shuju, 2014), 5:169–80. The first transcription was Mawangdui Han mu boshu zhengli xiaozu 馬王堆漢墓帛書整理小組, "Mawangdui Han mu boshu 'Xiangma jing' shiwen" 馬王堆漢墓帛書"相馬經"釋文, *Wenwu* 文物 8 (1977): 17–22; it was accompanied by Xie Chengxia 謝成俠, "Guanyu Mawangdui Han mu boshu 'Xiang ma jing' de tantao" 關於馬王堆漢墓帛書"相馬經"的探討, *Wenwu* 8 (1977): 23–26, an introductory article. For an overview of later scholarship, see Wang Shujin 王樹金, "Mawangdui Han mu boshu 'Xiang ma jing' yanjiu sanshinian" 馬王堆漢墓帛書 "相馬經"研究三十年, *Hu'nansheng bowuguan guankan* 湖南省博物館館刊 5 (2008): 241–48.

15. See Zhao Kuifu 趙逵夫, "Mawangdui Han mu chutu 'Xiang ma jing–Daguang po zhang gu xun zhuan'" 馬王堆漢墓出土 "相馬經·大光破章故訓傳" 發微, *Jiang-Han kaogu* 江漢考古 3 (1989): 48–51, 47; and Zhao Kuifu, "Mawangdui Han mu boshu 'Xiang ma jing' fawei" 馬王堆漢墓帛書 "相馬經" 發微, *Wenxian* 文獻 4 (1989): 262–68; see also Yu Xin 余欣, "Chutu wenxian suojian Han-Tang xiangma shu kao" 出土文獻所見漢唐相馬術考, *Xueshu yuekan* 學術月刊 2 (2014): 138 and passim.

16. See Richter, *The Embodied Text*, for discussion of related phenomena.

17. The explanatory commentary is lines 23–43 and the glossing commentary comes in lines 44–77. See discussion in Zhao Kuifu, "Mawangdui Han mu chutu," and Zhao Kuifu, "Mawangdui Han mu boshu," 262–68; see also Yu Xin, "Chutu wenxian suojian," 138; Wang Shujin, "Mawangdui Han mu boshu 'Xiang ma jing,'" 242–43; NB: the repetitions in the text were noted by Xie Chengxia, "Guanyu Mawangdui Han mu boshu 'Xiang ma jing,'" 24–26, already in 1977.

18. Li Ling, *Zhongguo fangshu kao*, 85.

19. A. F. P. Hulsewé, *Remnants of Ch'in Law: An Annotated Translation of the Ch'in Legal and Administrative Rules of the 3rd Century B.C. Discovered in Yün-meng Prefecture, Hu-pei Province, in 1975* (Leiden: E. J. Brill, 1985), 26n2, describes this as "a rather poetic (but also rather abstruse) text on the inspection of horses."

20. Zhao Kuifu, "Zaoci jueyu, yiyun hongshen–cong boshu 'Xiang ma jing–Daguang po zhang' kan Qufu biyu xiangzheng shoufa de xingcheng" 藻辭譎喻, 意蘊宏深–從帛書 "相馬經 · 大光破章"看屈賦比喻象徵手法的形成, *Liaoning shifan daxue xuebao (shekeban)* 遼寧師範大學學報(社科版) 3 (1988): 50–52.

21. Zhao Kuifu, "Zaoci jueyu," discusses the obscurity of the text generally, calling it something like a riddle and on page 52 likening it to a rhapsody; see also Wang Shujin, "Mawangdui Han mu boshu 'Xiang ma jing,'" 244–46. Cf. Xie Chengxia, "Guanyu Mawangdui Han mu boshu 'Xiang ma jing,'" 26, who accepts that the text has sections with poetic flavor but then notes that famous prose works do, too, and as such this is not a poem per se.

22. Mawangdui Han mu boshu zhengli xiaozu, "Mawangdui Han mu boshu 'Xiangma jing' shiwen," 17, line 4 of the manuscript; *Changsha Mangwangdui*, 169–70 (line 4); Wang Shujin, "Mawangdui Han mu boshu 'Xiang ma jing,'" 241.

23. *Zhoucao* 周草 appears in the glossing commentary in reference to the eye, which glosses the term, saying it "resides at the eye . . ." 居目, and which also says "must be complete" 必成, but the text is damaged there and none of these phrases is complete. I combine this with the literal sense of *zhoucao*, "surrounding grass," and the mention of the cheekbone just below to understand it tentatively as referring to the dark line on the edge of the eyelid, which is quite evident in foxes. "Eye socket" and "eye lashes" also seem like reasonable alternatives. Damage to the manuscript has destroyed the explanation of the term, leaving me unable to confirm or disprove any interpretation.

24. *Changsha Mawangdui*, 178 (lines 50–51).

25. *Changsha Mawangdui*, 171 (line 19).

26. *Changsha Mawangdui*, 180 (lines 72–73).

27. Fuyang Han jian zhenglizu 阜陽漢簡整理組 et al., "Fuyang Han jian jianjie" 阜陽漢簡簡介, *Wenwu* 文物 2 (1983): 23.

28. D. C. Lau and Roger T. Ames, *Sun Bin: The Art of Warfare: A Translation of the Classic Chinese Work of Philosophy and Strategy* (Albany: State University of New York Press, 2003), 1–4.

29. *Yinqueshan Han mu zhujian (er)* 銀雀山漢墓竹簡 (貳), ed. Yinqueshan Han mu zhujian zhengli xiaozu 銀雀山漢墓竹簡整理小組 (Beijing: Wenwu chubanshe, 2010), 253–54.

30. See Li Fang 李昉 (925–996) et al., eds., *Taiping yulan* 太平御覽 (Song woodblock edition; reprinted Taipei: Taiwan Shangwu yinshuguan, 1968), 4008–15.

31. *Yinqueshan Han mu zhujian (er)*, 253.

32. *Yinqueshan Han mu zhujian (er)*, 253.

33. See for example the breed standards for the Brazilian mastiff (fila brasileiro), online at http://www.filabrasileiroassn.com/breed-standard.html (accessed 21 May 2017).

34. Chen Enzhi 陳恩志, "Xiang ma shu yuanliu he gudai yangma wenming" 相馬術源流和古代養馬文明, *Nongye kaogu* 農業考古 2 (1987): 339–46.

35. He Runkun 賀潤坤, "Zhongguo gudai zui zao de xiangma jing–Yunmeng Qin jian 'Rishu–Ma' pian" 中國古代最早的相馬經–雲夢秦簡 "日書 • 馬" 篇, *Xibei nongye daxue xuebao* 西北農業大學學報 17.3 (1989): 9; see also Yu Xin, "Chutu wenxian," 137.

36. Discussed in Fu Junlian 伏俊璉 and Yang Xiaohua 楊曉華, "Dunhuang wenxue de shangyuan" 敦煌文學的上源, *Heilongjiang shehui kexue* 黑龍江社會科學 3 (2011): 82–84; and Yu Xin, "Chutu wenxian," 136–41.

37. *Dunhuang Han jian*, 250, photo 81 (no. 843).

38. A stricter translation might read: "Bole, in the evaluation of horses, had [consideration of] form: / The teeth [at age] fourteen or fifteen will be flat below" 伯樂相馬自有刑 (:形), 齒十四五當下平. There are a couple of difficulties with this text. One concerns the word choice, which seems clearly to have been tailored for the resulting rhyme. Another comes with the word *chi* 齒, which literally means "tooth, teeth" and is also used to refer to the age of horses. Here it blends both senses.

39. *Dunhuang Han jian*, 301, photo 185 (no. 2094). This reading and punctuation incorporates information from Luo Zhenyu and Wang Guowei, *Liusha zhuijian*, 95; Yu Xin, "Chutu wenxian," 136–37; and *Kankan goi*, s.vv., *wei* 胃 and *pi* 脾. The photograph in *Dunhuang Han jian* is unclear and there seems to be no better image available. As such, caution is warranted in interpreting this text—as Donald Harper reminded me in an email (11 July 2017).

40. Luo Zhenyu and Wang Guowei, *Liusha zhuijian* 流沙墜簡 (1914; Beijing: Zhonghua shuju, 1993), 95. On the *Qimin yaoshu*, see, for example, Shi Shenghan 石聲漢, ed., *Qimin yaoshu jinshi* 齊民要術今釋 (Beijing: Zhonghua shuju, 2009), 498.

41. The following incorporates information from my article on this text; see Charles Sanft, "Evaluating Swords: Introduction and Translation of a How-To Guide from the Han-Xin Period," *Early China* 39 (2016): 231–53.

42. Liu Jinhua 劉金華, "Han 'Xiang jian dao ce' lüeshuo" 漢 "相劍刀冊"略說, *Zhongguo lishi wenwu* 中國歷史文物 3 (2008): 58; Ma Mingda 馬

明達, *Shuo jian conggao* 說劍叢搞, revised edition (Beijing: Zhonghua shuju, 2007), 40–42.

43. *Hanshu*, 1775; and see, for example, Li Ling, *Zhongguo fangshu kao*, 86–87; Zhong Shaoyi 鐘少昊, "Gu xiang jian shu chu lun," 358–59; Han Hua 韓華 and Di Xiaoxia 狄曉霞, "Juyan Han jian 'Xiang bao jian dao' ce yanjiu zongshu" 居延漢簡 "相寶劍刀" 冊研究綜述, *Sichou zhi lu* 絲綢之路 20 (2009): 17.

44. Liu Jinhua, "Han 'Xiang jian dao ce' lüe shuo"; Gansusheng bowuguan Han jian zhenglizu, "Juyan Han jian 'Xiang jian dao' ce shiwen," 78.

45. Gansusheng bowuguan Han jian zhenglizu, "Juyan Han jian 'Xiang jian dao' ce shiwen,' 78; see, for example, Han Hua and Di Xiaoxia, "Juyan Han jian 'Xiang bao jian dao' ce yanjiu zongshu," 17; cf. also Liu Jinhua, "Han 'Xiang jian dao ce,'" 59, who himself disagrees.

46. He Maohuo 何茂活, "Juyan Han jian '相劍刀' 冊釋讀析疑," in *Jianduxue yanjiu* 簡牘學研究, no. 5, ed. Xibei shifan daxue lishi wenhua xueyuan 西北師範大學歷史文化學院 and Gansu jiandu bowuguan 甘肅簡牘博物館 (Lanzhou: Gansu renmin chubanshe, 2014), 96; Liu Jinhua, "Han 'Xiang jian dao ce,'" 59–60.

47. See the dates in the materials from that location in *Juyan xinjian shijiao*, 125–47; see also, for example, Ma Mingda, *Shuo jian conggao*, 40–42, who discusses the role of these materials as providing a terminus ante quem for "Evaluating Swords." See also Gansusheng bowuguan Han jian zhengli zu 甘肅省博物館漢簡整理組, "Juyan Han jian 'Xiang jian dao' ce shiwen" 居延漢簡 "相劍刀" 冊釋文, *Dunhuangxue jikan* 敦煌學輯刊 3 (1983): 78. See also Chen Li 陳力, "'Juyan xinjian' xiang lishan daojian zhujian xuanshi" "居延新簡"相利善刀劍諸簡選釋, *Kaogu yu wenwu* 考古與文物 6 (2002): 70; and Zhong Shaoyi 鐘少異, "Gu xiang jian shu chu lun" 古相劍術芻論, *Kaogu* 考古 4 (1994): 361, which cite this dating.

48. On this distinction in a somewhat different context, see Richter, *The Embodied Text*, 26–27 and passim.

49. This argued by Ma Mingda, *Shuo jian conggao*, 40–42. See also Donald B. Wagner, *Iron and Steel in Ancient China* (Leiden: Brill, 1996), 195–97; Zhong Shaoyi, "Gu xiang jian shu chu lun," 358–59, brings up the emergence of the *dao* in context of discussing the *Hanshu* "Yiwenzhi" listing of *Xiang bao jiandao*. Many scholars do not make the explicit division of manuscript and content with regard to periodization and generally date the Juyan sword text following the dates of other material in E.P.T. 40; see, for example, Zhong Shaoyi, "Gu xiang jian shu," 361; and Chen Li, "'Juyan xinjian' xiang lishan," 70.

50. Ma Mingda, "Zhongguo gudai de xiang jian fa" 中國古代的相劍法, *Wenshi zhishi* 文史知識 1 (2000): 59–61.

51. Ma Mingda, *Shuo jian conggao*, 35–36; cf. Liu Jinhua "Han 'Xiang jian dao ce,'" 60–61.

52. *Juyan Han jian jia yi bian*, 8, 81; *Juyan Han jiao shiwen hejiao*, 20–21, 192 (nos. 13.6, 118.18).

53. *Juyan xinjian shijiao*, 723–24 (E.P.T. 68.20, 68.25, 68.26A).

54. *Juyan Han jian jia yi bian*, 105 (no. 148.45); *Dunhuang Han jian*, 317, photo 187 (no. 2462).

55. *Juyan xinjian shijiao*, 727 (E.P.T. 68.72).

56. *Juyan Han jian jia yi bian*, 162; *Juyan Han jian shiwen hejiao*, 381 (no. 232.31).

57. *Dunhuang Han jian shiwen*, 111 (no. 1069).

58. *Juyan Han jian jia yi bian*, 7; *Juyan Han jian shiwen hejiao*, 17 (no. 10.37).

59. *Juyan Han jian jia yi bian*, 223, 227; *Juyan Han jian shiwen hejiao*, 524, 534 (nos. 334.33, 340.39).

60. See, for example, *Juyan Han jian jia yi bian*, 158, 200, 223; *Juyan Han jian shiwen hejiao*, 370, 470, 471, 525 (nos. 228.18, 280.4, 280.8, 334.47).

61. *Juyan xin jian shijiao*, 278 (E.P.T. 51:84).

62. *Juyan Han jian jia yi bian*, 194; *Juyan Han jian shiwen hejiao*, 455 (no. 271.1).

63. *Juyan Han jian jia yi bian*, 183; *Juyan Han jian shiwen hejiao*, 427 (no. 258.7).

64. See Sanft, "Evaluating Swords." The discussion here incorporates information from the introduction and notes there.

65. These are strips E.P.T.40:202–E.P.T.40:207; see *Juyan xinjian shijiao*, 145–46. My transcription and translation draw upon a number of sources, which I list here. In addition, my article "Evaluating Swords: Introduction and Translation of a How-To Guide from the Han-Xin Period" discusses in some detail particular problems and questions of interpretation. I refer the interested reader there. Transcription and photos of the original wooden strips are in Hu Zhi 胡之, ed., *Neimenggu Juyan Han jian (er)* 內蒙古居延漢簡(二) (Chongqing: Chongqing chubanshe, 2008), transcription and main photo 13, close-up photos 14–19; see also the transcription in *Juyan Xinjian shijiao*, loc. cit.; and He Maohuo 何茂活, "Juyan Han jian 'Xiang jian dao' ce shidu xiyi" 居延漢簡 "相劍刀"冊釋讀析疑, in *Jianduxue yanjiu* 簡牘學研究, no. 5, ed. Xibei shifan daxue lishi wenhua xueyuan 西北師大學歷史文化學院 and Gansu jiandu bowuguan 甘肅簡牘博物館 (Lanzhou: Gansu renmin chubanshe, 2014), 85–98, including his translation of the text on 97. The first published transcription of this text was in Gansusheng bowuguan Han jian zhenglizu 甘肅省博物館漢簡整理組, "Juyan Han jian 'Xiang jian dao' ce shiwen" 居延漢簡 "相劍刀"冊釋文, *Dunhuangxu jikan* 敦煌學輯刊 3 (1983): 78. In the course of reading the text, I referred also to Chen Li 陳力, " 'Juyan

xinjian' xiang lishan daojian zhujian xuanshi" "居延新簡"相利善刀劍諸簡選
釋, *Kaogu yu wenwu* 考古與文物 6 (2002): 70–73; and Ma Mingda, *Shuo jian conggao*, 27–44. For graphic and phonetic substitutions, I referred to Wang Hui, *Guwenzi tongjia shili*, and Gao Heng, *Guzi tongjia huidian*.

66. For the characteristics of and processes involved in creating steel in the Han period, see Wagner, *Iron and Steel in Ancient China*.

67. For citation information on this and subsequent sections of this text, see Sanft, "Evaluating Swords."

68. Ma and Zhang and others have 惡 here. All readers agree that in this context it is a form of ə/*wu* 惡, "bad; to be bad."

69. *Juyan xinjian*, 167, photo 375; *Juyan xin jian shi jiao*, 600 (EPT 59:343). I translate this with reference to the commentary on the parallel in *Liji zhushu*, 345; and Sun Xidan 孫希旦 (1736–1784), *Liji jijie* 禮記集解 (Beijing: Zhonghua shuju, 1989), 495–96. NB: Ma and Zhang have 齋 for the twenty-fourth character, whereas *Juyan xinjian* has 齊. The photograph of this fragment in *Juyan xinjian* supports the latter transcription and I follow it. Shen Songjin, *Ershi shiji jianboxue yanjiu*, 263, discusses this fragment.

70. For the processes of brewing beer (which he translates as "wine"), see H. T. Huang, *Science and Civilisation in China: Volume 6, Biology and Biological Technology, Part V: Fermentations and Food Science* (Cambridge: Cambridge University Press, 2000), 153–68. Huang discusses the workings of fermentation starter, which he calls "ferment," and also *nie* 糵 (written 蘖 in the fragment I consider), "sprouted grain," that is, "malt." What little understanding I have of modern beer-making I owe to Tore Olsson, my colleague and an accomplished home brewer.

71. *Liji zhushu*, 345. There are some very minor textual variations between the received *Liji* and this fragment, but nothing that creates doubt about the textual parallel.

72. See, for example, *Dunhuang Xuanquan Han jian shicui*, 148–49 (I 0112 3: 61–78), an accounting of provisions that refers to "self-made beer" 自治酒.

73. See Charles Sanft, "Environment and Law in Early Imperial China (3rd c. BCE–1st c. CE): Qin and Han Statutes Concerning Natural Resources," *Environmental History* 15.4 (2010): 701–21.

Chapter Seven. Cultural Texts

1. Martin Kern, "Ritual, Text, and the Formation of the Canon: Historical Transformations of *Wen* in Early China," *T'oung Pao* 87 (2001): 43–91; Beecroft, *Authorship and Cultural Identity in Early Greece and China*, 8–9, 188, 205–16, 280–81.

2. Johnson, "Chinese Popular Literature and Its Contexts."

3. For example, to the putative Qi *Lunyu* 齊論語; see Wang Chuning 王楚寧 and Zhang Yuzheng 張予正, "Jianshui jinguan Han jian 'Qi *Lunyu*' de zhengli" 肩水金關漢簡 "齊論語"的整理 (online at http://www.kaogu.cn/cn/kaoguyuandi/kaogusuibi/2017/0816/59268.html, dated 16 August 2017, accessed 5 December 2017); see also my discussion in Charles Sanft, "Questions about the Qi *Lunyu*," *T'oung Pao* 104.1–2 (2018): 189–94.

4. *Shangshu zhengyi* 尚書正義, 9.128, 2.21; for text and annotated translation, including information about paleographic aspects, see Sanft, "Edict," 178–79, lines 1 and 8, and accompanying notes.

5. I discuss this at length in Sanft, "Edict." In the appendix to that article I show the extant of overlap between the inscription and parallels in the *Record of Ritual* (*Li ji*) and other texts. The image accompanying the article shows the border, which was part of the original.

6. *Jianshui jinguan*, 5: 244 (73 EJC: 607); translated with reference to *Han shu*, 6.169, and Wang Xianqian, *Han shu bu zhu*, 61.

7. Wang Chuning and Zhang Yuzheng, "Jianshui jinguan Han jian 'Qi *Lunyu*' de zhengli"; Wang and Zhang acknowledge the connections to other classical texts that I discuss, but they prefer to attribute this fragment to a Qi version of *Analects*; see also discussion in my "Questions about the Qi *Lunyu*."

8. See the phonological information given in *Hanyu dacidian*, s.vv. *cuan* 篡 and *guan* 貫.

9. *Han shu*, 6.169.

10. *Maoshi zhengyi*, 12–1.400.

11. *Han shu*, 6.174.

12. *Maoshi zhengyi*, 7–1.252.

13. Nylan, *The Five "Confucian" Classics*, 91–104; Lewis, *Writing and Authority*, 163–76.

14. *Shangshu zhengyi*, 12.173; the text inserted into the translation is on the basis of the *Shangshu* parallel. The first part of this text is also quoted in *Zuozhuan zhushu* 左傳注疏, 29.501.

15. *Lunyu zhushu*, 16.146.

16. *Juyan xinjian shijiao*, 916 (E.S.C. 106A).

17. See *Lunyu zhushu*, 16.146.

18. Hebeisheng wenwu yanjiusuo 河北省文物研究所, *Dingzhou Han mu zhujian Lunyu* 定州漢墓竹簡論語 (Beijing: Wenwu chubanshe, 1997), 77.

19. Hunter, *Confucius Beyond the* Analects, 165–206.

20. Mark Csikszentmihalyi, "Confucius and the *Analects* in the Hàn," in *Confucius and the* Analects: *New Essays*, ed. Bryan W. Van Norden (Oxford: Oxford University Press, 2002), 145–49.

21. *Jianshui jinguan*, 3.21 (73 EJT 24:833); *Lunyu zhushu*, 17.157; translated with reference to Yang Bojun, *Lunyu yizhu*, 188.

22. The chapter is "Yang Huo" 陽貨; see *Lunyu zhushu*, 17.157 for both.

23. There are some thirty-two graphs between the two sections in the *Lunyu* version of this text; see *Lunyu zhushu*, 17.157. Some variation is likely due to varying conventions in textual reproduction.

24. Hu Pingsheng and Zhang Defang, *Dunhuang Xuanquan Han jian shicui*, 175 (no. 258); for the parallel, see *Lunyu zhushu*, 19.172–73; translated with reference to Yang Bojun, *Lunyu yizhu*, 202.

25. In the received version of this text, the phrase "I have heard it from the Master" is written in both instances 吾聞諸夫子, with *fuzi* 夫子 for Master instead of just *zi* 子. Also, the particles *ye zhe* 也者 are reversed in the received version, giving *zhe ye* 者也. Finally, the received version has the particle *ye* 也 after *xiao* 孝, "filial(ity)," which is absent from the Xuanquanzhi fragment. The semantic difference in context for all of these is negligible. In the textual note to his version of this text, Ruan Yuan points out that the Han dynasty "stone classics" (*shijing* 石經) version of the text writes just *zi* instead of *fuzi* at the first instance (he is silent about the second) and has *ye zhe*, not *zhe ye*; see *Lunyu zhushu*, 176.

26. See also Paul van Els, "Confucius' Sayings Entombed: On Two Han Dynasty Bamboo *Analects* Manuscripts," in *The Analects Revisited: New Perspectives on the Dating of a Classic*, ed. Michael Hunter and Martin Kern (Leiden: Brill, 2018); Kyung-ho Kim, "A Study of Excavated Bamboo and Wooden-Strip *Analects*: The Spread of Confucianism and Chinese Script," *Sungkyun Journal of East Asian Studies* 11.1 (2011): 59–88.

27. Hu Pingsheng and Zhang Defang, *Dunhuang Xuanquan Han jian shicui*, 176 (259, II 0114 5: 71). The absence of a larger context or received parallel makes my translation of this necessarily tentative. Cf. the translation of this fragment in Kim, "A Study of Excavated Bamboo and Wooden-Strip Analects," 68–69, and discussion throughout.

28. Wang Chuning and Zhang Yuzheng, "Jianshui jinguan Han jian 'Qi *Lunyu*' de zhengli."

29. Hebeisheng wenwu yanjiusuo, *Dingzhou Han mu zhujian Lunyu*, 73.

30. Cf. Wang Chuning and Zhang Yuzheng, "Jianshui jinguan Han jian 'Qi *Lunyu*' de zhengli," which asserts just that.

31. *Jianshui jinguan*, 3:135 (73 EJT 31:141); for the parallel, see *Maoshi zhengyi*, 17–2.600; cf. translation of the *Shijing* version in Arthur Waley, trans., *The Book of Songs*, ed. with additional translations by Joseph R. Allen (New York: Grove Press, 1996), 247.

32. *Xiaojing zhushu* 孝經注疏, 3.28–29; the parallel text comes on 28.

33. Rather than write *ni* 尼 (:昵), the received *Shijing* has *er* 爾. In context, both mean "close," so the sense is not altered by this shift.

34. See Wang Xianqian, ed., *Shi sanjia yi jishu* 詩三家義集疏 (Taipei: Mingwen shuju, 1988), 884–88.

35. Lai Guolong, "Lun Zhanguo Qin Han xieben wenhua zhong wenben de liudong yu guding" 論戰國秦漢寫本文化中文本的流動與固定, in *Jian bo* 簡帛, no. 2, ed. Wuhan daxue jianbo yanjiu zhongxin 武漢大學簡帛研究中心 (Shanghai: Shanghai guji chubanshe, 2007), 525–26; see also Chen Mengjia 陳夢家 (1911–1966), *Han jian zhuishu* 漢簡綴述 (Beijing: Zhonghua shuju, 1980), 302–3.

36. *Jianshui jinguan*, 3:128 (73 EJT 31:44A–B + T30:55A–B).

37. *Xiaojing zhushu*, 2.22.

38. From "Xiaomin" 小旻 (no. 195); *Maoshi zhengyi*, 12–2.414; cf. also the translation of these lines in Waley, *The Book of Songs*, 175.

39. *Jianshui jinguan*, 3:133 (73 EJT 31:102A–B). There are ditto marks on the original manuscript that I forgo here. Since their exact distribution does not fit with repetition as far as I can tell, I believe they serve here to mark emphasis. The poem is "Xiaowan" 小宛 (no. 196); *Maoshi zhengyi*, 12–3.419–20. My translation generally follows Cheng Junying 程俊英 and Jiang Jianyuan 蔣見元, *Shijing zhu xi* 詩經注析 (Beijing: Zhonghua shuju, 1991), 597–98; cf. also Waley, *The Book of Songs*, 176. For examples of citations in a variety of Han texts, see Wang Xianqian, *Shi sanjia yi jishu*, 694–95.

40. *Jianshui jinguan*, 3:135 (73 EJT 31:139).

41. The close parallel is found in *Fayan*; see Wang Rongbao 汪榮寶, ed., *Fayan yishu* 法言義疏 (Beijing: Zhonghua shuju, 1987), 18.515.

42. Wang Rongbao, *Fayan yishu*, 18.515, points to similar ideas and phrasings in the "Zi dao" 子道 chapter of *Xunzi* 荀子; see Wang Xianqian 王先謙 (1842–1918), ed., *Xunzi jijie* 荀子集解 (Beijing: Zhonghua shuju, 1988), 20.533.

43. See *Liji zhushu*, 24.474.

44. *Jianshui jinguan*, 3:14 (73 EJT 21:58).

45. Li Xiangfeng 梨翔鳳, ed., *Guanzi jiaozhu* 管子校注 (Beijing: Zhonghua shuju, 2004), 1.48; on the dating of *Guanzi*, see W. Allyn Rickett, "Kuan tzu," in *Early Chinese Texts: A Bibliographical Guide*, ed. Michael Loewe (Berkeley: Society for the Study of Early China, 1993), 247–48.

46. For example, *Shiji*, 31.1463, 78.2391, 86.2517; *Hou Han shu*, 28A.963, 75.2449; Zhang Lie 張烈, ed., *Liang Han ji* 兩漢紀 (Beijing: Zhonghua shuju, 2002), 15.266; and Shi Guangying 石光瑛, ed., *Xin xu jiaoshi* 新序校釋 (Beijing: Zhonghua shuju, 2001), 9.1206.

47. *Jianshui jinguan*, 3: 133 (73 EJT 31:101A–B).

48. Peng Duo 彭鐸, ed., *Qianfulun jiaozheng* 潛夫論校正 (Beijing: Zhonghua shuju, 1985), 36.473; *Guoyu* 國語, ed. Shanghai shifan daxue

guji zhenglizu 上海師範大學古籍整理組 (Shanghai: Shanghai guji chubanshe, 1978), 21.658.

49. *Jianshui jinguan*, 3:128 (73 EJT 31:42A–B).

50. See, for example, *Zuozhuan zhengyi*, 11.188; *Shiji*, 39.1642, 44.1835; Wang Liqi 王利器, ed., *Fengsu tongyi jiaozhu* 風俗通義校注 (Beijing: Zhonghua shuju, 1981), 1.34.

51. See Kim, "A Study of Excavated Bamboo and Wooden-Strip Analects."

52. See Olivia Milburn, *The Spring and Autumn Annals of Master Yan* (Leiden: Brill, 2016), particularly her discussion of recovered texts, 13–42. I learned much about Master Yan's ubiquity from Andrew Meyer, "Chronicle, Masters Text, or Other? The *Yanzi chunqiu* and the Question of Genre" (presentation at the Fifth Annual Conference of the Society for the Study of Early China, 16 March 2017); he also referred me to Milburn's work (email, 22 March 2017).

53. *Eji'na Han jian shiwen jiaozheng*, 29 (99ES18SH1:1–2). Note that I pass over the first few graphs of the fragment, which are impossible to render due to damage to the document.

54. Zhang Defang, "Qiantan Hexi Han jian he Dunhuang bianwen de yuanyuan guanxi" 淺談河西漢簡和敦煌變文的淵源關係, *Dunhuangxue jikan* 敦煌學輯刊 2 (2005): 52–56; see also Wu Zeyu 吳則虞, ed., *Yanzi chunqiu jishi* 晏子春秋集釋 (Beijing: Zhonghua shuju, 1982), 5.304.

55. *Juyan xinjian shijiao*, 316–17; *Juyan xin jian*, 86, photo volume 192 (E.P.T. 51:390); Milburn, *The Spring and Autumn Annals of Master Yan*, 24, mentions and translates this fragment; Li Zhenhong, "Handai Juyan tunshu lizu de jingshen wenhua shenghuo," 240–41, also discusses it.

56. Original transcription of this strip in *Dunhuan Han jian*, 238 (no. 496), photo 25. Qiu Xigui 裘錫圭, "Han jian zhong suojian Han Peng gushi de xin ziliao" 漢簡中所見韓朋故事的新資料, *Fudan xuebao (shehui kexue ban)* 復旦學報 (社會科學版) 3 (1999): 110, published a new transcription, which subsequent scholars have followed. The original version of the article had unclear reproductions of some characters, which are not present in the reprinted version; see Qiu Xigui, *Zhongguo chutu wenxian shijiang* 中國出土文現十講 (Shanghai: Fudan daxue chubanshe, 2004), 399. Qiu, "Han jian zhong," 111, discusses reading *can* 幹 as Han 韓 and *beng* 倗 as Peng 朋; on these borrowings, see also Wang Hui, *Guwenzi tonjia shili*, 393–94, 851–52; and Gao Heng, *Guzi tongjia hudian*, 43–44, 171.

57. Qiu Xigui, "Han jian zhong suojian Han Peng gushi de xin ziliao."

58. A number of scholars have treated these links, including Qiu Xigui, "Han jian zhong suojian Han Peng gushi de xin ziliao"; Fu Junlian 伏俊璉 and Yang Aijun 楊愛軍, "Han Peng gushi kaoyuan" 韓朋故事考源, 3 (2007): 91–93; Liu Yuejin 劉躍進, "Qin-Han jianbo zhong de wenxue shijie—Qin-

Han wenxue yanjiu xinziliao zhi yi" 秦漢簡帛中的文學世界—秦漢文學研究新資料之一, *Xinzhou shifan xueyuan xuebao* 忻州師範學院學報 17.2 (2001): 6–13, 37; Zong Fan 蹤凡, "Liang Han gushifu de biaoxian ticai ji wenxue chengjiu" 兩漢故事賦的表現題材及文學成就 1 (2005): 138–43; Shen Songjin 沈頌金, "Chutu jianbo yu wenxueshi yanjiu" 出土簡帛與文學史研究, *Qi-Lu xuekan* 齊魯學刊 6 (2004): 73–75; Pei Yongliang 裴永亮, "Han Peng gushi de wenxue chengchuan" 韓朋故事的文學承傳, *Yuwen jiaoxue tongxun* 語文教學通訊 2 (2015): 58–59.

59. Gan Bao 干寶 (fl. ca. early fourth century), *Soushenji*, *Siku quanshu* edition, 11.12a–13a.

60. Guo Tiena 郭鐵娜, "Handai minjian aiqing gushi de 'Han Peng moshi' yanjiu" 漢代民間愛情故事的 "韓朋模式," *Shenyang daxue xuebao* 沈陽大學學報 20.4 (2008): 63–66.

61. Fu Junlian and Yang Aijun, "Han Peng gushi kaoyuan"; Qiu Xigui, "Han jian zhong suojian Han Peng gushi de xin ziliao."

62. Fu Junlian and Yang Aijun, "Han Peng gushi kaoyuan"; cf. Zong Fan, "Liang Han gushifu," who acknowledges the same characteristics, but concentrates on them as reflecting the conventions of narrative rhapsody.

63. Qiu, "Han jian zhong," 111.

64. The number here is "ten thousand [times] ten thousand," which seems more easily understood if multiplied to give "one hundred million." Obviously no specific number is intended. "Miles" translates *li* 里, a unit of distance about one-third of a modern mile long, but is close enough in context.

65. This transcription is that of Qiu Xigui, "Tian Zhang jian bushi" 田章簡補釋, in *Zhongguo chutu wenxian shijiang* 中國出土文獻十講 (Shanghai: Fudan daxue chubanshe, 2004), 394; prior transcription in *Dunhuang Han jian*, 309; photo 71 (no. 2289).

66. For example, Zong Fan 蹤凡, "Liang Han gushifu de biaoxian ticai ji wenxue chengjiu" 兩漢故事賦的表現題材及文學成就, *Shehui kexue jikan* 社會科學輯刊 1 (2005): 39–41.

67. See Zhang Feng 張鳳, *Han-Jin xichui mujian huibian* 漢晉西陲木簡彙編, in *Hanjian wenxian yanjiu sizhong* 漢簡文獻研究四種 (Beijing: Beijing tushuguan chubanshe, 2007), 24; and Aurel Stein's notes in Maspero, *Les documents chinois*, 23.

68. *Eji'na Han jian*, 104 (2002ESCSF1:6).

69. See Liu Xiang 劉向 (ca. 77–ca. 6 BCE), ed., *Zhanguo ce* 戰國策 (Shanghai: Shanghai guji chubanshe, 1998), 4.163; and Chen Qiyou 陳奇猷, *Han Feizi xin jiaozhu* 韓非子新校注 (Shanghai: Shanghai guji chubanshe, 2000), 803, 820.

70. Pan Chonggui 潘重規, ed., *Dunhuang bianwen xinshu* 敦煌變文新書 (Taipei: Wenjin chubanshe, 1994), 1230–33.

71. Zhang Defang, "Qiantan Hexi Han jian he Dunhuang bianwen," 52–56; cf. Chen Pan 陳槃, Han-Jin yijian shixiao qizhong 漢晉遺簡識小七種 (Shanghai: Shanghai guji chubanshe, 2009), 248–56.

72. Chen Pan, Han Jin yijian, 251, notes the stories probably did not begin with set forms; see also discussion in Michael Nylan, "Manuscript Culture in Late Western Han, and the Implications for Authors and Authority," Journal of Chinese Literature and Culture 1.1–2 (2014): 155–85.

73. Qiu Xigui, "Tian Zhang jian bushi," 394–95 and passim.

74. While there is disagreement about whether most oracle bone inscriptions record queries and responses, scholars agree that at least some do; see Qiu Xigui, "An Examination of Whether the Charges in Shang Oracle-Bone Inscriptions Are Questions," Early China 14 (1989): 77–114.

75. See Huang Hui 黃暉, ed., Lunheng jiaoshi 論衡校釋 (Beijing: Zhonghua shuju, 1990), 11.469–84.

76. Chen Pan, Han-Jin yijian, 253–55, gives numerous examples.

77. Luo Zhenyu and Wang Guowei, Liusha zhuijian, 82–83.

78. Shi ji, 1.6.

79. Han shu, 30.1731, 30.1759.

80. Dunhuang Han jian, 301, photo 166 (no. 2103). Note that this text writes Li Mo 力墨, a variant of Li Mu; see Wang Hui, Guwenzi tongjia shili, 256.

81. Dunhuang Han jian, 300, no photo (no. 2069).

82. The discussion of poetry draws from Li Zhengyu 李正宇, "Shishi Dunhuang Han jian 'Jiao hui shi' " 試釋敦煌漢簡 "教誨詩," in Zhuanxingqi de Dunhuang yuyan wenxue–jinian Zhou Shaoliang xiansheng xianshi san zhounian xueshu yantaohui lunwenji 轉型期的敦煌語言文學—紀念周紹良先生仙逝三周年學術研討會論文集, ed. Yan Tingliang 顏廷亮 (Lanzhou: Gansu renmin chubanshe, 2010), 69–72; Liu Yuejin 劉躍進, "Qin-Han jianbo zhong de wenxue shijie—Qin-Han wenxue yanjiu xinziliao zhi yi" 秦漢簡帛中的文學世界—秦漢文學研究新資料之一, Xinzhou shifan xueyuan xuebao 忻州師範學院學報 17.2 (2001): 6–13, 37.

83. This transcription based on Dunhuang Han jian, 307, photo 169 (no. 2253); my reading, translation, and discussion are informed by Li Ling 李零, Jianbo gushu yu xueshu yuanliu 簡帛古書與學術源流 (Beijing: Sanlian shudian, 2004), 348; Li Zhengyu, "Shishi Dunhuang Han jian 'Jiaohui shi,' " 69–72; Xu Yunhe 許雲和, "Dunhuang Han jian 'Fengyu shi' shilun" 敦煌漢簡 "風雨詩" 試論, Shoudu shifan daxue xuebao (shehui kexueban) 首都師範大學學報(社會科學版) 2 (2011): 85–86; Long Wenling 龍文玲, "Lun Handai fengsui jiandu de wenxue shiliao jiazhi" 論漢代烽燧簡牘的文學史料價值, Xueshu luntan 學術論壇 11 (2014): 90–91.

84. On this loan, see Gao Heng, Guzi tongjia huidian, 596–97.

85. Wang Hui, Guwenzi tongjia shili, 223–24.

86. Shen Songjin 沈頌金, "Chutu jianbo yu wenxueshi yanjiu" 出土簡帛與文學史研究, *Qi-Lu xuekan* 齊魯學刊 6 (2004): 75.

87. Li Zhengyu, "Shishi Dunhuang Han jian 'Jiao hui shi'"; Xu Yunhe, "Dunhuang Han jian 'Fengyu shi' shilun."

88. *Dunhuang Han jian*, 297 (no. 2007); Fu Junlian 伏俊璉 and Yang Xiaohua 楊曉華, "Dunhuang wenxue de shangyuan" 敦煌文學的上源, *Heilongjiang shehui kexue* 黑龍江社會科學 3 (2011): 82; Li Zhengyu, "Shishi Dunhuang Han jian," 69.

89. *Juyan Xinjian shijiao*, 130 (E.P.T. 40.43); Long Wenling, "Lun Handai fengsui jiandu," 90.

90. See, for example, the discussion in Oliver Weingarten, "The Singing Sage: Rhymes in Confucius Dialogues," *Bulletin of the School of Oriental and African Studies* 79.3 (2016): 581–607.

91. Hayashi Minao 林巳奈夫, *Kandai no bunbutsu* 漢代の文物, second edition (Kyoto: Hoyu shoten, 1996), 98–100; Sun Ji 孫機, *Handai wuzhi wenhua ziliao tushuo* 漢代物質文化資料圖說, revised edition (Shanghai: Shanghai guji chubanshe, 2008), 467–68; Xi Wenqian 郗文倩, "Handai gangmao ji qi mingwen kaolun" 漢代剛卯及其銘文考論, *Fujian Jiangxia xueyuan xuebao* 福建江夏學院學報 4.4 (2014): 93–100; Zhao Chongliang, *Xingyi shubei*, 341–44; Harper, "Daybooks," 121–22. Qu Zhongrong 瞿中溶 (1769–1842), *Yizai tuyu tulu* 奕載古玉圖錄 (Rui'an: Dai Guochen 戴國琛 woodblock edition, postface dated 1930), 88a–94a, discusses *gangmao*, including on page 90 a detailed consideration of their rhymes. See also Derk Bodde, *Festivals in Classical China: New Year and Other Annual Observances During the Han Dynasty, 206 B.C.–A.D. 220* (Princeton: Princeton University Press, 1975), 304–6, who translates a fragment like the one I do; and Donald J. Harper, *Early Chinese Medical Literature: The Mawangdui Medical Manuscripts* (London: Kegan Paul International, 1997), 260n4.

Chapter Eight. Letters

1. In this chapter I provide translations of representative example letters, although in the interest of brevity I discuss some without translation. Han-time letters are numerous, if mostly fragmentary, and I discuss only a selection here. Those interested in examining more examples may wish to refer to Enno Giele's translation of a selection; see Giele, "Private Letter Manuscripts," 403–74.

2. See, for example, Ma Yi, "Juyan jian 'Xuan yu Yousun shaofu shu'–Han dai bianli de siren tongxin" 居延簡 "宣與幼孫少婦書"–漢代邊吏的私人通信, *Nandu xuetan (renwen shehui kexue xuebao)* 南都學壇(人文社會科學學報) 30.3 (2010): 1–9, and other articles cited in this chapter.

3. Li Xueqin 李學勤, "Chudu Liye Qin jian" 初讀里耶秦簡, *Wenwu* 文物 1 (2003): 74–76; Chen Zhiguo 陳治國, "Cong Liye Qin jian kan Qin de gongwen zhidu" 從里耶秦簡看秦的公文制度, *Zhongguo lishi wenwu* 中國歷史文物 1 (2007): 61–69; Chen Zhi, *Juyan Han jian yanjiu*, 48–51; Giele, "Private Letter Manuscripts," 403–17.

4. Liu Heng 劉恒, *Lidai chidu shufa* 歷代尺牘書法 (Beijing: Zhishi chubanshe, 1992), 6, notes that in early letters, it is difficult to distinguish personal and official natures, and that letters were written for both kinds of purposes. Cf. Li Baotong and Huang Zhaohong, *Jianduxue jiaocheng*, 269–71, who discuss excavated letters and on 270 propose a clear division between letters asking for or inquiring about official matters from others. See also discussion of this point in Antje Richter, *Letters and Epistolary Culture in Early Medieval China* (Seattle: University of Washington Press, 2013), 40–41, 166n119, although her resolution of this issue is different from mine; and Giele, "Private Letter Manuscripts," 412–15.

5. Cf. Zhang Guoyan 張國豔, *Juyan Han jian xuci tongshi* 居延漢簡虛詞通釋 (Beijing: Zhonghua shuju, 2012), 236, who calls this a "modifier" without further explanation, presumably taking it as "other." But the formula 毋它急 occurs in cases where there is no initial exigency named (e.g., later in this letter) suggesting that pure "other" is not sufficient. Zhang Guoyan notes that the types of usage that *tuo* sees is broad and that with the exception of this specific phrase, seldom repeated. This, combined with the fact that it occurs in places without a "first" urgency, suggests a lexicalization of the phrase in a more general sense. See also Shen Gang 沈剛, *Juyan Han jian yuci huishi* 居延漢簡語詞匯釋 (Beijing: Kexue chubanshe, 2008), 47, who glosses this as equivalent to "without worry" and "without illness." While those readings do not seem to fit here, they support my contention that this is a lexicalized wish.

6. Zhang Guoyan, *Juyan Han jian xuci tongshi*, 49–50, lists this type of usage of *bu* 不, although not this example. Cf. Lin Jianming 林劍鳴, "Han jian zhong yifeng qiguai de xin" 漢簡中一封奇怪的信, *Shaanxi lishi bowuguan guankan* 陝西博物館館刊 1 (1994): 81; and Chen Zhi 陳直, *Juyan Han jian yanjiu* 居延漢簡解要 (Beijing: Zhonghua shuju, 2009), 473; Chen proposes and Lin agrees that *bu* 不 here should be read *fou* 否, which is a possibility. The sense ends up the same whether one follows Zhang or Lin and Chen.

7. Following Ma Yi, I take this graph to be the surname Liu 劉. The original transcription has *dui* 對, a word with many meanings including "facing, reply(ing)."

8. *Juyan Han jian jiayi bian*, 5 (no. 10.16A–B), photos jia–15; see also *Juyan Han jian shiwen hejiao*, 15; *Zhongguo jiandu jicheng*, 5:27. I read this letter with reference to Ma Yi, "Juyan jian 'Xuan yu Yousun shaofu shu,'" including her transcription and modern Chinese paraphrase; I referred also

to Chen Zhi, *Juyan Han jian jieyao*, 472–74; and Lin Jianming, "Han jian zhong yifeng qiguai de xin," 78–82; see also the discussion and translation in Giele, "Private Letters," 450–56.

9. See, for example, Chen Zhi, *Juyan Han jian yanjiu*, 472–74.

10. Ma Yi, "Juyan jian 'Xuan yu Yousun shaofu shu.'"

11. Ma Yi, "Juyan jian 'Xuan yu Yousun shaofu shu,'" 3.

12. Cf. Giele, "Private Letter Manuscripts," 452, who understands Zhu Youji to be the same person as Xuan.

13. The postscript tells us Yousun's surname is Liu, so the additional letter is directed to someone else.

14. I follow Wang Guanying 王冠英, "Han Xuanquanzhi yizhi chutu Yuan yu Zifang boshu xinzha kaoshi" 漢懸泉置遺址出土元與子方帛書信札考釋, *Zhongguo lishi bowuguan guankan* 中國歷史博物館館刊 1 (1998): 59, to take Kudao 苦道 as a toponym.

Although Wang does not explain his reading, he presumably notes, as I do, parallel instances in which toponyms appear that support this reading. *Kankan goi kōshō* lists a Ku Prefecture 苦縣 and the toponym Xidao 西道. Those names indicate that this understanding of Kudao is entirely in keeping with attested contemporary practice. But cf. *Jianshui Jinguan Han jian*, 3:106 (73 EJT 30:27A + T2621A), which has the phrase *ku dao* 苦道 in the sense of "difficult road," which is how Giele, "Private Letter Manuscripts," 432, understands it in this letter.

15. Lü Zidu and Lü An are two names for the same person, the former a courtesy name.

16. Gansusheng wenwu kaogu yanjiusuo, "Dunhuang Xuanquan Han jian shiwen xuan" 敦煌懸泉漢簡釋文選, *Wenwu* 5 (2000): 39–40; *Dunhuang Xuanquan Han jian shicui*, 187–91 (II 0114 3: 611); Wang Guanying, "Han Xuanquanzhi yizhi chutu Yuan yu Zifang boshu xinzha kaoshi," 58–61. I previously published a translation of this letter, without annotations, in Sanft, "Send Shoes: A Letter from Yuan to Zifang," *Renditions: A Chinese-English Translation Magazine* 79 (2013): 7–10. See also Richter, *Letters and Epistolary Culture*, 20–22, which includes discussion and partial translation; and discussion and translation in Giele, "Private Letter Manuscripts," 430–35.

17. See Giele, "Private Letter Manuscripts," 407–11.

18. Dunhuang *Han jian*, 295–96 (no. 1965 A–B), photo plate 158; *Dunhuang Han jian shiwen*, 209; *Shulehe liuyu chutu Han jian*, 59 (no. 430). There the wife is referred to as "madam" (*furen* 夫人).

19. *Juyan Han jian jiayi bian*, 53 (no. 73.9, recto only); photo *yi*–65; *Juyan Han jian shiwen hejiao*, 128; *Zhongguo jiandu jicheng*, 5:209–210.

20. Clanchy, *From Memory to Written Record*, 8, 127–34, 272–73.

21. *Juyan Han jian jiayi bian*, 109 (nos. 157.10A–B), photo plate *yi*–113; *Juyan Han jian shiwen hejiao*, 257; *Zhongguo jiandu jicheng*, 6:130–31.

22. See Barbieri-Low and Yates, *Law, State, and Society*, 729–43.

23. On the sense of *tong* 通 as a "summary account," see *Hanyu dacidian*, s.v. *tong*.

24. After examining the photo, which shows a small part of this graph, and considering the later appearance of the name An 安, I believe this first character to be An. The published transcriptions mark it illegible.

25. *Dunhuang Han jian*, 282 (no. 1612A–B), photo plates 189; *Dunhuang Han jian shiwen*, 167–68; *Shulehe liuyu chutu Han jian*, 38 (no. 74).

26. On the sense of *shili* 士吏 in this context, see *Kankan goi*, s.v. *shili*.

27. Wang Hui, *Guwenzi tongjia shili*, 308.

28. *Dunhuang Han jian*, 229 (no. 244A–B), photo plates 26–27; *Dunhuang Han jian shiwen*, 23–24; *Zhongguo jiandu jicheng*, 3:34; there is also a punctuated version in Rao Zongyi and Li Junming, *Xin Mang jian jizheng*, 90.

29. It is theoretically possible that he is actually using a very unusual courtesy name, but the existence of the surname Ni and the appearance of Shang later indicate this is a surname-name combination.

30. Chen Pan 陳槃 (1905–1999), *Han-Jin yijian shixiao qizhong* 漢晉遺簡識小七種 (1975; Shanghai: Shanghai guji chubanshe, 2009), 25–26. For examples of surname and name used in conjunction with *baiji*, see *Juyan xinjian shijiao*, 126 (EPT 40:7), 503 (EPT 56:178), 593 (EPT 59:272A), 609 (EPT 59:409); for *baiji* used with an official title and surname, see *Juyan xinjian shijiao*, 251 (EPT 50:139), 619 (EPT 59:525). I also found examples of it together with a title and both surname and name; see *Juyan xinjian shijiao*, 703–4 (EPT 65:381); and *Juyan Han jian shiwen hejiao*, 600 (502.14A, 505.38A, 505.43A); cf. Giele, "Private Letter Manuscripts," 452.

31. *Juyan xinjian shijiao*, 294 (EPT 51:203A–B); *Zhongguo jiandu jicheng*, 10:94.

32. *Juyan Han jian jiayi bian*, 236–37 (nos. 408.2A–B); photo plate yi–250; *Juyan Han jian shiwen hejiao*, 555; *Zhongguo jiandu jicheng*, 8:29.

33. *Fei zi er* 非自二 is obscure and I have tried to render it in as straightforward a fashion as possible, taking *er* 二 as a verb, "to double, to match."

34. Both versions have this graph but it is not visible on the photo plate in *Juyan Han jian jiayi bian* (yi–51). Presumably those editors are deducing on the basis of the name Chu legible later.

35. See the "Online Dictionary of Character Variants" (http://140.111.1.40/yitia/fra/fra03759.htm; accessed 31 December 2017), s.v. *wa* 襪.

36. *Juyan Han jian jiayi bian*, transcription, 290; photo, yi–292; *Juyan Han jian shiwen hejiao*, 677; *Zhongguo jiandu jicheng*, 8:251.

37. For instance, the edict inscribed on the wall at Xuanquanzhi took more than three months to reach that post after initial dissemination; see Sanft, "Edict of Monthly Ordinances," 137n16.

Conclusion

1. *Hou Han shu*, 1629. I follow the *Hanyu dacidian*, s.v. *song* 誦, to understand *song* as "read aloud." See also chapter 1. This story about Wang Chong is a favorite of my former doctoral advisor, Reinhard Emmerich, who spoke to me about it more than once.

2. Lothar von Falkenhausen, "Die Seiden mit chinesischen Inschriften," in *Die Textilien aus Palmyra: neue und alte Funde*, ed. Andreas Schmidt-Colinet and Annemarie Stauffer, with Khaled Al-As'ad (Mainz am Rhein: Verlag Philipp von Zabern, 2000), 70 (the source of the quote) and passim. I am indebted to Olivier Venture for bringing these silks and Falkenhausen's article about them to my attention.

3. Yao, *The Ancient Highlands of Southwest China*, 217–26 and passim.

4. Tomiya, *Monjo gyōsei*, 151–54, 215–16, and passim.

5. Johnson, "Chinese Popular Literature and Its Contexts."

6. Smith, *Understanding Reading*, 2–4, 55–71, 212–32; Gould and Marler, "Learning by Instinct," 74–85.

7. Clanchy, *From Memory to Written Record*, 8, 272–73.

8. See Yates, "The Qin Slips and Boards from Well No. 1, Liye."

9. Hsing, "Handai biansai lizu de junzhong jiaoyu"; Miyake, "Shin-Kan jidai no moji to shikiji"; Yates, "Soldiers, Scribes"; see also Harper, "Daybooks in the Context," 100–1.

10. See Sanft, "Edict," 130; Hu Pingsheng, "Maquanwan mujian yu cejian" 馬圈灣木簡與廁簡, in *Hu Pingsheng jiandu wenwu lunji* 胡平生簡牘文物論集 (Taipei: Lantai, 2000), 96–98; and Huang Hailie 黃海烈, "Liye Qin jian yu Qin difang guanzhi" 里耶秦簡與秦地方官制, *Beifang luncong* 北方論叢 6 (2005): 7.

11. This is from Pope's "An Essay on Criticism"; see *Alexander Pope*, with an introduction by John Bailey (London and Edinburgh: Thomas Nelson and Sons, [1924?]), 59.

12. Ong, *Orality and Literacy*, 50.

13. Sanft, "Population Records from Liye."

14. Yates, "Soldiers, Scribes."

15. Sanft, *Communication and Cooperation*.

16. Michael Puett, "The Temptations of Sagehood, or: The Rise and Decline of Sagely Writing in Early China," in *Books in Numbers: Seventy-Fifth Anniversary of the Harvard-Yenching Library*, ed. Wilt L. Idema (Cambridge: Harvard-Yenching Library, 2007), 23–43; quote 43.

Bibliography

Transcription Conventions for Paleographic Text

Except for bullet points (•) and ditto marks (=), which appear in some paleographic materials, the punctuation and other marks in the paleographic texts this book treats are modern additions.

□ marks an illegible graph

( ) marks an alternate reading

(:) marks an alternate reading due to phonetic or graphic alternation

Note on the Translation of Terms and Titles

When practicable I follow the system of titles Hans Bielenstein laid out in *The Bureaucracy of Han Times* (Princeton: Princeton University Press, 1980). In cases where Bielenstein does not list a particular title or term, or his rendering does not work in this context, I used or developed other translations. In doing so I consulted Michael Loewe, *Records of Han Administration* (Cambridge: Cambridge University Press, 1967), and the entries in *Ciyuan* 辭源, *Hanyu dacidian* 漢語大詞典, and *Kankan goi: Chūgoku kodai mokkan jiten* 漢簡語彙: 中国古代木簡辞典, ed. Kyōto Daigaku Jinbun Kagaku Kenkyūsho Kantoku Kenkyūhan 京都大学人文科学研究所漢牘研究班 (Tokyo: Iwanami Shoten, 2015).

Anhuisheng wenwu kaogu yanjiusuo 安徽省文物考古研究所. *Tianchang Sanjiaowei mudi* 天長三角圩墓地. Beijing: Kexue chubanshe, 2013.

Anderson, Benedict. *Imagined Communities: Reflections on the Origin and Spread of Nationalism*. Revised edition. London: Verso, 1991.

Aqitu 阿其圖. "Shidu 'Eji'na Han jian' zhulu de dijiusui shiermei jianwen" 試讀 "阿濟納漢簡" 著錄的第九燧十二枚簡文. *Neimenggu shifan daxue xuebao (zhexue shehui kexue ban)* 內蒙古師範大學學報(哲學社會科學版) 1 (2007): 7–10.

Bagley, Robert W. "Anyang Writing and the Origin of the Chinese Writing System." In *The First Writing: Script Invention as History and Process*, edited by Stephen D. Houston, 51–84. Cambridge: Cambridge University Press, 2004.

Bagnall, Roger S. *Everyday Writing in the Graeco-Roman East*. Berkeley: University of California Press, 2011.

Bagnall, Roger S., and Raffaella Cribiore. *Women's Letters from Ancient Egypt, 300 BC–AD 800*. Ann Arbor: University of Michigan Press, 2006.

Bai Fang 白芳. "Lun Qin-Han shiqi 'zuxia' chengwei de shehui neihan" 論秦漢時期 "足下" 稱謂的社會內涵. *Bohai daxue xuebao* 渤海大學學報 1 (2009): 83–89.

Bai Yulan 白於藍. *Jiandu boshu tongjiazi zidian* 簡牘帛書通假字字典. Fuzhou: Fujian renmin chubanshe, 2008.

Barbieri-Low, Anthony. *Artisans in Early Imperial China*. Seattle: University of Washington Press, 2007.

———. "Craftsman's Literacy: Uses of Writing by Male and Female Artisans in Qin and Han China." In *Writing and Literacy in Early China: Studies from the Columbia Early China Seminar*, edited by Li Feng and David Prager Branner, 370–99. Seattle: University of Washington Press, 2012.

Barbieri-Low, Anthony J., and Robin D. S. Yates. *Law, State, and Society in Early Imperial China: A Study with Critical Edition and Translation of the Legal Texts from Zhangjiashan Tomb no. 247*. Leiden: Brill, 2015.

Beecroft, Alexander. *Authorship and Cultural Identity in Early Greece and China: Patterns of Literary Circulation*. Cambridge: Cambridge University Press, 2009.

Behr, Wolfgang. " 'To Translate' Is 'To Exchange' 譯者言易也: Linguistic Diversity and the Terms for Translation in Ancient China." In *Mapping Meanings: The Field of New Learning in Late Qing China*, edited by Michael Lackner and Natascha Vittinghoff, 199–235. Leiden: Brill, 2004.

Behr, Wolfgang, and Bernhard Führer. "Einführende Notizen zum Lesen in China mit besonderer Berücksichtigung der Frühzeit." In *Aspekte des Lesens in China in Vergangenheit und Gegenwart*, edited by Bernhard Führer, 1–42. Bochum: Projekt Verlag, 2005.

Bergman, Folke. "Travels and Archaeological Field-work in Mongolia and Sin-kiang: A Diary of the Years 1927–1934." In *History of the Expedition in Asia 1927–1935, Part IV General Reports of Travels and Field-work*, by Folke Bergman, Gerhard Bexell, Birger Bohlin, and Gösta Montell, 1–192. Göteborg: Elanders Boktryckeri Aktiebolag, 1945.

Bertrand, Arnaud. "La formation de le commanderie impériale de Dunhuang (Gansu) des Han antérieurs: l'apport des sources archéologiques." *Arts Asiatiques* 70 (2015): 63–76.

Bhatia, Varuni. "Six Blind Men and the Elephant: *Bhagavata Purana* in Colonial Bengal." In *Founts of Knowledge: Book History in India*, edited by Adhijit Gupta and Swapan Chakravorty, 110–39. New Delhi: Orient Blackswan, 2016.

Bielenstein, Hans. *The Bureaucracy of Han Times*. Cambridge: Cambridge University Press, 1980.

———. "Pan Ku's Accusations against Wang Mang." In *Chinese Ideas about Nature and Society: Studies in Honour of Derk Bodde*, edited by Charles Le Blanc and Susan Blader, 265–70. Hong Kong: Hong Kong University Press, 1987.

Bodde, Derk. *Festivals in Classical China: New Year and Other Annual Observances During the Han Dynasty, 206 B.C.–A.D. 220*. Princeton: Princeton University Press, 1975.

Boltz, William G. "The Composite Nature of Early Chinese Texts." In *Text and Ritual in Early China*, edited by Martin Kern, 50–78. Seattle: University of Washington Press, 2005.

Bottéro, Françoise. "Les 'manuels de caractères' à l'époque des Han occidentaux." In *Éducation et instruction en Chine*, edited by Christine Nguyen Tri and Catherine Despeux, 99–120. Paris: Peeters, 2003–2004.

Bowman, Alan K. *Life and Letters on the Roman Frontier*. New York: Routledge, 1998.

Brashier, K. E. *Public Memory in Early China*. Cambridge: Harvard University Asia Center, 2014.

Brindley, Erica. *Individualism in Early China: Human Agency and the Self in Thought and Politics*. Honolulu: University of Hawai'i Press, 2010.

———. "The Polarization of the Concepts *Si* (Private Interest) and *Gong* (Public Interest) in Early Chinese Thought." *Asia Major* (Third Series) 26.2 (2013): 1–31.

Brodkey, Linda. *Academic Writing as Social Practice*. Philadelphia: Temple University Press, 1987.

Brown, Miranda. " 'Medicine' in Early China." In *The Routledge Handbook of Early Chinese History*, edited by Paul R. Goldin, 459–72. London: Routledge, 2018.

Brown, Miranda, and Charles Sanft. "Categories and Legal Reasoning in Early Imperial China: The Meaning of *Fa* in Recovered Texts." *Oriens Extremus* 49 (2010): 283–305.

Brown, Miranda, and Zhang Zhongwei. "A Tale of Two Stones: Social Memory in Roman Greece and Han China." In *Citizens and Com-*

moners, edited by Hans Beck and Griet Vankeerberghen. Cambridge: Cambridge University Press, forthcoming.

Bu Xianqun 卜憲群. "Cong jianbo kan Qin Han xiangli de wenshu wenti" 從簡帛看秦漢鄉里的文書問題. *Wen shi zhe* 文史哲 6 (2007): 48–53.

Bu Xianqun and Cai Wanjin 蔡萬進. "Tianchang Jizhuang mudu ji qi jiazhi" 天長紀莊木牘及其價值. *Guangming ribao* 光明日報 15 June 2007. Online at http://www.gmw.cn/01gmrb/2007-06/15/content_623693.htm; accessed 14 February 2014.

Bu Xianqun and Liu Yang 劉楊. "Qin-Han richang zhixu zhong de shehui yu xingzheng guanxi chutan—guanyu 'ziyan' yici de jiedu" 秦漢日常秩序中的社會與行政關係初探—關於 "自言" 一詞的解讀. *Wenshizhe* 文史哲 4 (2013): 81–92.

Caulfeild, Sophia Frances Anne, and Blanche C. Saward. *The Dictionary of Needlework: An Encyclopaedia of Artistic, Plain and Fancy Needlework.* 1882; reprinted New York: Arno Press, 1972.

Changsha Mawangdui Han mu jianbo jicheng 長沙馬王堆漢墓簡帛集成. Edited by Qiu Xigui 裘錫圭. Beijing: Zhonghua shuju, 2014.

Chavannes, Édouard. *Les documents chinois découverts par Aurel Stein dans les sables du Turkestan oriental.* Oxford: Oxford University, 1913.

Chen Guoqing 陳國慶. *Han shu Yiwenzhi zhushi huibian* 漢書藝文志注釋彙編. Beijing: Zhonghua shuju, 1983.

Chen, Jack W. "On the Act and Representation of Reading in Medieval China." *Journal of the American Oriental Society* 129.1 (2009): 57–71.

Chen Lanlan 陳蘭蘭. "Handai jiandu zhong de siwenshu fazhan tezheng yanjiu" 漢代簡牘中的私文書發展特徵研究. *Sichuan wenwu* 四川文物 4 (2005): 57–63.

Chen Li 陳力. "'Juyan xinjian' xiang lishan daojian zhujian xuanshi" "居延新簡" 相利善刀劍諸簡選釋. *Kaogu yu wenwu* 考古與文物 6 (2002): 70–73.

Chen Mengjia 陳夢家 (1911–1966). *Han jian zhuishu* 漢簡綴述. Beijing: Zhonghua shuju, 1980.

Chen Pan 陳槃. *Han-Jin yijian shixiao qizhong* 漢晉遺簡識小七種. Shanghai: Shanghai guji chubanshe, 2009.

Chen Qiyou 陳奇猷, editor. *Han Feizi xin jiaozhu* 韓非子新校注. Shanghai: Shanghai guji chubanshe, 2000.

———. *Lüshi chunqiu xin jiaoshi* 呂氏春秋新校釋. Shanghai: Shanghai guji chubanshe, 2002.

Chen Zhi 陳直 (1901–1980). *Juyan Han jian yanjiu* 居延漢簡研究. Beijing: Zhonghua shuju, 2009.

Chen Zhiguo 陳治國. "Cong Liye Qin jian kan Qin de gongwen zhidu" 從里耶秦簡看秦的公文制度, *Zhongguo lishi wen* 中國歷史文物 1 (2007): 61–69.

Cheng Junying 程俊英 and Jiang Jianyuan 蔣見元. *Shijing zhu xi* 詩經注析. Beijing: Zhonghua shuju, 1991.

Chittick, Andrew. *Patronage and Community in Medieval China: The Xiang-yang Garrison, 400–600 CE*. Albany: State University of New York Press, 2009.

Chwe, Michael Suk-young. *Rational Ritual: Culture, Coordination, and Common Knowledge*. Princeton: Princeton University Press, 2001.

Clanchy, M. T. *From Memory to Written Record: England 1066–1307*. Third edition. Chichester: Wiley-Blackwell, 2013.

Coulmas, Florian. *Writing and Society: An Introduction*. Cambridge: Cambridge University Press, 2013.

Coupland, Justine, Nikolas Coupland, and Jeffrey D. Robinson. "'How Are You?' Negotiating Phatic Communication." *Language in Society* 21 (1992): 207–30.

Crespigny, Rafe de. "The Military Culture of Later Han." In *Military Culture in Imperial China*, edited by Nicola Di Cosmo, 90–111. Cambridge: Harvard University Press, 2009.

Crow, Graham. "Community." In *The Blackwell Encyclopedia of Sociology*, edited by George Ritzer, 617–20. Malden: Blackwell, 2007.

Csikszentmihalyi, Mark. "Confucius and the *Analects* in the Hàn." In *Confucius and the* Analects: *New Essays*, edited by Bryan W. Van Norden, 134–62. Oxford: Oxford University Press, 2002.

Dai Weihong 戴衞紅. "Tianchang Jizhuang Han mu mudu suojian 'tie-guancheng'" 天長紀莊漢墓木牘所見 "鐵官丞." In *Jianbo yanjiu erlinglingjiu* 簡帛研究二〇〇九, edited by Bu Xianqun 卜憲群 and Yang Zhenhong 楊振紅, 46–51. Guilin: Guangxi shifan daxue chubanshe, 2011.

Dehaene, Stanislas. *Reading in the Brain: The New Science of How We Read*. New York: Penguin, 2009.

Despeux, Catherine. "Physiognomonie." In *Divination et société dans le Chine médiéval: Étude des manuscrits de Dunhuang de la Bibliothèque nationale de France et de la British Library*, edited by Marc Kalinowski, 513–38. Paris: Bibliothèque nationale de France, 2003.

Di Cosmo, Nicola. *Ancient China and Its Enemies: The Rise of Nomadic Power in East Asian History*. Cambridge: Cambridge University Press, 2002.

———. "Han Frontiers: Toward an Integrated View." *Journal of the American Oriental Society* 129.2 (2009): 199–214.

Dictionary of Character Variants. By the Ministry of Education, R.O.C. Online at http://140.111.1.40.

Drège, Jean-Pierre. "La lecture et l'écriture en Chine et la xylographie." *Études chinoises* 10, nos. 1–2 (1991): 77–111.

Dunhuang Han jian 敦煌漢簡. Edited by Gansusheng wenwu kaogu yanjiusuo 甘肅省文物考古研究所. Beijing: Zhonghua shuju, 1991.

Dunhuang Xuanquan Han jian shicui 敦煌懸泉漢簡釋萃. Edited by Hu Pingsheng and Zhang Defang 張德芳. Shanghai: Shanghai guji chubanshe, 2001.

Durrant, Stephen. "Histories (*shi* 史)." In *The Oxford Handbook of Classical Chinese Literature (1000 BCE—900 CE)*, edited by Wiebke Denecke, Wai-yee Li, and Xiaofei Tian, 184–200. Oxford: Oxford University Press, 2017.

Ebrey, Patricia Buckley. *The Aristocratic Families of Early Imperial China: A Case Study of the Po-ling Ts'ui Family.* Cambridge: Cambridge University Press, 1978.

Eji'na Han jian shiwen jiaoben 額濟納漢簡釋文校本. Edited by Sun Jiazhou 孫家洲. Beijing: Wenwu chubanshe, 2007.

Els, Paul van. "Confucius' Sayings Entombed: On Two Han Dynasty Bamboo *Analects* Manuscripts." In *The Analects Revisited: New Perspectives on the Dating of a Classic*, edited by Michael Hunter and Martin Kern. Leiden: Brill, 2018.

Eno Gīre エノ・ギーレ (Giele, Enno). "Kodai no shikiji nōryoku o ikani hantei suru no ka—Kandai gyōsei monjo no jirei kenkyū –" 古代の識字能力を如何に判定するのか—漢代行政文書の事例研究 –." In *Kanji bunka sanzennen* 漢字文化三千年, edited by Takata Tokio 高田時雄, 133–54. Kyoto: Rinsen Shoten, 2009.

Erickson, Susan N. "Han Dynasty Tomb Structures and Contents." In *China's Early Empires: A Re-appraisal*, edited by Michael Nylan and Michael Loewe, 13–81. Cambridge: Cambridge University Press, 2010.

Falkenhausen, Lothar von. *Chinese Society in the Age of Confucius (1000–250 BC): The Archaeological Evidence.* Los Angeles: Cotsen Institute, University of California Press, 2006.

———. "Die Seiden mit chinesischen Inschriften." In *Die Textilien aus Palmyra: neue und alte Funde*, edited by Andreas Schmidt-Colinet and Annemarie Stauffer, with Khaled Al-As'ad, 58–81. Mainz am Rhein: Verlag Philipp von Zabern, 2000.

Fan Changxi 范常喜. "Anhui Tianchang Jizhuang Han mu shudu kaoshi shiyi" 安徽天長紀莊漢墓書牘考釋拾遺. Online at www.bsm.org.cn/show_article.php?id=910; posted 20 December 2008; accessed 6 January 2015.

Fang Shiming 方詩銘. "Xihan Wudi wanqi de 'wugu zhi huo' ji qi qianhou—jianlun Yumen Han jian 'Han Wudi yizhao'" 西漢武帝晚期的 "巫蠱之禍" 及其前後—兼論玉門漢簡 "漢武帝遺詔." *Guankan* 館刊 4 (1987): 357–69.

Finnegan, Ruth. *Literacy and Orality: Studies in the Technology of Communication.* Oxford: Basil Blackwell, 1988.

Foster, Christopher. "Study of the *Cang Jie pian*: Past and Present." PhD dissertation, Harvard University, 2017.

Fu Junlian 伏俊璉 and Yang Aijun 楊愛軍. "Han Peng gushi kaoyuan" 韓朋故事考源, *Dunhuang yanjiu* 敦煌研究 3 (2007): 91–93.

Fu Junlian and Yang Xiaohua 楊曉華. "Dunhuang wenxue de shangyuan" 敦煌文學的上源. *Heilongjiang shehui kexue* 黑龍江社會科學 3 (2011): 82–85.

Fuyang Han jian zhenglizu 阜陽漢簡整理組 et al. "Fuyang Han jian jianjie" 阜陽漢簡簡介. *Wenwu* 文物 2 (1983): 21–23.

Gan Bao 干寶 (fl. ca. early fourth century). *Soushenji* 搜神記. *Siku quanshu* 四庫全書 edition.

Gansu jiandu baohu yanjiu zhongxin 甘肅簡牘保護研究中心 et al. *Jianshui Jinguan Han jian* 肩水金關漢簡. Five volumes. Shanghai: Zhongxi shuju, 2011–2016.

Gansusheng bowuguan 甘肅省博物館. "Gansusheng Wuwei Mozuizi Han mu fajue" 甘肅省武威磨咀子漢墓發掘. *Kaogu* 考古 9 (1960): 15–28.

Gansusheng bowuguan 甘肅省博物館 et al., editors. *Wuwei Han jian* 武威漢簡. Beijing: Zhonghua shuju, 2005.

Gansusheng bowuguan Han jian zhenglizu 甘肅省博物館漢簡整理組. "Juyan Han jian 'Xiang jian dao' ce shiwen" 居延漢簡 "相劍刀" 冊釋文. *Dunhuangxu jikan* 敦煌學輯刊 3 (1983): 78.

———. "'Yongshi sannian zhaoshu' jiance shiwen" "永始三年詔書" 簡冊釋文. *Xibei shiyuan xuebao (shehui kexueban)* 西北師院學報(社會科學版) 4 (1983): 61.

Gansusheng wenwu gongzuodui Juyan jian zhenglizu 甘肅省文物工作隊居延簡整理組. "Juyan jian 'Yongshi sannian zhaoshu' ce shiwen" 居延簡 《永始三年詔書》冊釋文. *Dunhuangxue jikan* 敦煌學輯刊 2 (1984): 171–73.

Gansusheng wenwu kaogu yanjiusuo 甘肅省文物考古研究所, editor. *Dunhuang Han jian* 敦煌漢簡. Beijing: Zhonghua shuju, 1991.

———. "Dunhuang Xuanquan Han jian shiwen xuan" 敦煌懸泉漢簡釋文選. *Wenwu* 5 (2000): 27–45.

Gao Heng 高亨. *Guzi tongjia huidian* 古字通假會典. Ji'nan: Qi-Lu shushe, 1997.

Giele, Enno. "Evidence for the Xiongnu in Chinese Wooden Documents from the Han Period." In *Xiongnu Archaeology: Multidisciplinary Perspectives of the First Steppe Empire in Inner Asia*, edited by Ursula Brosseder and Bryan K. Miller, 49–75. Bonn: Rheinische Friedrich-Wilhelms-Universität Bonn, 2011.

———. "Excavated Manuscripts: Context and Methodology." In *China's Early Empires: A Re-appraisal*, edited by Michael Nylan and Michael Loewe, 114–34. Cambridge: Cambridge University Press, 2010.

———. "The Geographical Origins of the Han Time Northwestern Border Society According to Excavated Documents." In *International Conference: Military Control on Multi-Ethnic Society in Early China*, edited by Kim Byung-Joon and Miyake Kiyoshi, 61–105. Seoul: Seoul National University, 2015.

———. "Private Letter Manuscripts from Early Imperial China." In *A History of Chinese Letters and Epistolary Culture*, edited by Antje Richter, 403–74. Leiden: Brill, 2015.

———. "Signatures of 'Scribes' in Early Imperial China." *Asiatischen Studien* 59.1 (2005): 353–87.

———. "Using Early Chinese Manuscripts as Historical Source Materials." *Monumenta Serica* 51 (2003): 409–38.

———. See also Eno Gīre エノ・ギーレ.

Goldin, Paul R. "Steppe Nomads as a Philosophical Problem in Classical China." In *Mapping Mongolia: Situating Mongolia in the World from Geologic Time to the Present*, edited by Paula L. W. Sabloff, 220–46. Philadelphia: University of Pennsylvania Museum of Archaeology and Anthropology, 2011.

Gould, James J., and Peter Marler. "Learning by Instinct." *Scientific American* 256.1 (1987): 74–85.

Gumbrecht, Cordula. "Die Physiognomie von vier Kaiserinnen im China der späten Han-Zeit (25–220)." *Monumenta Serica* 50 (2002): 171–214.

Guo Bingjie 郭炳潔. "Handai jiandu shuxin zhong de 'wuyang'" 漢代簡牘書信中的 "無恙." *Shixue yuekan* 史學月刊 12 (2011): 125–28.

———. "Handai shuxin de chengwei" 漢代書信的稱謂. *Lantai shijie* 蘭臺世界 11 (2010): 62.

Guo Qingfan 郭慶藩 (1844—ca. 1896), editor. *Zhuangzi jishi* 莊子集釋. Beijing: Zhonghua shuju, 1961.

Guo Tiena 郭鐵娜. "Handai minjian aiqing gushi de 'Han Peng moshi' yanjiu" 漢代民間愛情故事的 "韓朋模式." *Shenyang daxue xuebao* 沈陽大學學報 20.4 (2008): 63–66.

Guoyu 國語. Edited by Shanghai shifan daxue guji zhenglizu 上海師範大學古籍整理組. Shanghai: Shanghai guji chubanshe, 1978.

Han Hua 韓華 and Di Xiaoxia 狄曉霞. "Juyan Han jian 'Xiang bao jian dao' ce yanjiu zongshu" 居延漢簡 "相寶劍刀" 冊研究綜述. *Sichou zhi lu* 絲綢之路 20 (2009): 13–17.

Han shu 漢書. By Ban Gu 班固 (32–92). Beijing: Zhonghua shuju, 1962.

Hao Jianping 郝建平. "Jin 30 nian lai Juyan Han jian yanjiu zongshu" 近30年來居延漢簡研究綜述. *Ludong daxue xuebao (zhexue shehui kexue ban)* 魯東大學學報 (哲學社會科學版) 29.3 (2012): 61–66.

Hao Shusheng 郝樹聲. "Cong Xibei Han jian he Chaoxian bandao chutu 'Lunyu' jian kan Handai Rujia wenhua de liubu" 從西北漢簡和朝鮮半島出土 "論語" 簡看漢代儒家文化的流布. *Dunhuang yanjiu* 敦煌研究 3 (2012): 63–68.

———. "Jianlun Dunhuang Xuanquan Han jian 'Kangju wang shizhe ce' ji Xi-Han yu Kangju de guanxi" 簡論敦煌懸泉漢簡 "康居王使者冊" 及西漢與康居的關係. *Dunhuang yanjiu* 敦煌研究 1 (2009): 53–58.

Harper, Donald. "Daybooks in the Context of Manuscript Culture and Popular Culture Studies." In *Books of Fate and Popular Culture in Early China*, edited by Donald Harper and Marc Kalinowski, 91–137. Leiden: Brill, 2017.

———. *Early Chinese Medical Literature: The Mawangdui Medical Manuscripts.* London: Kegan Paul International, 1997.

Harper, Donald, and Marc Kalinowski. "Introduction." In *Books of Fate and Popular Culture in Early China: The Daybook Manuscripts of the Warring States, Qin, and Han,* edited by Donald Harper and Marc Kalinowski, 1–10. Leiden: Brill, 2017.

Hayashi Minao 林巳奈夫. *Kandai no bunbutsu* 漢代の文物. Second edition. Kyoto: Hoyu shoten, 1996.

He Maohuo 何茂活. "Juyan Han jian 'Xiang jian dao' ce shidu xiyi" 居延漢簡 "相劍刀" 冊釋讀析疑. In *Jianduxue yanjiu* 簡牘學研究, no. 5, edited by Xibei shifan daxue lishi wenhua xueyuan 西北師範大學歷史文化學院 and Gansu jiandu bowuguan 甘肅簡牘博物館, 85–98. Lanzhou: Gansu renmin chubanshe, 2014.

He Ning 何寧, editor *Huainanzi jishi* 淮南子集釋. Beijing: Zhonghua shuju, 1998.

He Runkun 賀潤坤. "Zhongguo gudai zui zao de xiangma jing—Yunmeng Qin jian 'Rishu—Ma' pian" 中國古代最早的相馬經—雲夢秦簡 "日書 • 馬" 篇. *Xibei nongye daxue xuebao* 西北農業大學學報 17.3 (1989): 9.

He Shuangquan 何雙全. "'Han jian—xiangli zhi' ji qi yanjiu" 《漢簡・鄉里志》及其研究. In *Qin-Han jiandu lunwenji* 秦漢簡牘論文集, edited by Gansu wenwu kaogu yanjiusuo 甘肅文物考古研究所, 145–235. Lanzhou: Gansu renmin chubanshe, 1989.

———. *Jiandu* 簡牘. Lanzhou: Dunhuang wenyi chubanshe, 2003.

———. "Juyan Han jian yanjiu" 居延漢簡研究. *Guoji jiandu xuehui huikan* 國際簡牘學會會刊 2 (1996): 1–114.

———. "'Saishang fenghuo pinyue' quanshi" "塞上烽火品約" 詮釋. *Kaogu* 考古 9 (1985): 843–47.

He Youzu 何有祖. "Tianchang Han mu suo jian shuxindu guankui" 天長漢墓所見書信牘管窺. In *Jianbo* 簡帛, no. 3, edited by Wuhan daxue jianbo yanjiu zhongxin 武漢大學簡帛研究中心, 261–68. Shanghai: Shanghai guji chubanshe, 2008.

Hebeisheng wenwu yanjiusuo 河北省文物研究所. *Dingzhou Han mu zhujian Lunyu* 定州漢墓竹簡論語. Beijing: Wenwu chubanshe, 1997.

Hinsch, Bret. *Women in Imperial China.* Lanham: Rowman & Littlefield, 2016.

Hirschler, Konrad. *The Written Word in the Medieval Arabic Lands.* Edinburgh: Edinburgh University Press, 2012.

Hou Han shu 後漢書. By Fan Ye 范曄 (398–445). Beijing: Zhonghua shuju, 1965.

Hou Pixun 侯丕勛. "Xibei suo chutu jiandu de tedian" 西北所出土簡牘的特點. In *Jianduxue yanjiu* 簡牘學研究, no. 1, edited by Xibei shifan daxue lishixi 西北師範大學歷史系 et al., 98–104. Lanzhou: Gansu renmin chubanshe, 1996.

Hsing I-t'ien 邢義田. "Handai biansai lizu de junzhong jiaoyu—du 'Juyan xinjian' zhaji zhi san" 漢代邊塞吏卒的軍中教育—讀 "居延新簡" 札記 之三. In *Jianbo yanjiu* 簡帛研究, no. 2, edited by Li Xueqin 李學勤, 273–78. Beijing: Falü chubanshe, 1996.

———. "Qin-Han pingmin de duxie nengli—shiliao jiedu pian zhi yi" 秦漢 平民的讀寫能力—史料解讀篇之一. In *Gudai shumin shehui: Disijie guoji Hanxue huiyi lunwenji* 古代庶民社會: 第四屆國際漢學會議論文集 · 古代 庶民社會, edited by Hsing I-t'ien and Liu Zenggui 劉增貴, 241–88. Taipei: Zhongyang yanjiuyuan, 2013.

Hu Pingsheng 胡平生. "'Bianshu,' 'Dabianshu' kao" 扁書、 "大扁書" 考. In *Dunhuang Xuanquan Yueling zhaotiao* 敦煌懸泉月令詔條, edited by Zhong-guo wenwu yanjiusuo 中國文物研究所 and Gansusheng wenwu kaogu yanjiusuo 甘肅省文物考古研究所, 48–54. Beijing: Zhonghua shuju, 2001.

———. "Han jian 'Cang Jie pian' xin ziliao yanjiu" 漢簡 "蒼頡篇" 新資料研 究. In *Hu Pingsheng jiandu wenwu lungao* 胡平生簡牘文物論稿, 11–25. Shanghai: Zhongxi shuju, 2012.

———. *Hu Pingsheng jiandu wenwu lunji* 胡平生簡牘文物論集. Taipei: Lantai, 2000.

———. "Tianchang Anle Han jian 'hukou bu' 'Yuanyong' kao" 天長安樂漢 簡《戶口簿》 "垣雍" 考. Online at http://www.bsm.org.cn/show_article. php?id=1215; posted 3 February 2010, accessed 21 January 2015.

———. "Xie zai mugu shang de Xi-Han yizhao" 寫在木觚上的西漢遺詔. *Wenwu tiandi* 文物天地 6 (1987): 31, 33.

———. "Yingguo guojia tushuguan cang Sitanyin suohuo weikan Han wen jiandu zhong 'Cang Jie pian' canpian yanjiu" 英國國家圖書館藏 斯坦因所獲未刊漢文簡牘中 "蒼頡篇" 殘片研究. In *Hu Pingsheng jiandu wenwu lungao* 胡平生簡牘文物論稿, 26–41. Shanghai: Shanghai wenyi chubanshe, 2012.

———. "Yumen, Wuwei xin huo jiandu wenzi jiaoshi—du 'Hanjian yanjiu wenji' zhaji" 玉門、武威新獲簡牘文字校釋—讀 "漢簡研究文集" 札記. in *Hu Pingsheng jiandu wenwu lungao* 胡平生簡牘文物論稿, 215–27. Shanghai: Zhongxi shuju, 2012.

Hu Pingsheng and Han Ziqiang 韓自強. "'Cang Jie pian' de chubu yanjiu" "蒼頡篇" 的初步研究. *Wenwu* 2 (1983): 35–40.

Hu Zhi 胡之, editor. *Neimenggu Juyan Han jian (er)* 內蒙古居延漢簡(二). Chongqing: Chongqing chubanshe, 2008.

Huang Bosi 黃伯思 (1079–1118). *Dongguan yulun* 東觀餘論. *Siku quanshu* edition.

Huang Chunping 黃春平. "Cong chutu jiandu kan Han diguo zhongyang de xinxi fabu—jian ping Zhang Tao xiansheng de 'fubao' shuo" 從出 土簡牘看漢帝國中央的信息發布—兼評張濤先生的 "府報" 說. *Xinwen yu chuanbo yanjiu* 新聞與傳播研究 4 (2006): 2–11.

Huang Hailie 黃海烈. "Liye Qin jian yu Qin difang guanzhi" 里耶秦簡與秦地方官制. *Beifang luncong* 北方論叢 6 (2005): 6–10.

Huang Hui 黃暉, editor. *Lunheng jiaoshi* 論衡校釋. Beijing: Zhonghua shuju, 1990.

Hulsewé, A. F. P. "Han China: A Proto 'Welfare State'? Fragments of Han Law Discovered in North-West China." *T'oung Pao* 73.4/5 (1987): 265–85.

———. *Remnants of Ch'in Law: An Annotated Translation of the Ch'in Legal and Administrative Rules of the 3rd Century B.C. Discovered in Yün-meng Prefecture, Hu-pei Province, in 1975*. Leiden: E. J. Brill, 1985.

Hunter, Michael. *Confucius Beyond the* Analects. Leiden: Brill, 2017.

Idema, Wilt L. "Elite versus Popular Literature." In *The Oxford Handbook of Classical Chinese Literature (1000 BCE—900 CE)*, edited by Wiebke Denecke, Wai-yee Li, and Xiaofei Tian, 258–72. Oxford: Oxford University Press, 2017.

Jacobs, Justin. "Confronting Indiana Jones: Chinese Nationalism, Historical Imperialism, and the Criminalization of Aurel Stein and the Raiders of Dunhuang, 1899–1944.' In *China on the Margins*, edited by Sherman Cochran and Paul G. Pickowicz, 65–90. Ithaca: Cornell University Press, 2010.

Ji Shimei 吉仕梅. "Wang Mang gai zhi zai Juyan Dunhuang Han jian cihui zhong de fanying" 王莽改制在居延敦煌漢簡詞匯中的反應. *Xueshu jiaoliu* 學術交流 4 (2008): 129–32.

Jia Liying 賈麗英. "Cong Juyan Han jian kan Handai suijun xiaceng funü shenghuo" 從居延漢簡漢代隨軍下層婦女生活. *Shijiazhuang shifan zhuanke xuexiao xuebao* 石家莊師範專科學校學報 6.1 (2004): 56–60.

Jiayuguanshi wenwu baoguansuo 嘉峪關市文物保管所. "Yumen Huahai Han dai fengsui yizhi chutu de jiandu" 玉門花海漢代烽燧遺址出土的簡牘. In *Han jian yanjiu wenji* 漢簡研究文集, edited by Gansusheng wenwu gongzuodui 甘肅省文物工作隊 and Gansusheng bowuguan 甘肅省博物館, 15–33. Lanzhou: Gansu renmin chubanshe, 1984.

Johnson, David. "Chinese Popular Literature and Its Contexts." *Chinese Literature: Essays, Articles, Reviews* 3.2 (1981): 225–33.

Juyan Han jian jiayi bian 居延漢簡甲乙編. Edited by Zhongguo shehui kexue yuan kaogu yanjiusuo 中國社會科學院考古研究所. Beijing: Zhonghua shuju, 1980.

Juyan Han jian shiwen hejiao 居延漢簡釋文合校. Edited by Xie Guihua 謝桂華 et al. Beijing: Wenwu chubanshe, 1987.

Juyan xin jian 居延新簡. Edited by Gansusheng wenwu kaogu yanjiusuo et al. Beijing: Zhonghua shuu, 1994.

Juyan xin jian shijiao 居延新簡釋校. Edited by Ma Yi and Zhang Rongqiang 張榮強. Tianjin: Tianjin guji chubanshe, 2013.

Kadota Akira 門田明. "Henkyō bōei no naka de no seikatsu" 辺境のなかで
  の生活. In Mokkan—kodai kara no messēji 木簡—古代からのメッセージ,
  edited by Ōba Osamu 大庭脩, 135–80. Tokyo: Taishūkan Shoten, 1998.

Kalinowski, Marc. "Diviners and Astrologers under the Eastern Zhou: Trans-
  mitted Texts and Recent Archaeological Discoveries." In Early Chinese
  Religion, Part One: Shang through Han (1250 BC–220 AD), edited by
  John Lagerwey and Marc Kalinowski, 341–52. Leiden: Brill, 2009.

———. "Hémérologie." In Divination et société dans la Chine médiévale: Étude
  des manuscrits de Dunhuang de la Bibliothèque nationale de France et de la
  British Library, edited by Marc Kalinowski, 213–99. Paris: Bibliothèque
  nationale de France, 2003.

———. "Technical Traditions in Ancient China and Shushu Culture in
  Chinese Religion." In Religion and Chinese Society: A Centennial Conference of the École française d'Extrême-Orient, edited by John Lagerwey,
  223–48. Paris: École française d'Extrême-Orient, 2004.

Kankan goi: Chūgoku kodai mokkan jiten 漢簡語彙: 中国古代木簡辞典. Edited
  by Kyōto Daigaku Jinbun Kagaku Kenkyūsho Kantoku Kenkyūhan 京
  都大学人文科学研究所漢牘研究班. Tokyo: Iwanami Shoten, 2015.

Kaogu yanjiusuo bianjishi 考古研究所編輯室. "Wuwei Mozuizi Han mu chutu
  wangzhang shijian shiwen" 武威磨咀子漢墓出土王杖十簡釋文. Kaogu 考
  古 9 (1960): 29–30.

Kern, Martin. "Methodological Reflections on the Analysis of Textual Variants and the Modes of Manuscript Production in Early China." Journal
  of East Asian Archaeology 4 (2002): 143–81.

———. "The Performance of Writing in Western Zhou China." In Poetics
  of Grammar and the Metaphysics of Sound and Sign, edited by Sergio La
  Porta and David Shulman, 109–75. Leiden: Brill, 2007.

———. "Ritual, Text, and the Formation of the Canon: Historical Transformations of Wen in Early China." T'oung Pao 87 (2001): 43–91.

Kim, Kyung-ho. "A Study of Excavated Bamboo and Wooden-Strip Analects:
  The Spread of Confucianism and Chinese Script." Sungkyun Journal
  of East Asian Studies 11.1 (2011): 59–88.

Kirkham, Alexander James, Julian Michael Breeze, and Paloma Marí-Beffa.
  "The Impact of Verbal Instructions on Goal-Directed Behaviour." Acta
  Psychologica 139 (2012): 212–19.

Knechtges, David R. "Culling the Weeds and Selecting Prime Blossoms:
  The Anthology in Early Medieval China." In Culture and Power in the
  Reconstitution of the Chinese Realm, 200–600, edited by Scott Pearce
  et al., 200–41. Cambridge: Harvard University Asia Center, 2001.

———. "The Problem with Anthologies: The Case of the 'Bai yi' Poems
  of Ying Qu (190–252)." Asia Major (third series) 23.1 (2010): 173–
  99.

———, translator. *Wen xuan or Selections of Refined Literature, Volume 1: Rhapsodies on Metropolises and Capitals.* Princeton: Princeton University Press, 1982.

Kneib, André. "Le *Sitishu shi* de Wei Heng (252–291)—Première traité chinois de calligraphie." *Cahiers d'Extrême-Asie* 9 (1996): 99–129.

Korolkov, Maxim. "'Greeting Tablets' in Early China: Some Traits of the Communicative Etiquette of Officialdom in Light of Newly Excavated Inscriptions." *T'oung-Pao* 98.4–5 (2012): 295–348.

Lai Guolong 來國龍. "Lun Zhanguo Qin Han xieben wenhua zhong wenben de liudong yu guding" 論戰國秦漢寫本文化中文本的流動與固定. In *Jian bo* 簡帛, no. 2, edited by Wuhan daxue jianbo yanjiu zhongxin 武漢大學簡帛研究中心, 515–27. Shanghai: Shanghai guji chubanshe, 2007.

Lai Ming-chiu 黎明釗. "Shili de zhize yu gongzuo: Eji'na Han jian duji" 士吏的職責與工作: 額濟納漢簡讀記. *Zhongguo wenhua yanjiusuo xuebao* 中國文化研究所學報 48 (2008): 15–33.

Lau, D. C., and Roger T. Ames. *Sun Bin: The Art of Warfare: A Translation of the Classic Chinese Work of Philosophy and Strategy.* Albany: State University of New York Press, 2003.

Leung, Vincent S. "Bad Writing: Cursive Calligraphy and the Ethics of Orthography in the Eastern Han Dynasty." In *Behaving Badly in Early and Medieval China*, edited by N. Harry Rothschild and Leslie V. Wallace, 106–21. Honolulu: University of Hawai'i Press, 2017.

Lewis, Mark Edward. "The Han Abolition of Universal Military Service." In *Warfare in Chinese History*, edited by Hans van den Ven, 33–76. Leiden: Brill, 2000.

———. *The Early Chinese Empires: Qin and Han.* Cambridge: Belknap Press, 2007.

———. "Public Spaces in Cities in the Roman and Han Empires." In *State Power in Ancient China and Rome*, ed. Walter Scheidel, 204–29. New York: Oxford University Press, 2014.

———. *Writing and Authority in Early China.* Albany: State University of New York Press, 1999.

Li Baotong 李寶通 and Huang Zhaohong 黃兆宏, editors. *Jianduxue jiaocheng* 簡牘學教成. Lanzhou: Gansu renmin chubanshe, 2011.

Li Fang 李昉 (925–996) et al., editors. *Taiping guangji* 太平廣記. Beijing: Zhonghua shuju, 1961.

———. *Taiping yulan* 太平御覽. Song woodblock edition; reprinted Taipei: Taiwan Shangwu yinshuguan, 1968.

Li Feng. "Literacy and Social Contexts of Writing in the Western Zhou." In *Writing and Literacy in Early China: Studies from the Columbia Early China Seminar*, edited by Li Feng and David Prager Branner, 271–301. Seattle: University of Washington Press, 2012.

Li Hengquan 李恒全. "Cong Tianchang Jizhuang mudu kan Handai de yaoyi zhidu" 從天長紀莊木牘看漢代的徭役制度. *Shehui kexue* 舍會科學 10 (2012): 159–66.

Li Junming 李均明. *Chuxuelu* 初學錄. Taipei: Lantai chubanshe, 1999.

———. "Eji'na Han jian fazhi shiliao kao" 額濟納漢簡法制史料考. In *Eji'na Han jian* 額濟納漢簡, edited by Wei Jian 魏堅, 54–70. Guilin: Guangxi shifan daxue chubanshe, 2005.

———. "Eji'na Han jian fazhi shiliao kao" 額濟納漢簡法制史料考. In *Eji'na Han jian shiwen jiaoben* 額濟納漢簡釋文校本, edited by Sun Jiazhou 孫家洲, 215–31. Beijing: Wenwu chubanshe, 2007.

———. "Xin-Mang jian shidai tezheng suoyi" 新莽簡時代特徵瑣議. *Wenwu chunqiu* 文物春秋 4 (1989): 1–3.

Li Junming and Liu Jun 劉軍. "Wuwei Hantanpo chutu Han jian kaoshu" 武威漢灘坡出土漢簡考述. *Wenwu* 文物 10 (1993): 34–39.

Li Ling 李零. *Jianbo gushu yu xueshu yuanliu* 簡帛古書與學術源流. Beijing: Sanlian shudian, 2004.

———. *Zhongguo fangshu kao* 中國方術考. Revised edition. Beijing: Dongfang chubanshe, 2001.

Li Tianhong 李天虹. "Juyan Han jian suojian houguan shaoli de renyong yu bamian" 居延漢簡所見侯官少吏的任用與罷免. *Shixue jikan* 史學集刊 3 (1996): 66–72, 65.

Li Xiangfeng 梨翔鳳, editor. *Guanzi jiaozhu* 管子校注. Beijing: Zhonghua shuju, 2004.

Li Xueqin 李學勤. "Chudu Liye Qin jian" 初讀里耶秦簡. *Wenwu* 文物 1 (2003): 73–81.

Li Zhengyu 李正宇. "Shishi Dunhuang Han jian 'Jiao hui shi'" 試釋敦煌漢簡 "教誨詩." In *Zhuanxingqi de Dunhuang yuyan wenxue—jinian Zhou Shaoliang xiansheng xianshi san zhounian xueshu yantaohui lunwenji* 轉型期的敦煌語言文學—紀念周紹良先生仙逝三周年學術研討會論文集, edited by Yan Tingliang 顏廷亮, 69–72. Lanzhou: Gansu renmin chubanshe, 2010.

Li Zhenhong 李振宏. "Handai Juyan tunshu lizu de jingshen wenhua shenghuo" 漢代居延屯戍吏卒的精神文化生活. In *Jianduxue yanjiu* 簡牘學研究, no. 3, edited by Xibei shifan daxue wenxueyuan lishixi 西北師範大學文學院歷史系 et al., 233–47. Lanzhou: Gansu renmin chubanshe, 2002.

Liao Boyuan 廖伯源. *Jiandu yu zhidu: Yinwan Han mu jiandu guanwenshu kaozheng* 簡牘與制度: 尹灣漢墓簡牘官文書考證. Revised edition. Guilin: Guangxi shifan daxue chubanshe, 2005.

Lin Jianming 林劍鳴. "Han jian zhong yifeng qiguai de xin" 漢簡中一封奇怪的信. *Shaanxi lishi bowuguan guankan* 陝西博物館館刊 1 (1994): 78–82.

Lin Suqing 林素清. "Cang Jie pian yanjiu" 蒼頡篇研究. *Hanxue yanjiu* 漢學研究 5.1 (1987): 53–72.

Ling Yun 凌雲. "Shi 'qiang fan zi ai'" 釋 "強飯自愛." *Sichuan zhiye jishu xueyuan xuebao* 四川職業技術學院學報 4 (2006): 63–64.

Liu Heng 劉恒. *Lidai chidu shufa* 歷代尺牘書法. Beijing: Zhishi chubanshe, 1992.

Liu Jinhua 劉金華. "Han 'Xiang jian dao ce' lüeshuo" 漢 "相劍刀冊" 略說. *Zhongguo lishi wenwu* 中國歷史文物 3 (2008): 58–64.

Liu Lexian 劉樂賢. "Tianchang Jizhuang Han mu 'Bing Chongguo' shudu bushi" 天長紀莊漢墓 "丙充國" 書牘補釋. In *Jianbo* 簡帛, no. 3, edited by Wuhan daxue jianbo yanjiu zhongxin 武漢大學簡帛研究中心, 269–73. Shanghai: Shanghai guji chubanshe, 2008.

Liu Xi 劉熙 (ca. second–third c.). *Shiming* 釋名. *Siku quanshu* 四庫全書 edition.

Liu Xiang 劉向 (ca. 77—ca. 6 BCE), editor. *Zhanguo ce* 戰國策. Shanghai: Shanghai guji chubanshe, 1998.

Liu Yuejin 劉躍進. "Qin-Han jianbo zhong de wenxue shijie—Qin-Han wenxue yanjiu xinziliao zhi yi" 秦漢簡帛中的文學世界—秦漢文學研究新資料之一. *Xinzhou shifan xueyuan xuebao* 忻州師範學院學報 17.2 (2001): 6–13, 37.

Loewe, Michael. *Dong Zhongshu, a 'Confucian' Heritage and the Chunqiu Fanlu*. Leiden: Brill, 2011.

———. "Liu Xiang and Liu Xin." In *Chang'an in 26 BCE: An Augustan Age in China*, edited by Michael Nylan and Griet Vankeerberghen, 369–89. Seattle: University of Washington Press, 2015.

———. *Records of Han Administration*. Cambridge: Cambridge University Press, 1967.

———. "Wang Mang and His Forebears: The Making of the Myth." *T'oung Pao* 80.4–5 (1994): 197–222.

———. "The Western Han Army: Organization, Leadership, and Operation." In *Military Culture in Imperial China*, edited by Nicola Di Cosmo, 65–89. Cambridge: Harvard University Press, 2009.

———. "Wood and Bamboo Administrative Documents of the Han Period." In *New Sources of Early Chinese History: An Introduction to the Reading of Inscriptions and Manuscripts*, edited by Edward L. Shaughnessy, 161–92. Berkeley: Society for the Study of Early China and the Institute of East Asian Studies, University of California, Berkeley, 1997.

———. "The Wooden and Bamboo Strips Found at Mo-chü-tzu (Kansu)." *Journal of the Royal Asiatic Society* 1/2 (1965): 13–26.

Long Wenling 龍文玲. "Lun Handai fengsui jiandu de wenxue shiliao jiazhi" 論漢代烽燧簡牘的文學史料價值. *Xueshu luntan* 學術論壇 11 (2014): 86–92.

Lunyu zhushu 論語注疏. See *Shisanjing zhushu*.

Luo Zhenyu 羅振玉 and Wang Guowei 王國維. *Liusha zhuijian* 流沙墜簡. 1914; reprinted Beijing: Zhonghua shuju, 1993.

Ma Manli 馬曼麗. "Cong Han jian kan Handai xibei biansai shouyu zhidu" 從漢簡看漢代西北邊塞守御制度. *Zhongguo bianjiang shidi yanjiu* 中國邊疆史地研究 1 (1992): 68–74.

Ma Mingda 馬明達. *Shuo jian conggao* 說劍叢搞. Revised edition. Beijing: Zhonghua shuju, 2007.

———. "Zhongguo gudai de xiang jian fa" 中國古代的相劍法. *Wenshi zhishi* 文史知識 1 (2000): 59–63.

Ma, Tsang Wing. "Scribes, Assistants, and the Materiality of Administrative Documents in Qin-Early Han China: Excavated Evidence from Liye, Shuihudi, and Zhangjiashan." *T'oung-Pao* 103-104-105 (2017): 297–333.

Ma Yi 馬怡. "Bianshu shi tan" 扁書試探. In *Jian bo (di yi ji)* 簡帛(第一輯), edited by Wuhan daxue jian bo yanjiu zhongxin 武漢大學簡帛研究中心, 415–28. Shanghai: Shanghai guji chubanshe, 2006.

———. "Du Dongpailou Han jian 'Chi yu duyou shu'—Handai shuxin geshi yu xingzhi de yanjiu" 讀東牌樓漢簡 "侈與督郵書"—漢代書信格式與形制的研究. In *Jianbo yanjiu 2005* 簡帛研究2005, edited Bu Xianqun 卜憲群 and Yang Zhenhong 楊振紅, 173–86. Guilin: Guangxi shifan daxue chubanshe, 2008.

———. "Handai zhaoshu zhi sanpin" 漢代詔書之三品. In *Tian Yuqing xiansheng jiushi huadan songshou lunwenji* 田餘慶先生九十華誕頌壽論文集, edited by Beijing daxue Zhongguo gudaishi yanjiu zhongxin 北京大學中國古代史研究中心, 65–83. Beijing: Zhonghua shuju, 2014.

———. "Juyan jian 'Xuan yu Yousun shaofu shu'—Handai bianli de siren tongxin" 居延簡 "宣與幼孫少婦書"—漢代邊吏的私人通信. *Nandu xuetan (renwen shehui kexue xuebao)* 南都學壇(人文社會科學學報) 30.3 (2010): 1–9.

———. " 'Shijianguo ernian zhaoshu' ce suojian zhaoshu zhi xiaxing" "始建國二年詔書" 冊所見詔書之下行. *Lishi yanjiu* 歷史研究 5 (2006): 166–71.

———. "Tianchang Jizhuang Han mu suo jian 'feng ye qing bing' mudu—jian tan jiandu shidai de ye yu ci" 天長紀莊漢漢墓所見 "奉謁請病" 木牘—兼談簡牘時代的謁與刺. In *Jianbo yanjiu erlinglingjiu* 簡帛研究二〇〇九, edited by Bu Xianqun 卜憲群 and Yang Zhenhong 楊振紅, 14–39. Guilin: Guangxi shifan daxue chubanshe, 2011.

———. "Xuanquan Han jian 'Shiwang zhuanxin ce' bukao" 懸泉漢簡 "失亡傳信冊" 補考. In *Chutu wenxian yanjiu* 出土文獻研究, no. 8, edited by Zhongguo wenwu yanjiusuo 中國文物研究所, 111–16. Shanghai: Shanghai guji chubanshe, 2007.

———. "Zao nang yu Han jian suojian zao wei shu" 皂囊與漢簡所見皂緯書. In *Jiandu yu gudaishi yanjiu* 簡牘與古代史研究, edited by Wu Rongzeng 吳榮曾 and Wang Guihai 汪桂海, 128–44. Beijing: Beijing daxue chubanshe, 2012.

———. " 'Zhao Xian jie ru shu' yu 'Zhao Junhao cunwu shu'—Jinguan Han jian siwenshu shikao erze" "趙憲借襦書" 與 "趙君勢存物書"—金關漢簡私文書釋考二則. In *Jianduxue yanjiu* 簡讀學研究, no. 5, edited by Xibei shifandaxue lishi wenhua xueyuan 西北師範大學歷史文化學院 and Gansu jiandu bowuguan 甘肅簡牘博物館, 29–37. Lanzhou: Gansu renmin chubanshe, 2014.

Macdonald, M. C A. "Literacy in an Oral Environment." In *Writing and Near East Society*, edited by E. A. Slater, Piotr Bienkowski, and C. B. Mee, 49–118. New York: T & T Clark International, 2005.

Macdonald, Michael C. A. "On the Uses of Writing in Ancient Arabia and the Role of Paleography in Studying Them." *Arabian Epigraphic Notes* 1 (2015): 1–50.

Mair, Victor H. "Buddhism and the Rise of the Written Vernacular in East Asia: The Making of National Languages." *Journal of Asian Studies* 53.3 (1994): 707–51.

Maoshi zhengyi 毛詩正義. See *Shisanjing zhushu*.

Martin, François. "Les anthologies dans la Chine antique et médiévale: De la genèse au déploiement." *Extrême-Orient, Extrême-Occident* 25 (2003): 13–38.

Maspero, Henri, editor and translator. *Les documents chinois de la troisième expédition de Sir Aurel Stein en Asie centrale*. London: Trustees of the British Museum, 1953.

Mawangdui Han mu boshu zhengli xiaozu 馬王堆漢墓帛書整理小組. "Mawangdui Han mu boshu 'Xiangma jing' shiwen" 馬王堆漢墓帛書 "相馬經"釋文. *Wenwu* 文物 8 (1977): 17–22.

McKnight, Brian. *The Quality of Mercy: Amnesties and Traditional Chinese Justice*. Honolulu: University of Hawai'i Press, 1981.

Meyer, Andrew. "Chronicle, Masters Text, or Other? The *Yanzi chunqiu* and the Question of Genre.' Presentation at the Fifth Annual Conference of the Society for the Study of Early China, 16 March 2017.

Milburn, Olivia. *The Spring and Autumn Annals of Master Yan*. Leiden: Brill, 2016.

———. "Palace Women in the Former Han Dynasty (202 BCE–CE 23): Gender and Administrative History in the Early Imperial Era." *Nan Nü* 18 (2016): 195–223.

Miyake Kiyoshi 宮宅潔. "Shin-Kan jidai no moji to shikiji—chikukan, mokkan kara mita" 秦漢時代の文字と識字—竹簡、木簡からみた. In *Kanji no Chūgoku bunka* 漢字の中国文化, edited by Tomiya Itaru 冨谷至, 191–223. Kyoto: Showado, 2009.

Momiyama Akira 籾山明. "Ōjō mokkan saikō" 王杖木簡再考. *Tōhōshi kenkyū* 東方史研究 65 (2006): 1–36.

Narain, A. K. "Indo-Europeans in Inner Asia." In *The Cambridge History of Early Inner Asia*, edited by Denis Sinor, 151–76. Cambridge: Cambridge University Press, 1990.

Newell, Aimee E. *A Stitch in Time: The Needlework of Aging Women in Antebellum America*. Athens: Ohio University Press, 2014.

Nylan, Michael. "Introduction." In *Chang'an 26 BCE: An Augustan Age in China*, edited by Michael Nylan and Griet Vankeerberghen, 3–52. Seattle: University of Washington Press, 2015.

———. *The Five "Confucian" Classics*. New Haven: Yale University Press, 2001.

———. "Manuscript Culture in Late Western Han, and the Implications for Authors and Authority." *Journal of Chinese Literature and Culture* 1.1–2 (2014): 155–85.

———. *Yang Xiong and the Pleasures of Reading and Classical Learning in China*. New Haven: American Oriental Society, 2011.

Ōba Osamu 大庭脩. "Lun Jianshui Jinguan chutu de 'Yongshi sannian zhaoshu' jiance" 論肩水金關出土的 "永始三年詔書" 簡冊. Translated by Jiang Zhenqing 姜鎮慶. *Dunhuangxue jikan* 敦煌學輯刊 2 (1984): 174–84.

———. "Lun Jianshui Jinguan chutu de 'Yongshi sannian zhaoshu' jiance" 論肩水金關出土的 "永始三年詔書" 簡冊. Translated by Jiang Zhenqing 姜鎮慶. *Dunhuangxue jikan* 敦煌學輯刊 2 (1984): 174–84.

———. *Tonkō Kan kan: Tai Ei toshokan zō* 敦煌漢簡: 大英図書館蔵. Kyoto: Dōhōsha, 1990.

———. "Yuankang wunian (qian 61 nian) zhaoshuce de fuyuan he yushi dafu de yewu" 元康五年(前61年)詔書冊的復原和御史大夫的業務. *Qi-Lu xuekan* 齊魯學刊 2 (1988): 3–8.

Ong, Walter J. *Orality and Literacy: The Technologizing of the Word*. Revised edition. London: Routledge, 2002.

Orme, Nicholas. *Medieval Children*. New Haven: Yale University Press, 2001.

Owen, Stephen. *Readings in Chinese Literary Thought*. Cambridge: Harvard University Press, 1996.

Pan Chonggui 潘重規, editor. *Dunhuang bianwen xinshu* 敦煌變文新書. Taipei: Wenjin chubanshe, 1994.

Pei Yongliang 裴永亮. "Han Peng gushi de wenxue chengchuan" 韓朋故事的文學承傳. *Yuwen jiaoxue tongxun* 語文教學通訊 2 (2015): 58–59.

Peng Duo 彭鐸, editor. *Qianfulun jiaozheng* 潛夫論校正. Beijing: Zhonghua shuju, 1985.

Peng Hao 彭浩, Chen Wei 陳偉, and Kudo Mutoo 工藤元男, editors. *Ernian lüling yu Zouyanshu: Zhangjiashan ersiqihao Han mu chutu falü wenxian shidu* 二年律令與奏讞書: 張家山二四七號漢墓出土法律文獻釋讀. Shanghai: Shanghai guji, 2007.

Pitner, Mark. "Disability in Early China." Unpublished paper, 2015.

Pope, Alexander. *Alexander Pope*. With an introduction by John Bailey. London and Edinburgh: Thomas Nelson and Sons, [1924?].

Puett, Michael. *The Ambivalence of Creation: Debates Concerning Innovation and Artifice in Early China*. Stanford: Stanford University Press, 2001.

———. "Centering the Realm: Wang Mang, the *Zhouli*, and Early Chinese Statecraft." In *Statecraft and Classical Learning: The Rituals of Zhou in East Asian History*, edited by Benjamin Elman and Martin Kern, 129–54. Leiden: Brill, 2010.

———. "The Temptations of Sagehood, or: The Rise and Decline of Sagely Writing in Early China." In *Books in Numbers: Seventy-Fifth Anniver-*

sary of the Harvard-Yenching Library, edited by Wilt L. Idema, 23–43. Cambridge: Harvard-Yenching Library, 2007.

Qian Mu 錢穆 (1395–1990). *Qin-Han shi* 秦漢史. Taipei: Dongda tushu gongsi, 2001.

Qiu Xigui 裘錫圭. "An Examination of Whether the Charges in Shang Oracle-Bone Inscriptions Are Questions." *Early China* 14 (1989): 77–114.

———. "Han jian zhong suojian Han Peng gushi de xin ziliao" 漢簡中所見韓朋故事的新資料. *Fudan xuebao (shehui kexue ban)* 復旦學報 (社會科學板) 3 (1999): 109–13.

———. "Tian Zhang jian bushi" 田章簡補釋. In *Jianbo yanjiu (di san ji)* 簡帛研究(第三集), edited by Li Xueqin 李學勤 et al., 455–58. Guilin: Guangxi jiaoyu chubanshe, 1998.

———. *Zhongguo chutu wenxian shijiang* 中國出土文獻十講. Shanghai: Fudan daxue chubanshe, 2004.

Qu Zhongrong 瞿中溶 (1769–1842). *Yizai tuyu tulu* 奕載古玉圖錄. Rui'an: Dai Guochen 戴國琛 woodblock edition, ca. 1930.

Rao Zongyi 饒宗頤 and Li Junming 李均明. *Xin-Mang jian jizheng* 新莽簡輯證. Taipei: Xinwenfeng chubangongsi, 1995.

Rawski, Evelyn Sakakida. *Education and Popular Literacy in Ch'ing China.* Ann Arbor: University of Michigan Press, 1979.

Ray, Larry. "Society" In *The Blackwell Encyclopedia of Sociology*, edited by George Ritzer, 4581–83. Malden: Blackwell, 2007.

Richter, Antje. *Letters and Epistolary Culture in Early Medieval China.* Seattle: University of Washington Press, 2013.

Richter, Matthias L. *The Embodied Text: Establishing Textual Identity in Early Chinese Manuscripts.* Leiden: Brill, 2013.

Rickett, W. Allyn. "Kuan tzu." In *Early Chinese Texts: A Bibliographical Guide*, edited by Michael Loewe, 244–51. Berkeley: Society for the Study of Early China, 1993.

Rong Zhaozu 容肇祖. "Xichui mujian zhong suo ji de 'Tian Zhang'" 西陲木簡中所記的 "田章." *Lingnan xuebao* 嶺南學報 2.3 (1931): 125–31.

Rothenbuhler, Eric W. "Communication as Ritual." In *Communication As—: Perspectives on Theory*, ed. Gregory J. Shepherd, Jeffrey St. John, and Ted Striphas, 13–21.Thousand Oaks: Sage, 2005.

Salinger, J. D. *The Catcher in the Rye.* Boston: Little, Brown, 1951.

Sanft, Charles. *Communication and Cooperation in Early Imperial China: Publicizing the Qin Dynasty.* Albany: State University of New York Press, 2014.

———. "Edict of Monthly Ordinances for the Four Seasons in Fifty Articles from 5 C.E.: Introduction to the Wall Inscription Discovered at Xuanquanzhi, with Annotated Translation." *Early China* 32 (2008–9): 125–208.

———. "Environment and Law in Early Imperial China (3rd c. BCE–1st c. CE): Qin and Han Statutes Concerning Natural Resources." *Environmental History* 15.4 (2010): 701–21.

———. "Evaluating Swords: Introduction and Translation of a How-To Guide from the Han-Xin Period." *Early China* 39 (2016): 231–53.

———. "Interacting with Text in Early China and Beyond." *Fragments: Interdisciplinary Approaches to the Ancient and Medieval Pasts*. Forthcoming.

———. "The Moment of Dying: Representations in Liu Xiang's Anthologies *Xin xu* and *Shuo yuan*." *Asia Major* (third series) 24.1 (2011): 127–58.

———. "Paleographic Evidence of Qin Religious Practice from Liye and Zhoujiatai." *Early China* 37 (2014): 327–58.

———. "Population Records from Liye: Ideology in Practice." In *Ideology of Power and Power of Ideology in Early China*, edited by Yuri Pines, Paul R. Goldin, and Martin Kern, 249–69. Leiden: Brill, 2015.

———. "Questions about the Qi *Lunyu*." *T'oung Pao* 104.1–2 (2018): 189–94.

———. "Send Shoes: A Letter from Yuan to Zifang." *Renditions: A Chinese-English Translation Magazine* 79 (2013): 7–10.

Satō Tatsurō 佐藤達郎. "Kandai no hensho, kabegaki—toku ni chihō teki kyōrei to no kakei de—" 漢代の扁書・壁書—特に地方的教令との関係で—. *Kansai gakuin shigaku* 関西學院史學 35 (2008): 83–98.

Schaberg, David. *A Patterned Past: Form and Thought in Early Chinese Historiography*. Cambridge: Harvard University Asia Center, 2001.

Schoeler, Gregor. *The Genesis of Literature in Islam: From the Aural to the Read*. Revised edition, in collaboration with and translated by Shawkat M. Toorawa. Edinburgh: Edinburgh University Press, 2009.

Schwermann, Christian. "Anecdote Collections as Argumentative Texts: The Composition of the *Shuoyuan*." In *Between History and Philosophy: Anecdotes in Early China*, edited by Paul van Els and Sarah Queen, 147–92. Albany: State University of New York Press, 2017.

Shangguan Xuzhi 上官續智 and Huang Jinyan 黃今言. "Handai fengsui zhong de xinxi qiju yu fenghuo pinyue zhiyong kaolun" 漢代烽燧中的信息器具與烽火品約置用考論. *Shehui kexue jikan* 社會科學輯刊 5 (2004): 93–98.

Shangshu zhengyi 尚書正義. See *Shisanjing zhushu*.

Shen Gang 沈剛. "'Eji'na Han jian' Wang Mang zhaoshu lingce pailie cixu xinjie" "額濟納漢簡" 王莽詔書令冊排列次序新解. *Beifang wenwu* 北方文物 2 (2007): 75–77.

———. *Juyan Han jian yuci huishi* 居延漢簡語詞匯釋. Beijing: Kexue chubanshe, 2008.

———. "Juyan Han jian zhong de xizijian shulüe" 居延漢簡中的習字簡述略. *Guji zhengli yanjiu xuekan* 古籍整理研究學刊 1 (2006): 29–31.

Shen Songjin 沈頌金. "Chutu jianbo yu wenxueshi yanjiu" 出土簡帛與文學史研究. *Qi-Lu xuekan* 齊魯學刊 6 (2004): 71–76.

———. *Ershi shiji jianboxue yanjiu* 二十世紀簡帛學研究. Beijing: Xueyuan chubanshe, 2003.

Shi Guangying 石光瑛, editor. *Xin xu jiaoshi* 新序校釋. Beijing: Zhonghua shuju, 2001.

Shiji 史記. By Sima Qian 司馬遷 (ca. 145–ca. 86 BCE). Beijing: Zhonghua shuju, 1959.

Shisanjing zhushu 十三經注疏. ed. Ruan Yuan 阮元 (1764–1849). Taipei: Yiwen yinshuguan, 200□.

Sima Guang 司馬光 (1019–1036). *Zizhi tongjian* 資治通鑑. Beijing: Zhonghua shuju, 1956.

Smith, Frank. *Understanding Reading: A Psycholinguistic Analysis of Reading and Learning to Read*. Sixth edition. Mahwah: Lawrence Erlbaum Associates, 2004.

Sommarström, Bo. *Archaeological Researches in the Edsen-gol Region Inner Mongolia: Together with the Catalogue Prepared by Folke Bergman*. Stockholm: Statens Etnografiska Museum, 1956.

Song Chao 宋超. "'Xiangnu' yu 'Gongnu'—lüe lun Xin-Mang shiqi Xiongnu chengwei de bianhua" "降奴" 與 "恭奴"—略論新莽時期匈奴稱謂的變化. In *Gansusheng dierjie jianduxue guoji xueshu yantaohui lunwenji* 甘肅省第二屆簡牘學國際學術研討會論文集, edited by Zhang Defang 張德芳, 75–86. Shanghai: Shanghai guji chubanshe, 2012.

Song Yanping 宋艷萍 "Tianchang Jizhuang Han mu mudu suojian 'waichu' kaoxi" 天長紀莊漢墓木牘所見 "外廚" 考析. *Zhongguoshi yanjiu* 中國史研究 4 (2012): 200–4.

Stein, M. Aurel. *On Ancient Central-Asian Tracks: Brief Narrative of Three Expeditions in Innermost Asia and North-Western China*. London: Macmillan and Col, 1933.

———. *Ruins of Desert Cathay. Personal Narrative of Explorations in Central Asia and Westernmost China*. 2 volumes. 1912; reprinted New York: Benjamin Blom, 1968.

———. "A Third Journey of Exploration in Central Asia, 1913–16." *The Geographical Journal* 48.2 (August 1916): 97–130.

———. "A Third Journey of Exploration in Central Asia, 1913–16." *The Geographical Journal* 48.3 (September 1916): 193–225.

Stock, Brian. *The Implications of Literacy: Written Language and Models of Interpretation in the Eleventh and Twelfth Centuries*. Princeton: Princeton University Press, 1983.

Sun Ji 孫機. *Handai wuzhi wenhua ziliao tushuo* 漢代物質文化資料圖說. Revised edition. Shanghai: Shanghai guji chubanshe, 2008.

Sun Rui 孫瑞 and Chen Lanlan 陳蘭蘭. "Handai jiandu siwenshu suofanying de jizhong shehui xianxiang" 漢代簡牘私文書所反映的幾種舍會現象. *Shehui kexue zhanxian* 合會科學戰線 2 (2007): 119–21.

———. "Handai jiandu zhong suojian siren shuzha ji buji" 漢代簡牘中所見私人書札及簿籍. *Dongbei shidaxue bao (zhexue shehui kexue ban)* 東北師大學報 (哲學社會科學版) 1 (2012): 69–74.

Sun Shuxia 孫淑霞. "'Cang Jie pian' yanjiu zongshu" "倉頡篇" 研究綜述. *Mianyang shifan xueyuan xuebao* 綿羊師範學院院報 32.4 (2013): 36–39, 43.

Sun Wenbo 孫聞博. "Hexi Han sai junren de shenghuo shijianbiao" 河西漢塞軍人的生活時間表. In *Jianbo yanjiu. 2015. Chunxia juan* 簡帛研究. 2015. 春夏卷, edited by Yang Zhenhong 楊振紅 and Wu Wenling 鄔文玲, 152–83. Guilin: Guangxi shifan daxue chubanshe, 2015.

Sun Yirang 孫詒讓 (1848–1908). *Mozi jiangu* 墨子閒詁. Beijing: Zhonghua shuju, 2001.

Sun Zhanyu 孫占宇. "Maquanwan Hanjian suojian yici fasheng zai Jushi de zhanzheng" 馬圈灣漢簡所見一次發生在車師的戰爭. *Dunhuangxue jikan* 敦煌學輯刊 3 (2006): 51–57.

Svarvarud, Rune. "Body and Character: Physiognomical Descriptions in Han Dynasty Literature." In *Minds and Mentalities in Traditional Chinese Literature*, ed. Halvor Elfring, 120–46. Beijing: Culture and Art Publishing House, 1999.

Tan Qixiang 譚其驤. *Zhongguo lishi dituji* 中國歷史地圖集. Beijing: Zhongguo ditu chubanshe, 1982.

Tang Kejing 湯可敬. *Shuowen jiezi jinshi* 說文解字今釋. Changsha: Yuelu shushe, 1997.

Tao Quyong 陶曲勇. "Anhui Tianchang Han mu mudu 'shouji' shijie" 安徽天長漢墓木牘 "綬急" 試解. *Huainan shifan xueyuan xuebao* 淮南師範學院學報 14.1 (2012): 121–22.

Tavor, Ori. "Religious Thought." In *Routledge Handbook of Early Chinese History*, edited by Paul R. Goldin, 261–79. London: Routledge, 2018.

Taylor, Insup, and Martin M. Taylor. *Writing and Literacy in Chinese, Korean and Japanese*. Amsterdam: John Benjamins, 1995.

Terigele 特日格樂. "'Eji'na Han jian' suojian Wang Mang jian lüe kao" "額濟納漢簡" 所見王莽簡略考. *Chutu wenxian yanjiu* 出土文獻研究 7 (2005): 185–93.

Thote, Alain. "Daybooks in Archaeological Context." In *Books of Fate and Popular Culture in Early China: The Daybook Manuscripts of the Warring States, Qin, and Han*, edited by Donald Harper and Marc Kalinowski, 11–56. Leiden: Brill, 2017.

Tian Yuqing 田余慶. *Qin-Han Wei-Jin shi tanwei* 秦漢魏晉史探微. Beijing: Zhonghua shuju, 2008.

Tianchangshi wenwu guanlisuo 天長市文物管理所 and Tianchangshi bowuguan 天長市博物館. "Anhui Tianchang Xihan mu fajue jianbao" 安徽天長西漢墓發掘簡報. *Wenwu* 文物 11 (2006): 4–21.

Tomiya Itaru 冨谷至. "Gaisetsu" 概説. In *Kankan goi kōshō* 漢簡語彙考証. Edited by Tomiya Itaru, 1–44. Tokyo: Iwanami Shoten, 2015.

———. *Monjo gyōsei no Kan teikoku: mokkan, chikukan no jidai* 文書行政の漢帝国: 木簡・竹簡の時代. Nagoya: Nagoya Daigaku Shuppansha, 2010.

———. "Ōjō jukkan" 王杖一簡. *Tōhō gakuhō* 東方學報 64 (1992): 61–113.

———. *Shin-Kan keibatsu seido no kenkyū* 秦漢刑罰制度の研究. Kyoto: Dōhōsha, 1998.

Tomiya Itaru, editor. *Kankan goi kōshō* 漢簡語彙考証. Tokyo: Iwanami Shoten, 2015.

Tsien, Tsuen-Hsü. *Written on Bamboo and Silk*. Second edition. Chicago: University of Chicago Press, 2004.

Twitchett, Denis. "Chinese Social History from the Seventh to the Tenth Centuries: The Tunhuang Documents and Their Implications." *Past and Present* 35 (1966): 28–53.

Wagner, Donald B. *Iron and Steel in Ancient China*. Leiden: Brill, 1996.

Waley, Arthur. *The Book of Songs*. Edited, with additional translations, Joseph R. Allen. New York: Grove Press, 1996.

Wang Bing 王冰. "Tianchang Jizhuang Han mu 'Benqie zhi Xie Meng shu' du kaoshi" 天長紀莊漢墓 "貫且致謝孟書" 牘考釋. *Jianbo* 簡帛 6 (2011): 421–26.

Wang Chuning 王楚寧 and Zhang Yuzheng 張予正. "Jianshui jinguan Han jian 'Qi *Lunyu*' de zhengli" 肩水金關漢簡 "齊論語" 的整理. Online at http://www.kaogu.cn/cn/kaoguyuandi/kaogusuibi/2017/0816/59268.html; dated 16 August 2017, accessed 5 December 2017.

Wang Guanying 王冠英. "Han Xuanquanzhi yizhi chutu Yuan yu Zifang boshu xinzha kaoshi" 漢懸泉置遺址出土元與子方帛書信札考釋. *Zhongguo lishi bowuguan guankan* 中國歷史博物館館刊 1 (1998): 58–61.

Wang Guihai 王桂海. *Qin-Han jiandu tanyan* 秦漢簡牘探研. Taipei: Wenjin chubanshe, 2009.

Wang Guiyuan 王貴元. "Anhui Tianchang Han mu mudu chutan" 安徽天長漢墓木牘初探. In *Guwenzixue lungao* 古文字學論稿, edited by Zhang Guangyu 張光裕 et al., 465–71. Hefei: Anhui daxue chubanshe, 2008.

Wang Haicheng. *Writing and the Ancient State: Early China in Comparative Perspective*. Cambridge: Cambridge University Press, 2014.

Wang Hui 王輝. *Guwenzi tongjia shili* 古文字通假釋例. Taipei: Yiwen yinshuguan, 1993.

Wang Liqi 王利器, editor. *Fengsu tongyi jiaozhu* 風俗通義校注. Beijing: Zhonghua shuju, 1981.

Wang Lunxin 王倫信. "'Gu' yu jiandu shidai de xizi cailiao" "觚" 與簡牘時代的習字材料. *Jichu jiaoyu* 基礎教育 8.6 (2011): 120–24.

Wang Mo 王謨 (ca. eighteenth c.), editor. *Han-Wei yishu chao* 漢魏遺書鈔. Kyoto: Chubun shuppansha, 1981.

Wang Rongbao 汪榮寶, editor. *Fayan yishu* 法言義疏. Beijing: Zhonghua shuju, 1987.

Wang Shuanghuai 王雙懷, editor. *Zhonghua rili tongdian* 中華日曆通典. Jilin: Jilin wenshi chubanshe, 2006.

Wang Shujin 王樹金. "Mawangdui Han mu boshu 'Xiang ma jing' yanjiu sanshinian" 馬王堆漢墓帛書 "相馬經" 研究三十年. *Hu'nansheng bowuguan guankan* 湖南省博物館館刊 5 (2008): 241–48.

Wang Xianqian 王先謙 (1842–1918). *Han shu bu zhu* 漢書補注. 1900 woodblock edition; reprinted Yangzhou: Guangling shushe, 2006.

———. *Hou Han shu jijie* 後漢書集解. 1915 woodblock edition; reprinted Yangzhou: Guangling shushe, 2006.

———. *Shi sanjia yi jishu* 詩三家義集疏. Taipei: Mingwen shuju, 1988.

———. *Xunzi jijie* 荀子集解. Beijing: Zhonghua shuju, 1988.

Wang Xiaoguang 王曉光. "Tianchang Jizhuang mudu moji yanjiu ji shuxie shijian xintan" 天長紀莊木牘墨迹研究及書寫時間新探. In *Jianbo yanjiu erlingyiling* 簡帛研究二〇一〇, edited by Bu Xianqun 卜憲群 and Yang Zhenhong 楊振紅, 89–98. Guilin: Guangxi shifan daxue chubanshe, 2012.

Wang Zhenya 王震亞 and Zhang Xiaofeng 張小鋒. "Han jian zhong de shuzu shenghuo" 漢簡中的戍卒生活. In *Jianduxue yanjiu* 簡牘學研究, no. 2, edited by Gansusheng wenwu kaogu yanjiusuo 甘肅省文物考古研究所 et al., 101–18. Lanzhou: Gansu renmin chubanshe, 1998.

Wang Zijin 王子今. "Eji'na 'Zhuan bu shili dian quzhe' jiance shiming" 額濟納 "專部士吏典趣輒" 簡冊釋名. In *Eji'na Han jian shiwen jiaoben* 額濟納漢簡釋文校本, edited by Sun Jiazhou 孫家洲, 165–69. Beijing: Wenwu chubanshe, 2007.

———. *Hanjian Hexi shehui shiliao yanjiu* 漢簡河西社會史料研究. Beijing: Shangwu yinshuguan, 2017.

———. "Juyan Han jian suojian 'mingfu' chengwei" 居延漢簡所見 "明府" 稱謂. In *Jianbo yanjiu erlinglingqi* 簡帛研究二〇〇七, edited by Bu Xianqun 卜憲群 and Yang Zhenhong 楊振紅, 89–98. Guilin: Guangxi shifan daxue chubanshe, 2010.

———. *Qin-Han chengwei yanjiu* 秦漢稱謂研究. Beijing: Zhongguo shehui kexue chubanshe, 2014.

Wei Yanli 魏燕利. "'Wang zhang' kaobian" "王杖" 考辨. *Jianduxue yanjiu* 簡牘學研究, no. 4, edited by Xibei shifan daxue wenxueyuan lishixi 西北師範大學文學院歷史系 et al., 147–59. Lanzhou: Gansu renmin chubanshe, 2004.

Wenwuju guwenxian yanjiushi 文物局古文獻研究室 and Anhuisheng Fuyang diqu bowuguan 安徽省阜陽地區博物館. "Fuyang Han jian 'Cang Jie pian'" 阜陽漢簡 "蒼頡篇." *Wenwu* 2 (1983): 24–34.

Wolf, Maryanne. *Proust and the Squid: The Story and Science of the Reading Brain*. New York: Harper Perennial, 2007.

Wu Dexu 伍德煦. "Xin faxian de yifen Xihan zhaoshu—'Yongshi sannian zhaoshu jiance' kaoshi he youguan wenti" 新發現的一份西漢詔書—《永始三年詔書簡冊》考釋和有關問題. *Xibei shiyuan xuebao (shehui kexue ban)* 西北師院學報(社會科學版) 4 (1983): 62–69.

Wu Rengxiang 吳礽驤. *Hexi Han sai diaocha yu yanjiu* 河西漢塞調查與研究. Beijing: Wenwu chubanshe, 2005.

Wu Rengxiang, Li Yongliang 李永良, and Ma Jianhua 馬建華, editors. *Dunhuang Han jian shiwen* 敦煌漢簡釋文. Lanzhou: Gansu renmin chubanshe, 1991.

Wu Shuping 吳樹平, editor. *Dongguan Han ji jiaozhu* 東觀漢記校注. Zhengzhou: Zhongzhou guji chubanshe, 1987.

Wu Wangzong 吳旺宗. "Xihan yu Xin-Mang shiqi zhengfu xinxi chuanbo meijie—Eji'na Han jian 'bianshu' tanxi" 西漢與新莽時期政府信息傳播媒介—額濟納漢簡 "扁書" 探析. In *Eji'na Han jian shiwen jiaoben* 額濟納漢簡釋文校本, edited by Sun Jiazhou 孫家洲, 184–87. Beijing: Wenwu chubanshe, 2007.

Wu Wenling 鄔文玲. "Ejian Shijianguo ernian zhaoshuce 'yi gong' shijie" 額簡始建國二年詔書冊 "壹功" 試解. In *Eji'na Han jian shiwen jiaoben* 額濟納漢簡釋文校本, edited by Sun Jiazhou 孫家洲, 137–39. Beijing: Wenwu chubanshe, 2007.

———. "Shijianguo ernian Xin-Mang yu Xiongnu guanxi shishi kaobian" 始建國二年新莽與匈奴關係史事考辨. *Lishi yanjiu* 歷史研究 2 (2006): 177–81.

———. "Tianchang Jizhuang Han mu muzhuren xingming shitan" 天長紀莊漢墓墓主人姓名試探. In *Jianbo* 簡帛, no. 3, edited by Wuhan daxue jianbo yanjiu zhongxin 武漢大學簡帛研究中心, 40–45. Shanghai: Shanghai guji chubanshe, 2008.

Wu Zeyu 吳則虞, editor. *Yanzi chunqiu jishi* 晏子春秋集釋. Beijing: Zhonghua shuju, 1982.

Wuwei diqu bowuguan 武威地區博物館. "Gansu Wuwei Hantanpo Donghan mu" 甘肅武威旱灘坡東漢墓. *Wenwu* 文物 10 (1993): 28–33.

Wuweixian bowuguan 武威縣博物館. "Wuwei xinchu Wang zhang zhaoling ce" 武威新出王杖詔令冊. In *Hanjian yanjiu wenji* 漢簡研究文集, edited by Gansusheng wenwu gongzuodui 甘肅省文物工作隊 et al., 34–61. Lanzhou: Gansu renmin chubanshe, 1984.

Xi Wenqian 郗文倩. "Handai gangmao ji qi mingwen kaolun" 漢代剛卯及其銘文考論. *Fujian Jiangxia xueyuan xuebao* 福建江夏學院學報 4.4 (2014): 93–100.

Xiaogan diqu dierqi yigong yinong wenwu kaogu xunlianban 孝感地區第二期亦工亦農文物考古訓練班. "Hubei Yunmeng Shuihudi shiyi hao Qin mu fajue jianbao" 湖北雲夢睡虎地十一號秦墓發掘簡報. *Wenwu* 文物 6 (1976): 1–10.

Xiaojing zhushu 孝經注疏. See *Shisanjing zhushu*.

Xie Chengxia 謝成俠. "Guanyu Mawangdui Han mu boshu 'Xiang ma jing' de tantao" 關於馬王堆漢墓帛書 "相馬經" 的探討. *Wenwu* 文物 8 (1977): 23–26.

Xie Guihua. "Han Bamboo and Wooden Medical Records Discovered in Military Sites from the Northwestern Frontier Region." In *Medieval Chinese Medicine: The Dunhuang Medical Manuscripts*, edited by Vivienne Lo and Christopher Cullen, 78–106. London: Routledge Curzon, 2005.

Xu Pingfang 徐苹芳. "Juyan, Dunhuang faxian de 'Saishang fenghuo pinyue'—jian shi Handai de fenghuo zhidu" 居延、敦煌發現的 "塞上蓬火品約"—兼釋漢代的蓬火制度. *Kaogu* 考古 5 (1979): 445–54.

Xu Shen 許慎 (fl. ca. 100 CE). *Shuowen jiezi* 說文解字. Beijing: Zhonghua shuju, 1963.

Xu Weiyu 許維遹, editor. *Hanshi waizhuan jishi* 韓詩外傳集釋. Beijing: Zhonghua shuju, 1980.

Xu Yanbin 徐燕斌. "Han jian bianshu jikao—jian lun Handai falü chuanbo de lujing" 漢簡扁書輯考—兼論漢代法律傳播的路徑. *Huadong zhengfa daxue xuebao* 華東政法大學學報 2 (2013): 50–62.

Xu Yunhe 許雲和. "Dunhuang Han jian 'Fengyu shi' shilun" 敦煌漢簡 "風雨詩" 試論. *Shoudu shifan daxue xuebao (shehui kexueban)* 首都師範大學學報(社會科學版) 2 (2011): 84–92.

Xue Yingqun 薛英群. *Juyan Han jian tonglun* 居延漢簡通論. Lanzhou: Gansu jiaoyu chubanshe, 1991.

———. "Juyan 'Saishang fenghuo pinyue'" 居延 "塞上烽火品約" 冊. *Kaogu* 4 (1979): 361–64.

Xue Yingqun, He Shuangquan 何雙全, Li Yongliang 李永良, et al. *Juyan xinjian shicui* 居延新簡釋粹. Lanzhou: Lanzhou daxue chubanshe, 1988.

Yamada Katsuyoshi 山田勝芳. "Zen-Kan Butei dai no chiiki shakai to josei youeki—Ankishō Tenchōshi Anrakuchin jūkyūgō Kan bo mokutoku kara kangaeru" 前漢武帝代の地域社會と女性徭役—安徽省天長市安樂鎮十九號漢墓木牘から考える. *Shūkan Tōyōgaku* 集刊東洋學 97 (2007): 1–19.

Yan Gengwang 嚴耕望. *Zhongguo dingfang xingzheng zhidushi—Qin-Han difang xingzheng zhidu* 中國地方行政制度史—秦漢地方行政制度. Shanghai: Shanghai guji chubanshe, 2007.

Yang Bojun 楊伯峻. *Lunyu yizhu* 論語譯注. Beijing: Zhonghua shuju, 1980.

Yang Dianyue 楊典岳. "Handai guanliao sishu wanglai ji qi yingxiang" 漢代官僚私書往來及其影響. MA thesis, National Taiwan Normal University, 2007.

Yang Fen 楊芬. "Du Dunhuang boshu 'Zheng yu Youqing, Junming shu' zhaji" 讀敦煌帛書 "政與幼卿、君明書." *Dunhuangxue jikan* 敦煌學輯刊 1 (2011): 119–26.

Yang Hongnian 楊鴻年. *Han-Wei zhidu congkao* 漢魏制度叢考. Second edition. Wuhan: Wuhan daxue chubanshe, 2005.

Yang Jidong. "Transportation, Boarding, Lodging, and Trade along the Early Silk Road: A Preliminary Study of the Xuanquan Manuscripts." *Journal of the American Oriental Society* 135.3 (2015): 421–32.

Yang Jiping 楊際平. "Xi Changsha Zoumalou Sanguo Wujian zhong de 'tiao'—jian tan hutiaozhi de qiyuan" 析長沙走馬樓三國吳簡中的 "調"—兼談戶調制的起源. *Lishi yanjiu* 歷史研究 3 (2006): 39–58.

Yang Yiping 楊以平 and Qiao Guorong 喬國榮. "Tianchang Xihan mudu shulüe" 天長西漢木牘述略. In *Jianbo yanjiu erlinglingliu* 簡帛研究二〇〇六, edited by Bu Xianqun 卜憲群 and Qiao Guorong 喬國榮, 195–202. Guilin: Guangxi shifan daxue chubanshe, 2009.

Yang Zhenhong 楊振紅. "Jizhuang Han mu 'Biqie' shudu de shidu ji xiangguan wenti—Jizhuang Han mu mudu suo fanying de Xihan difang shehui yanjiu zhi yi" 紀莊漢墓 "貰且" 書牘的釋讀及相關問題—紀莊漢墓木牘所反映的西漢地方社會研究之一. In *Jianbo yanjiu erlinglingjiu* 簡帛研究二〇〇九, edited by Bu Xianqun 卜憲群 and Yang Zhenhong, 1–13. Guilin: Guangxi shifan daxue chubanshe, 2011.

———. "Tianchang Jizhuan Han mu Xie Meng de ming, zi, shenfen ji yu muzhuren guanxi lice—Jizhuang Han mu mudu suo fanying de Xihan difang shehui yanjiu zhi er" 天長紀莊漢墓謝孟的名、字、身份及與墓主人關係蠡測—紀莊漢墓木牘所反映的西漢地方社會研究之二. *Zhejiang xuekan* 浙江學刊 6 (2011): 42–49.

Yao, Alice. *The Ancient Highlands of Southwest China: From the Bronze Age to the Han Empire*. Oxford: Oxford University Press, 2016.

Yao Zhenzong 姚振宗 (1843–1906). *Sui shu jingji zhi kaozheng* 隋書經籍志考證. *Xuxiu Siku quanshu* 續修四庫全書 edition. Shanghai: Shanghai guji chubanshe, 2002.

Yates, Robin D. S. "Purity and Pollution in Early China." In *Zhongguo kaoguxue yu lishixue zhi zhenghe yanjiu* 中國考古學與歷史學之整合研究, edited by Zang Zhenhua 臧振華, 479–536. Taipei: Zhongyang yanjiuyuan lishi yuyan yanjiusuo, 1997.

———. "The Qin Slips and Boards from Well No. 1, Liye, Hunan: A Brief Introduction to the Qin Qianling County Archives." *Early China* 35–36 (2012–2013): 291–329.

———. "Soldiers, Scribes, and Women: Literacy among the Lower Orders in Early China." In *Writing and Literacy in Early China: Studies from the Columbia Early China Seminar*, edited by Li Feng and David Prager Branner, 339–69. Seattle: University of Washington Press, 2012.

Yinqueshan Han mu zhujian (er) 銀雀山漢墓竹簡 (貳). Edited by Yinqueshan Han mu zhujian zhengli xiaozu 銀雀山漢墓竹簡整理小組. Beijing: Wenwu chubanshe, 2010.

Yu Shinan 虞世南 (558–638), editor. *Beitang shuchao* 北堂書鈔. Taipei: Wen-
    hai chubanshe, 1978.
Yu Xin 余欣. "Chutu wenxian suojian Han-Tang xiangma shu kao" 出土文
    獻所見漢唐相馬術考. *Xueshu yuekan* 學術月刊 2 (2014): 135–43.
Yu Zhenbo 于振波. "Qin-Han shiqi de youren" 秦漢時期的郵人. In *Jianduxue
    yanjiu* 簡牘學研究, no. 4, edited by Gansusheng kaogu yanjiusuo 甘
    肅省考古研究所 and Xibei shifan daxue wenxueyuan lishixi 西北師
    範大學文學院歷史系, 28–33. Lanzhou: Gansu renmin chubanshe,
    2004.
———. *Jiandu yu Qin-Han shehui* 簡牘與秦漢社會. Changsha: Hunan daxue
    chubanshe, 2012.
Yuan Yahao 袁雅浩. "Handai Juyan tunshu jigou neibu baoli chongtu
    yuanyin chutan" 漢代居延屯戍機構內部暴力衝突原因初探. *Dang'an* 檔
    案 11 (2014): 41–45.
Zadneprovskiy, Y. A. "The Nomads of Northern Central Asia after the Inva-
    sion of Alexander." In *History of Civilizations of Central Asia, Volume
    2, The Development of Sedentary and Nomadic Civilizations: 700 B.C. to
    A.D. 250*, edited by János Harmatta, 457–72. Paris: United Nations
    Educational, Scientific and Cultural Organization, 1994.
Zhang Defang 張德芳. "Cong Xuanquan Hanjian kan Xi-Han Wu-Zhao shiqi
    he Xuan-Yuan shiqi jingying xiyu de butong zhanlüe" 從懸泉漢簡看
    西漢武昭時期和宣元時期經營西域的不同戰略. In *Han diguo de zhidu yu
    shehui zhixu* 漢帝國的制度與社會秩序, edited by Lai Ming-chiu 黎明釗,
    277–316. Hong Kong: Oxford University Press, 2012.
———. "Qiantan Hexi Han jian he Dunhuang bianwen de yuanyuan
    guanxi" 淺談河西漢簡和敦煌變文的淵源關係. *Dunhuangxue jikan* 敦煌
    學輯刊 2 (2005): 52–56.
———. "Xuanquan Han jian zhong de 'zhuanxin jian' kaoshu" 懸泉漢簡
    中的 "傳信簡" 考述. In *Chutu wenxian yanjiu* 出土文獻研究, no. 7,
    edited by Zhongguo wenwu yanjiusuo, 65–81. Shanghai: Shanghai
    guji chubanshe, 2005.
Zhang Feng 張鳳. *Han-Jin xichui mujian huibian* 漢晉西陲木簡彙編. In *Hanjian
    wenxian yanjiu sizhong* 漢簡文獻研究四種. Beijing: Beijing tushuguan
    chubanshe, 2007.
Zhang Guoyan 張國豔. *Juyan Han jian xuci tongshi* 居延漢簡虛詞通釋. Beijing:
    Zhonghua shuju, 2012.
Zhang Jinguang. *Qin zhi yanjiu* 秦制研究. Shanghai: Shanghai guji chuban-
    she, 2004.
Zhang Junmin 張俊民. "Xuanquan Han jian suojian wenshu geshi jian" 懸
    泉漢簡所見文書格式簡. In *Jianbo yanjiu erlinglingjiu* 簡帛研究二〇〇九,
    ed. Bu Xianqun 卜憲群 and Yang Zhenhong 楊振紅, 120–41. Guilin:
    Guangxi shifan daxue chubanshe, 2011.

———. "Gansu chutu de Handai boshu" 甘肅出土的漢代帛書. *Sichou zhi lu* 絲綢之路 3 (1997): 38–39.

Zhang Lie 張烈, editor. *Liang Han ji* 兩漢紀. Beijing: Zhonghua shuju, 2002.

Zhang Xiaofeng 張小鋒. *Xi-Han houqi zhengju yanbian tanwei* 西漢後期政局演變探微. Tianjin: Tianjin guji chubanshe, 2007.

Zhangsun Wuji 長孫無忌 (d. 659). *Sui shu*. Beijing: Zhonghua shuju, 1973.

Zhao Chongliang 趙寵亮. "Juyan xinjian 'Nüzi Qi Tongnai suo ze Qin Gong gu shi' cance fuyuan yu yanjiu" 居延新簡 "女子齊通耐所責秦恭鼓事" 殘冊復原與研究. In *Jianbo* 簡帛, no. 5, edited by Wuhan daxue jianbo yanjiu zhongxin 武漢大學簡帛研究中心, 403–13. Shanghai: Shanghai guji chubanshe, 2010.

———. *Xingyi shubei: Hexi Han sai lizu de tunshu shenghuo* 行役戍備—河西漢塞吏卒的屯戍生活. Beijing: Kexue chubanshe, 2012.

Zhao Huacheng 趙化成, Gao Chongwen 高崇文, et al. *Qin-Han kaogu* 秦漢考古. Beijing: Wenwu chubanshe, 2002.

Zhao Kuifu 趙逵夫. "Mawangdui Han mu chutu 'Xiang ma jing—Daguang po zhang gu xun zhuan'" 馬王堆漢墓出土 "相馬經・大光破章故訓傳" 發微. *Jiang-Han kaogu* 江漢考古 3 (1989): 48–51, 47.

———. "Mawangdui Han mu boshu 'Xiang ma jing' fawei" 馬王堆漢墓帛書 "相馬經" 發微. *Wenxian* 文獻 4 (1989): 262–68.

———. "Zaoci jueyu, yiyun hongshen—cong boshu 'Xiang ma jing—Daguang po zhang' kan Qufu biyu xiangzheng shoufa de xingcheng" 藻辭譎喻, 意蘊宏深—從帛書 "相馬經・大光破章" 看屈賦比喻象徵手法的形成. *Liaoning shifan daxue xuebao (shekeban)* 遼寧師範大學學報(社科版) 3 (1988): 50–55.

Zhao Ping'an 趙平安. "'Zuxia' yu 'mazuxia'—Yinwan Han jian ciyu zhaji zhi yi" "足下" 與 "馬足下"—尹灣漢簡詞語札記之一. *Yuwen jianshe* 語文建設 12 (1998): 32–33.

Zhao Yan 趙岩. "Handai jianbo cihui yanjiu de huigu yu zhanwang" 漢代簡帛詞匯研究的回顧與展望. *Leshan shifan xueyuan xuebao* 樂山師範學院學報 25.8 (2010): 55–59.

Zhao Yi 趙壹 (d. ca. 185). "Fei caoshu" 非草書. In *Quan Shanggu Sandai Qin Han Sanguo Liuchao wen* 全上古三代秦漢三國六朝, edited by Yan Kejun 嚴可均 (1762–1843), 82.916–917. Beijing: Zhonghua shuju, 1958.

Zheng Youguo 鄭有國. *Zhongguo jianduxue zonglun* 中國簡牘學綜論. Shanghai: Huadong shifan daxue chubanshe, 1989.

Zhong Shaoyi 鐘少異. "Gu xiang jian shu chu lun" 古相劍術芻論. *Kaogu* 考古 4 (1994): 368–62.

Zhongguo jiandu jicheng: biao zhu ben 中國簡牘集成: 標註本. Edited by Zhongguo jiandu jicheng bianji weiyuanhui 中國簡牘集成編輯委員會. Lanzhou: Dunhuang wenyi chubanshe, 2001–2005.

Zhou Zhenhe 周振鶴. "Qindai Dongting, Cangwu liangjun xuanxiang" 秦
代洞庭、蒼梧兩郡懸想. *Fudan xuebao (shehui kexue ban)* 復旦學報 (社
會科學版) 5 (2005): 63–67.

Zhou Zuliang 周祖亮. "Han jian shouyi ziliao ji qi jiazhi kaolun" 漢簡獸醫
資料及其價值考論. *Nongye kaogu* 農業考古 4 (2011): 457–60.

Zhuang Xiaoxia 莊小霞. "Jiandu suojian Handai siren shuxin zhisong xinxi
shitan—yi Tianchang Jizhuang Han mu shuxin du wei zhongxin" 簡
牘所見漢代私人書信致送信息試探——以天長紀莊漢墓書信牘為中心. In
Gansusheng dierjie jianduxue guoji xueshu yantaohui lunwenji 甘肅省第二屆
簡牘學國際學術研討會論文集, edited by Zhang Defang 張德芳, 249–55.
Shanghai: Shanghai guji chubanshe, 2012.

———. "Tianchang Jizhuang Han mu shuxin mudu suojian 'yuti' kao—jianji
Wuwei chutu 'wangzhang' jian de shidu" 天長紀莊漢墓書信木牘所見
"玉體" 考——兼及武威出土 "王杖" 簡的釋讀. In *Jianbo yanjiu erlinglingjiu*
簡帛研究二〇〇九, edited by Bu Xianqun 卜憲群 and Yang Zhenhong
楊振紅, 52–56. Guilin: Guangxi shifan daxue chubanshe, 2011.

Zong Fan 蹤凡. "Liang Han gushifu de biaoxian ticai ji wenxue chengjiu"
兩漢故事賦的表現題材及文學成就. *Shehui kexue jikan* 社會科學輯刊 1
(2005): 39–41.

Zuozhuan zhushu 左傳注疏. See *Shisanjing zhushu.*

Index